HAWAII ✓ W9-AZE-224

TRAVEL+SMART™ TRIP PLANNER

HAWAII

TRAVEL✦SMART™ TRIP PLANNER

Arnold Schuchter

John Muir Publications
Santa Fe, New Mexico

John Muir Publications
P.O. Box 613, Santa Fe, New Mexico 87504
© 1996 Arnold Schuchter
Cover and maps © 1996 John Muir Publications
All rights reserved.

Printed in the United States of America.
First printing July 1996.

Parts of this book were originally published in *2 to 22 Days in Hawaii*, © 1988, 1989, 1991, 1992, 1993, 1994, and 1995 by Arnold Schuchter.

ISSN 1086-8135
ISBN 1-56261-255-7

Cover photo: Leo de Wys Inc./Lynn Pelham
Back cover photos: *top*—Leo de Wys Inc./R. Vanderbes;
                    bottom—Leo de Wys Inc./Sunstar
Map Design: American Custom Maps—Albuquerque, NM USA
Editors: Dianna Delling, Peggy Schaefer, Elizabeth Wolf
Design: Janine Lehmann, Linda Braun
Typesetting: Kathleen Sparkes
Graphics Manager: Sarah Horowitz
Production: Janine Lehmann, Nikki Rooker
Printing: Publishers Press

Distributed to the book trade by
Publishers Group West
Emeryville, California

HOW TO USE THIS BOOK

The *Hawaii Travel•Smart™ Trip Planner* is organized in 18 destination chapters, each covering the best sights and activities, restaurants, and lodging available in that specific destination. Thanks to thorough research and experience, the author is able to bring you only the best options, saving you time and money in your travels. The chapters are presented in geographic sequence so you can follow an easy route from one to the next. If you were to visit each destination in chapter order, you'd enjoy a complete tour of the best of Hawaii.

Each chapter contains:

• User-friendly maps of the area, showing all recommended sights, restaurants, and accommodations.

• "A Perfect Day" description—how the author would spend his time if he had just one day in that destination.

• Sightseeing highlights, each rated by degree of importance: ★★★ Don't miss; ★★ Try hard to see; ★ See if you have time; and No stars—Worth knowing about.

• Selected restaurant, lodging, and camping recommendations to suit a variety of budgets.

• Helpful hints, fitness and recreation ideas, insights, and random tidbits of information to enhance your trip.

The Importance of Planning. Developing an itinerary is the best way to get the most satisfaction from your travels, and this guidebook makes it easy. First, read through the book and choose the places you'd most like to visit. Then, study the color map on the inside cover flap to determine which you can realistically see in the time you have available and at the travel pace you prefer. Using the Planning Map (pages 10–11), map out your route. Finally, use the lodging recommendations to determine your accommodations.

Some Suggested Itineraries. To get you started, six itineraries of varying lengths and based on specific interests follow. Mix and match according to your interests and time constraints, or follow a given itinerary from start to finish. The possibilities are endless. *Aloha!*

SUGGESTED ITINERARIES

With the *Hawaii Travel•Smart™ Trip Planner* you can plan a trip of any length—a one-day excursion, a getaway weekend, or a three-week vacation—around any special interest. To get you started, the following pages contain six suggested itineraries geared toward a variety of interests. You can follow a suggested itinerary in its entirety, or shorten, lengthen, or combine parts of each, depending on your starting and ending points.

Discuss alternative routes and schedules with your travel companions—it's a great way to have fun, even before you leave home. And remember: don't hesitate to change your itinerary once you're on the road. Careful study and planning ahead of time will help you make informed decisions as you go, but spontaneity is the extra ingredient that will make your trip memorable.

Jean Higgins/Unicorn Stock Photos

Hawaii in One to Three Weeks

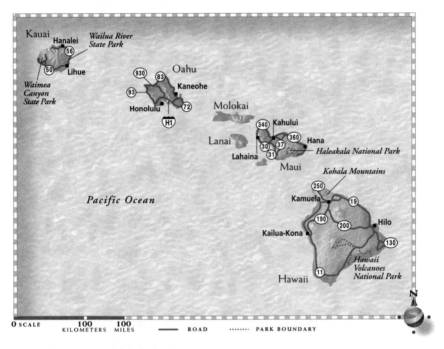

If you have one week in Hawaii:
- Spend 5 days on either Oahu or Maui, plus 2 days in Molokai or Lanai;
- Spend a week fully exploring The Big Island; or
- Spend 4 days on Kauai and add a day or two for extended hiking on the Kalalau Trail and Waimea Canyon.

If you have 2 weeks in Hawaii, combine 2 of the above suggestions.

If you have 3 weeks, you can see a great deal of Hawaii but you won't have the luxury of spending too much time in any one place. Arnold suggests:
- 4 days in Oahu;
- 5 days in Maui;
- 2 days in Lanai and/or Molokai (see West Maui chapter);
- 6 days on the Big Island; and
- 4 days in Kauai

The Nature Lover's Tour

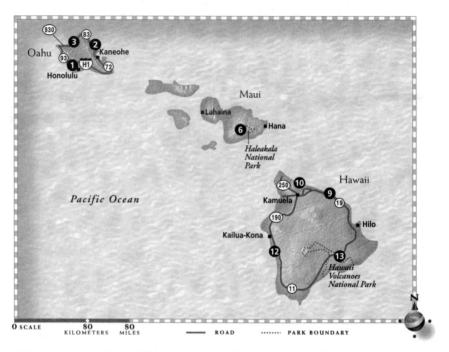

Nature lovers will find hiking trails and public gardens on all of the islands. Here are the best destinations for adventurers, birdwatchers, and nature enthusiasts and a quick run-down of the best each has to offer.

❶ Honolulu (Aiea Heights, Foster Botanical Garden, Lyon Arboretum, Puu Ohia Trail, Tantulus Drive)

❷ Windward Coast (Haiku Gardens, Senator Fong's Plantation and Gardens)

❸ North Shore (Kaena Point, Makaha Beach, Mokuleia Beach)

❻ Haleakala Volcano and Upcountry (Haleakala crater and trails, Iao Needle State Park, Olinda Road area, Kula Botanical Garden, Polipoli Springs)

❾ Hamakua Coast (Waipio Valley, Waimanu Valley, Hamakua Coast, Akaka Falls State Park, Hawaii Tropical Botanical Gardens)

❿ Kamuela and North Kalala (Kohala Mountains)

⓬ Kona Coast (Kealakekua Bay)

⓭ Hawaii Volcanoes National Park (Manua Loa, heli tour)

The Art and Culture Lover's Tour

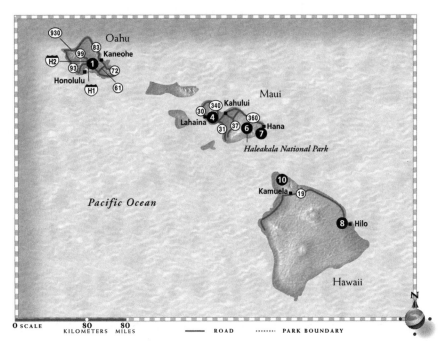

Galleries, rather than museums, are the places to see contemporary Hawaiian art. You'll find galleries concentrated in Chinatown on Oahu; Lahaina on Maui; and in Hilo, Volcano, and Kamuela on the Big Island.

❶ Honolulu (Bishop Museum, Contemporary Arts Museum, Chinatown)
❹ West Maui (Lahaina)
❻ Haleakala Volcano and Upcountry (Paia's Maui Craft Guild, Makaweo's Hui Noeau Visual Arts Center)
❼ Hana (Hana Cultural Center, Coast Gallery in the Hana-Maui Hotel)
❽ Hilo (various galleries)
❿ Kamuela and North Kohala (various galleries in Kamuela)

The Family Fun Tour

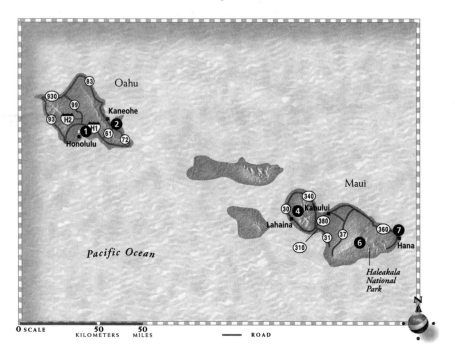

With dozens of beaches and tropical hikes to choose from, few families will return bored from any Hawaiian island. Manmade attractions include two very different zoos—one in Oahu, the other on the Big Island—and an outstanding sea life park in Oahu; train rides on Maui; exciting helicopter rides; and boat rides of many kinds, from submarines and ferries to pontoon boats and charters. The biggest and best family attraction, Polynesian Cultural Center on Windward Oahu, is well worth its high admission fee.

❶ **Honolulu** (Waikiki Aquarium, Honolulu Zoo, Sea Life Park, Waikiki and other beaches)

❷ **Windward Coast** (Polynesian Cultural Center, Nuuanu Pali Lookout)

❹ **West Maui** (Lahaina-Hawaii Experience Domed Theater, Lahaina-Kaanapali and Pacific Railroad)

❻ **Haleakala Volcano And Upcountry** (biking, hiking in national park)

❼ **Hana** (Seven Sacred Pools)

Culinary Tour

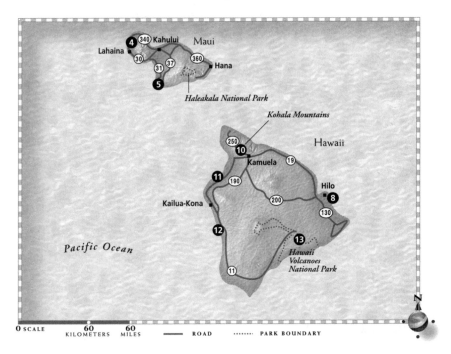

Along with an amazing assortment of ethnic restaurants, Hawaii has its own multicultural cuisine that relies on fresh island food products and borrows from both East and West. Some call it Pacific Rim; most call it deliciously different, creative, and memorable. Here are some of the islands' best.

④ **West Maui** (Old Lahaina Cafe, Gerard's, Avalon Restaurant, David Paul's Lahaini Grill, Roy's Kahana Bar and Grill, Bay Club, Plantation House Restaurant)

⑤ **The Wailea Coast** (Sea Watch, Hakone, Cafe Kiowai, Kincha)

⑧ **Hilo** (Roussel's, The Seaside, Pescatore, Soontaree's)

⑩ **Kamuela** (Merriman's, Mean Cuisine, Bamboo, Tropical Dreams Ice Cream Factory)

⑪ **South Kohala** (Bistro at Hapuna Beach Prince Hotel, The Dining Room at Ritz-Carlton Mauna Lani, Canoe House, Le Soleil)

⑫ **Kona Coast** (Sam Choy's Restaurant)

⑬ **Hawaii Volcanoes National Park** (Kilauea Lodge Restaurant)

The Beach Lover's Tour

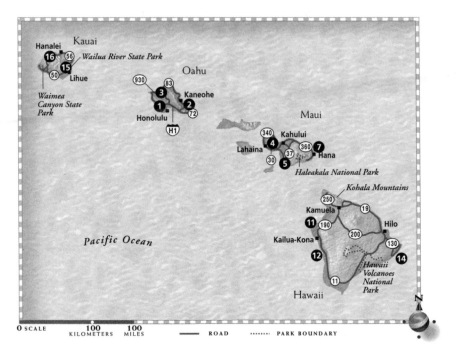

With a week to spend, you can explore and enjoy a different white or black sand beach every day on each island, all of which look and feel quite different.

❶ **Honolulu** (Waikiki and Makapuu Beaches)

❷ **The Windward Coast** (Goat Island, Kailua Beach Park, Lanikai, Malaekahana Bay, Pounders Beach)

❸ **The North Shore** (Makaha, Makua, and Mokoleia Beaches; Pokai Bay Beach Park; Waimea Bay; Yokohama Bay)

❹ **West Maui** (D.T. Fleming Beach Park, Honolua Bay, Kaanapali Beach, Kapalua Beach, Windmill Beaches)

❺ **Wailea Coast** (Kihei, Makena, Oneloa, and Wailea Beaches)

❼ **Hana** (Hamoa and Red Sand Beaches)

⓫ **South Kohala** (Anaehoomalu, Hapuna Beach, Mauna Kea and Mauna Lani Resort Beaches, Puako, "69" Beach, Spencer Beach, Waikaloa Resort Beach)

⓬ **Kona Coast** (Green Sand Beach, Magic Sands, Napoopoo Beach Park, Punaluu Beach Park)

⓮ **Puna Coast** (Kehena Beach)

⓯ **Lihue and Wailua River State Park** (Kealia and Poipu Beaches)

⓰ **North Shore and Hanalei Valley** (Anahola, Anini, Haena, Hanalei, Kee, Kalihiwai, Larson's, Lumahai, Moloaa, and Secret Beaches)

USING THE PLANNING MAP

A major aspect of itinerary planning is determining your mode of transportation and the route you will follow as you travel from destination to destination. The Planning Map on the following pages will allow you to do just that.

First, read through the destination chapters carefully and note the sights that intrigue you. Then, photocopy the Planning Map so you can try out several different routes that will take you to these destinations. Decide where you will be starting your tour of Hawaii. Will you fly into Honolulu? How many islands will you visit, and in what order? The answers to these questions will form the basis for your travel route design.

Once you have a firm idea of where your travels will take you, copy your route onto the additional Planning Map in the Appendix. You won't have to worry about where your map is, and the information you need on each destination will always be close at hand.

Joe Sohm, Unicorn Stock Photos

Planning Map: Hawaii

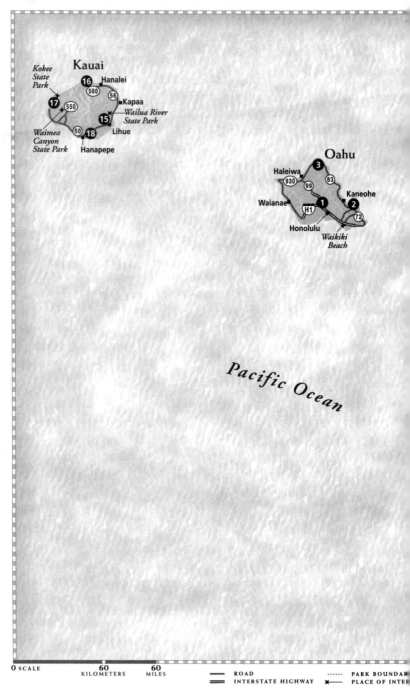

Kauai

Kokee State Park

16 Hanalei

560

56 Kapaa

Wailua River State Park

550

17

15

Waimea Canyon State Park

50 18 Lihue

Hanapepe

Oahu

Haleiwa

3

930

83

99

Kaneohe

Waianae

1

2

H1

72

Honolulu

Waikiki Beach

Pacific Ocean

0 SCALE   60   60
KILOMETERS   MILES

ROAD
INTERSTATE HIGHWAY

PARK BOUNDAR
PLACE OF INTER

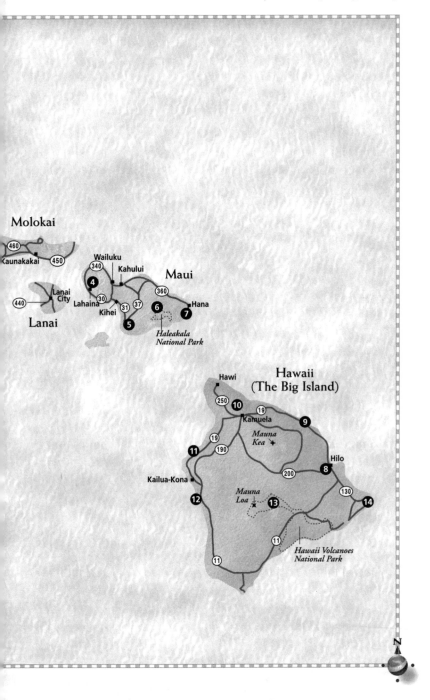

WHY VISIT HAWAII?

Welcome to Hawaii, where ancient sacrificial temples share the lush landscape with opulent resorts and simple tents pitched on stunning white sand. With its dramatic volcanic origins and rich Polynesian, Hawaii is a land of both simple and lavish vacation pleasures. The *Hawaii Travel•Smart™ Trip Planner* takes you to six of the 132 islands, reefs, and shoals that make up the Hawaiian archipelago: Oahu, Maui, Molokai, Lanai, Hawaii, and Kauai.

We begin with Oahu, where the windward and north coasts completely contrast with the capital city of Honolulu. Don't bypass Oahu because you mistakenly equate the whole island with Waikiki's commercialization—it is rich in history and culture and, although more crowded, as beautiful as the other islands.

Maui, the second-largest island, is Hawaii's fastest-growing tourist destination. Its highlights include Lahaina, the splendidly rejuvenated historic whaling town; Haleakala, a huge, dormant volcano; the blissful town of Hana; and remote western beaches. From Maui, take a side trip to Molokai for a taste of old Hawaii, or to Lanai, where you'll find some of Hawaii's remote beaches and two outstanding resorts.

The Big Island is dominated by two 13,000-foot volcanoes. (After ten years of volcanic activity, Kilauea may still be spouting lava when you arrive.) The Big Island has a half-dozen of Hawaii's most dazzling beaches, both white- and black-sand; its largest and best-preserved historic sites; North America's largest ranch; and North America's only commercial coffee-growing farms. The Big Island's windward and leeward coasts are perfect for hiking and exploring.

Kauai has incredibly varied climates and terrain for such a small island. It also boasts some of the best hidden beaches and hiking trails in the chain, and unforgettable mountain and valley jungle scenery. Calling spectacular Waimea Canyon the "Grand Canyon" of Hawaii is no exaggeration. In combination with the adjoining Na Pali mountains and coastline, Waimea Canyon can be counted as one of the wonders of the world.

Take your time as you explore the islands—you can fly between any two for about the same price. You'll be surprised and startled by the differences, both obvious and subtle, as you travel from one island to another. And remember, when asking for directions you'll sound like a local when you ask, "On the *makai* (toward the sea) or the *mauka* (toward the mountains) side?"

HISTORY

The Hawaiian islands, all 132 points of land now visible in the Pacific, rose from the bottom of the ocean, about 40 million years ago. Geologists describe the process with precision. The movement of tectonic plates, the shifting of the earth's crust, resulted in a series of volcanoes, one after another, emerging from the sea just south of the last one. The newest volcanoes are on the southern end of the archipelago. Kilauea on the Big Island's Mauna Loa is the most active volcanic peak. Other dormant volcanoes on the Big Island, Mauna Kea and Hualalai, and Haleakala on neighboring Maui to the north could be hot spots, too.

Remarkably seaworthy double-hulled canoes from the Marquesas Islands arrived on these islands sometime between 500 and 800 A.D. Perhaps these settlers were the *Menehune*, the legendary "little people" on Kauai. About 500 to 600 years later a second wave of settlers arrived in "Burning Hawaii," probably near South Point on the Big Island, this time from the Tahitian Islands.

This second group's culture, gods, and way of life prevailed. Along with Hawaii's indigenous flora, fauna, birds, and marine life, they had the entire island to themselves. The Hawaiians brought with them and developed exquisite artwork, wood and stone sculpture, featherwork and *tapa*-making, equal to any tribal or national group in the world.

Life may have been simple, but Hawaiian culture was comparatively complex, caste relationships tight, and the powers of the nobility and kings protected by rigid taboos. Sacrifices to deities at temples (*heiau*) were common. This feudal society saw frequent, brutal wars of succession and conquest, which lasted until Kamehameha beat everyone else and brought the Hawaiian islands into one kingdom.

In 1778, while searching for an Arctic route to the Atlantic, Captain James Cook, commanding the H.M.S. *Resolution* and *Discovery*, stumbled onto what he named the Sandwich Islands. These "floating islands," as the natives called them, stopped at today's Waimea on Kauai. Cook's men left behind gifts of goats, pigs, seeds, and venereal diseases. Within 80 years, the Hawaiian population shrank from about 300,000 to 60,000.

Cook and his ships returned at the end of 1778 and put into Kealakekua on the Big Island on January 17, 1779. A series of mishaps led to Cook's death weeks later. Subsequently, Hawaii became a regular stopping place for ships from many nations, including ships from the U.S. sailing to China to trade pelts for silks and tea. During the 1790s, Kamehameha enlisted the aid of westerners to wage war against Maui, the Big Island, and Oahu. It wasn't until 1810 that, after several failed invasions, Kamehameha could negotiate a treaty with Kaumualii, king of Kauai and Niihau.

After Kamehameha's death in 1819 his favorite wife, Kaahumanu, forced Liholiho, his heir, to share power. At this time, the first missionaries arrived on the Kona Coast, bringing a new god.

Liholiho, Kamehameha II, sailed to London in 1825, contracted measles and died. Kauikeaouli, Kamehameha III, became king at ten years of age. During his reign the missionaries acquired increasing political power and advisory and cabinet posts. The whaling industry had become the biggest business in the kingdom. Lahaina had become the biggest port in the Pacific and the nation's capitol until it was moved to Honolulu, the second biggest port, in 1845.

Kamehameha III lived until December 1854, by which time the whaling industry was dying and a Constitution had been adopted (1852) that left the monarchy vulnerable to overthrow. The California Gold Rush of 1849 created a seemingly insatiable demand for Hawaiian sugar and turned Hawaii's former whaling ports to servicing hordes of Western gold miners. By the time Alexander Liholiho took office as Kamehameha IV, Hawaii already had started importing Chinese laborers who would be followed by the Japanese, Filipino, Portuguese, and other nationalities.

Kamehameha IV's ill-fated reign ended with his unexpected death at age 29. His elder brother and former minister of the interior, Lot Kamehameha, took over and pursued anti-American and nativist sentiments he shared with his brother. After calling a Constitutional Convention in 1864, Kamehameha impatiently abolished the old constitution and revamped the legislature to ensure loyalist control. The sugar business had tripled by this time and more than tripled again by the time Kamehameha V died in 1872 without an heir.

Like Kamehameha V, his successor, Lunalilo, died a bachelor; his previous competitor for the throne, Kalakaua, was then elected by the legislature. Hawaii's "Merry Monarch" built the grand Iolani Palace, circled the globe to meet and charm other monarchs, and devoted much attention to restoring Hawaiian cultural traditions, including the *hula*.

Kalakaua's diplomatic success secured a long-sought-after Reciprocity Treaty with the U.S. that had eluded his predecessors and increased revenues and power for Hawaiian sugar growers. The ultimate aim of these landowners and businessmen was annexation of Hawaii to the U.S., which wanted to control Hawaii for strategic military reasons.

Several of Kalakaua's misjudgments fueled his *haole* (white foreign) opposition, which staged a revolt in 1887 and forced him to accept a "Bayonet Constitution" that greatly reduced the King's powers. A figurehead until he died while on a trip to the States, his sister, Princess Lydia Liliuokalani, became Hawaii's first reigning Queen and last monarch.

A strong advocate of the rights of native Hawaiians, the new Queen was determined to restore monarchical power. With the assistance of a pro-annexation U.S. Minister and a contingent of U.S. Marines, in 1893 annexation advocates forced Liliuokalani to abdicate.

Congress refused to accept President Cleveland's recommendation that the legitimate government of Hawaii be restored. These were the heady days of expansionist U.S. policy that history would refer to as "Manifest Destiny." The "Provisional Government" of Hawaii declared itself the Republic of Hawaii in 1894. Queen Liliuokalani supported a failed insurrection in 1895 and was arrested.

Election of Republican William McKinley to the U.S. presidency sealed Hawaii's fate. In 1898 Congress passed a Joint Resolution of Annexation. Old Glory's raising over Iolani Palace signaled the transfer of power. The U.S. Army occupied "Camp McKinley" in Kapiolani Park.

Less than two years later, Chinatown was inadvertently burned down by the Honolulu Fire Department, who set a blaze to eradicate bubonic plague. Between this disaster and the bombing of Pearl Harbor on December 7, 1941, perhaps the most significant event in Hawaii was the 1935 arrival of a Pan American Airlines Clipper from San Francisco en route across the Pacific. Regular jet service to Hawaii would begin 24 years later in 1959, the same year that Hawaii was admitted to the Union. Hawaiian tourism would shape its history for the rest of the twentieth century and probably beyond.

CULTURE & ART

Hawaiian culture developed largely in isolation from other Polynesian cultures. Thus Hawaii's traditional artistic styles and techniques developed without outside influences. Until the first Europeans arrived, the Hawaiian Islands were home to a people with a complex and sophisticated social order. It was a world of powerful *kahunas* (priests) in touch with the cosmic order, its strict taboos and numerous deities.

With no written language, the history, beliefs, and culture of ancient Hawaiians were passed from generation to generation through chant and the *hula*. In ancient Hawaii, the *hula* was a religious ritual, a way of establishing contact between man and god. Traditionally dances mimed wished-for events, like a successful hunt or fertility. Long chants were recited or sung, sometimes accompanied by drums made from coconut trees, calabash gourds, bamboo rattles and pipes, nose flutes, sticks, pebble castanets, and other *hula* implements made from plant material.

Thus *hula* fostered development of crafts to produce the implements associated with dance. The making of the *ipu* (Hawaiian gourd drum), the *ului'uli* (a gourd or coconut filled with shells or pebbles, usually decorated with beautiful feathers and sometimes *tapa* cloth), and other *hula* instruments is becoming a lost art. Sadly, the natural materials necessary for making these instruments are also disappearing.

Hawaiians observed their natural environment closely, interpreting it and the powers inherent in it. The origin and creation of the universe and all it contains, man-made and natural, have meaning in the Hawaiian order of things. That order is to be disturbed as little as possible.

Natural objects have an inherent beauty. All objects made by people out of natural objects should retain, and disturb as little as possible, their natural beauty. Utility and beauty go together, as *hula* instruments, calabashes, and traditional Hawaiian carving clearly show.

Hawaiians went beyond geometric form to the shape of the natural object as the determinant of form. Wood-carvers to this day spend a great deal of time finding and choosing wood that, according to these craftspeople, wants to be shaped in a certain way. The Hawaiian artist's job, therefore, is to discover that inner beauty and the form it should take—for example, as a polished wooden bowl.

The artist's work is to bring out an object's natural beauty. The material and its qualities are sacred and the Hawaiian artist's goal is to unleash natural forces that minimally change the essential characteristics of the object. Thus, the Hawaiian artist must search the materials' qualities deeply and sensitively enough to discover their primary and secondary natures.

Look at each material that the Hawaiian artist shapes or uses—such as wood, feather, *kapa*—and you will find a remarkable technical inventiveness and an unrivaled esthetic achievement.

Making *tapa* or *kapa* cloth from bark was one of the highest achievements of Hawaiian artists. The bark of the mulberry tree was turned into a gauzy cloth unequaled before or since. *Kapa* fibers from the mulberry's inner bark was softened by soaking and then beaten together into sections that were sewn together and beautifully decorated. Intricately carved beaters were used in order to give *kapa* distinctive surface patterns. Even after European contact, *kapa* designs and kapa-making continued to develop until the art died out in the nineteenth century.

At the Bishop Museum you can see extensive *tapa* collections and inventive featherwork for capes, helmets, and *kahilis* (cylinders mounted on poles). Some feather art is still created today; this ancient art is being revived using the peacock and pheasant feathers. Beautiful feather-lei work can cost up to $1,000. *Lauhala* woven from the *pandanus* tree are still made into table mats, textured hats, baskets, and other small items.

New England missionaries introduced quilt-making which acquired a Hawaiian style of motifs and colors prized for the last hundred years. The best place to find the most beautiful Hawaiian quilts is in Waimea on the Big Island and the Bishop Museum.

Although many of the most important aspects of Hawaiian culture may be lost or dormant forever, the making, giving, and wearing of *leis* lives on at the heart of the Hawaiian culture and experience. *Leis* of sweet-scented *maile* leaves picked in the mountains are the traditional offering to Laka, goddess of dance, venerated by *hula* dancers.

The *lei* is a token of love and a very special way to say hello or good-bye, to give thanks, to pray, or to mark a special event or achievement. Like the word *aloha*, it means many things, from joy to sorrow. Some of the most prized *leis* are made of tiny shells washed up on the shores of Nihau, the private island next to Kauai. Nihau leis range from elegantly simple to complicated and expensive designs.

FLORA AND FAUNA

B efore colonization by Hawaiians, the islands had no vegetables, fruits, edible animals, amphibians, reptiles, palm trees, or most other plants common to today's Hawaii. Taro, breadfruit, yams, coconut, sugarcane, and other foods were brought to Hawaii by Polynesians. Non-Hawaiians brought mangoes, papayas, pineapples, passion fruit, and the "Hawaiian" flowers we admire, including orchids, anthuriums, heliconia, hibiscus, and ginger. In other words, most of the flora that we associate with Hawaii's tropical abundance have come from elsewhere.

The arrival of native plants, flowers, and especially 1,000 varieties of snails in the Hawaiian Islands, thousands of miles from any land, is as mysterious as the arrival of people. Most of these species are threatened and face extinction, including the 70 species of birds that were native to the islands before Hawaiians came. Half of the endangered birds in the U.S. inhabit Hawaii.

Close to 2,000 species of plants existed in Hawaii before the Polynesians arrived. Some, like the silversword, found only at the top of Maui's Haleakala, exist nowhere else on earth. *Koa* and *ohia* growth, two of the most important native trees for carvers and canoe builders, have also been greatly reduced. (The more versatile *ohia* has survived better.)

Most of Hawaii's endemic plants came with the tides as spores and seeds from Asia and Indonesia; *koa*, for instance, resembles trees in Australia. But why does *koa* appear only in Hawaii when there are many islands between Australia and Hawaii that have no *koa* trees?

Whatever the reasons, these plant travelers had to be incredibly hardy and tenacious, to adapt quickly or perish. For humans, flora and fauna, and birds, the isolation was advantageous and had a remarkable impact. First, specialization. Where flora or birds landed, they stayed, adapted, and specialized.

Sometimes adaptation was so amazing that later versions of the same species became unrecognizable, like the 40 distinct varieties of honeycreeper that evolved from one species. Honeycreepers' body types and bills looked nothing like their ancestors'.

Hawaii today has more than 10,000 insect species. Amazingly, most of these appear nowhere else on earth and evolved from about 150 original species. However, over 700 species have been imported in recent years, including cockroaches and mosquitoes.

Large numbers of native Hawaiian birds have been destroyed by agriculture, by tree-cutting, and for their prized feathers. After Capt.ain Cook's arrival, mongeese, rats, and diseases spread from exotic (introduced) birds took their toll on birdlife. Most remaining species of endemic Hawaiian birds, like the yellowish-green *amakihi* and bright red *iiwi*, live in forests above 2,000 feet.

The almost extinct *nene*, or Hawaiian goose, is making a comeback in Haleakala Crater on Maui and on the slopes of Mauna Kea and Mauna Loa on the Big Island. Look for the distinctive heart-shaped face of the legendary *pueo*, the Hawaiian owl, in Haleakala Crater. In Hawaiian mythology, the *pueo* can be counted on to come to the aid of defeated and pursued warriors.

Hawaii's agricultural crops are not doing well. Pineapple, native to Latin America, is produced more profitably in the Philippines, Taiwan, and elsewhere. Hawaii once produced more sugar per acre than anywhere else on earth but most of Hawaii's sugarcane plantations have closed down. Hawaii's delicious bananas can be produced more cheaply elsewhere, and likewise papayas, mangoes, avocados, and other produce.

Stop by the Guava Kai Plantation on the North Shore of Kauai. Macadamia nuts are still grown in large orchards on the Big Island. In fact most of the former sugarcane land south of Hilo on the Big Island has switched to macadamia nut orchards. Visit the Mauna Loa Macadamia Nuts center en route from Hilo to the Puna coast or Volcano.

The best places to see Hawaii's flora—growing wild and

cultivated—and its bird population is in Waimea Falls Park and Valley (where you can see *nene*, too) and along the Koolau Range's trails on Oahu, in Waipio Valley and on the slopes of Mauna Kea and Mauna Loa on the Big Island, on Upcountry slopes and in Haleakala National Park on Maui, along Na Pali Coast State Park's trails and in the National Tropical Botanical Garden on Kauai, and on the Wailau Trail and in the Kamakou Preserve and Halawa Valley on Molokai.

CUISINE

You can find Hawaiian home-cooking at a few small eating places around Hawaii, such as the Aloha Diner in Waipouli Complex in Kapaa. The best way to experience the local color and variety of Hawaiian home-cooking is at a *luau*. *Luaus* are expensive; you'll probably attend only one. The best one in Hawaii is at the Old Lahaina Cafe and *Luau* (667-1998) in Lahaina. The feast itself, the music and *hula*, and the atmosphere are all exceptional and authentic.

You'll soon realize that much of Hawaiian food is an acquired taste—it takes time to appreciate. *Luaus* feature *poi*, an *imu*, baked pork, and other items such as *haupia*, a coconut custard desert. Purplish-colored *poi* is made by pounding taro into a paste and letting it ferment a little (sometimes for a whole day, which gives it an acid taste). *Poi* is a very healthy starch rich in vitamins.

Poi comes in three consistencies: "one-, two-, and three-finger" *poi*—the fewer fingers you need to eat the gooey stuff, the thicker it is. There's also a steamed taro pudding called *kukolo*. Understand that taro is not only a staple of traditional Hawaii but, according to Hawaiians, it is the food created by the gods when they created mankind.

Centerpiece of a *luau* is an *imu*, the underground oven filled with hot rocks used to steam-bake *kalua* pork and other dishes. You'll see a whole pig (*puaa*) wrapped in ti and banana leaves and its stomach filled with hot stones after it is set on the fire's coals. Placed around the pig are little bundles (*laulau*) of chicken, breadfruit, sweet potatoes (*uala*), and other delicacies, also wrapped in ti leaves. Pig and *laulau* are covered with banana or ti leaves and earth. Water for steam is added through a bamboo tube.

You may be served *lomilomi*, raw salmon made into a vinegar salad with chopped onion, tomatoes, and spices, and another *luau* favorite, *limu*, an edible seaweed. Sometimes *limu* is mixed with ground *kukui* nuts and salt as a relish.

Where do you find Hawaiian home-cooking? Fresh *poi*? *Kalau* pig?

Lomi salmon and, of course, laulau? On the Big Island, join Hilo's natives at Kimo's Ono Hawaiian Food (935-3111) in Walakea Village Food Court. On The Big Island, try Sam Choy's Restaurant (326-1545), in an industrial park near the airport. For breakfast, load up on fat and calories with *loco moco*—fried rice topped with a hamburger patty, fried egg, and gravy. Better still, for dinner order Sam's seafood *laulau, ono* with vegetables steamed in *ti* leaves with soy sauce.

You have to know your fish in Hawaii: *Ahi* (yellowfin tuna); *aku* (skipjack tuna) and *akule* (a species of jack); *ahipalaha* (albacore); *au* (swordfish); *ehu* (a variety of snapper); *kumu* (a redfish); *mahimahi* (sometimes called dolphin, but it isn't); *oama* (baby weke); *ono* (also called wahoo); opakakaka (variety of blue snapper); opelu (species of Jack); *ulua* (a type of Jack); and *opihi*, a limpet painstakingly gathered from rocks, a very expensive delicacy eaten raw.

"Home-cooking" that you experience while moving around Hawaii more often than not means a plate lunch. *Kaukau* means food and "*kaukau* wagons" sell plate lunches, *huli huli* (barbecue), chicken (*moa*), or meat dishes. (Any barbecued food is *kaola*.)

Plate lunches frequently are served by short-order places that offer breakfast, lunch, and dinner Hawaiian-style, like teriyaki and breaded fish with two scoops of rice and macaroni salad, tripe stew, or meat-loaf sandwiches.

What do plate lunches have to do with Hawaiian culinary traditions? Not much. Hawaiians are actually among the world's best multiethnic cooks. They can mix Japanese and Chinese vegetables with Asian spices and Portuguese seafood-making techniques and still preserve each ingredient's texture, nutrients, color, and taste. In other words, the Rainbow State shows up most clearly in Hawaii's cuisine.

Hawaii is one of the most fabulous multiethnic societies in the world. During the last two centuries, workers and businesspeople, artists and chefs from France, England, Russia, China, Japan, the Philippines, Spain, Portugal, and many other places have moved to Hawaii and created an East-and-West culture, especially in food.

At the other end of the spectrum from plate lunches, and deeply rooted in traditional Hawaiian cuisine, is Pacific Rim cuisine. In Kapaa at A Pacific Café, Jean-Marie Josselin, the winner of the Hawaii Seafood Championship, absolutely knows how to prepare and present Hawaiian fish. His Hawaiian cuisine can be characterized as healthy and low-fat because of all the natural ingredients in Hawaiian cooking.

Rice is the island's staple. Chinese spices, steaming, roasting, and stir-fry techniques prevail. The Japanese have made their contribution with soy sauce, sashimi, broiling, grilled fish, noodle soups, soybeans, tempura, and the ubiquitous *bento* (boxed lunch).

Korean barbecues and Filipino fish, meat, and chicken stews are more easily found than Hawaiian meals. Thai and Vietnamese restaurants and cooking are becoming increasingly familiar and popular on all of the islands.

Mediterranean dishes bring French and Portuguese gusto to soups and other dishes that feature fresh vegetables. Hawaiians are outstanding farmers. Waimea on the Big Island, Upcountry on Maui, Kilauea on Kauai, and elsewhere grow mouthwatering fruits and vegetables: passion fruit, mangoes, guavas, bananas (more than 70 varieties), countless different types of avocados, and, of course, pineapples, limes, oranges, and other fruits.

OUTDOOR ACTIVITIES

The Hawaiian Islands are an outdoor-lover's paradise. Opportunities for land and sea activities abound, from diving, snorkeling, and surfing, to hiking, biking, and golfing.

You don't have to leave Oahu or even Waikiki for great bodysurfing. Just head for the Diamond Head end of Prince Kuhio Beach. For a combination of scenery and bodysurfing, the famous Makapuu Beach on the Windward Shore is among the best in Hawaii. At Makapuu, bodysurf in the early morning and hang-glide later on. No surf compares with Oahu's North Shore, but Oahu's Waianae Coast and Waikiki will satisfy most surfers, as will East and West Maui and Kauai's North Shore.

In winter, however, watch out at Makapuu and almost anywhere else in Hawaii—winter surfing and bodysurfing can be bad for your body.

Underwater terrain in Hawaii is even more fascinating than the landforms. Better still, crowds consist mainly of curious, colorful fish. Divers prefer the Waianae shore on Oahu, the Big Island's Kona Coast, and all of Kauai's shores except west of *Poipu*. Diving is sensational on Oahu's North Shore late spring to late summer but can be lethal or at least unsafe at any speed in winter. Instead, play it safe and dive or snorkel in Hanauma Bay, safe year-round. Year-round windsurfing action is found at Kailua Beach Park.

Sharks are rarely sighted and usually don't bother divers. (I hope that's sufficiently reassuring.) Not everyone is ready to plunge into the surf and paddle-board toward crashing waves or look for marine life at 60 feet. Skim in comfort over the waves on boats of all kinds that cruise out of Kewalo Basin on Oahu, Lahaina on Maui, and Kailua Pier on the Big

Island. For those who prefer not to dive, board the *Atlantic Submarine* in Oahu and Kailua-Kona to view reefs and sealife along the ocean floor from portholes.

Most hikers coming to Hawaii head for the outer islands. True, Oahu doesn't offer any smoking volcanoes, spouting lava, or desolate calderas. Otherwise, in my opinion, there's no better hiking in Hawaii than on Oahu. Hike all day along Lanipo Trail on the *pali* overlooking the Windward Coast and you may agree. Or start at Kahana Valley State Park and work your way up into the Koolaus on a trail that starts at the beach (where you can camp). On Mount Tantalus, minutes from Waikiki, you'll think you're on Kauai hiking trails.

One of the best aspects of hiking and camping in Hawaii is the variety of places to enjoy these activities within a short distance of each other. About 50 miles of trails meandering at 5,000 feet in Kokee State Park on Kauai are above several beautiful beaches near Waimea that offer beach-combers solitude. After hiking in Oahu's Koolau Range, you can camp (on weekends) on the white sand of Bellows Field Beach Park or on Kahana Bay Beach. Both places also are safe for swimming and enjoyed by snorkelers.

Several islands offer serious treks, like the Wailau Trail on Molokai and the Kalalau Trail on Kauai. Most hiking areas on Hawaii's islands, including the most spectacular ones, are only moderately strenuous. The miles of trails in Hawaii Volcanoes National Park on the Big Island and Haleakala National Park on Maui are easy to moderate. Even the first few miles of the mostly difficult Kalalau Trail along the Na Pali Coast State Park on Kauai are an incredible day-trip for any walker in reasonable shape.

Each island has its own very special and fantastic hiking and walking experiences, unlike any of the other islands. Waipio Valley on the Big Island is totally unlike Halawa Valley on Molokai. The ancient King's Walking Trail on the Kohala Coast of the Big Island doesn't at all resemble the lava and cliffside King's Trail that connects Waianapanapa State Park and Hana on Maui.

Most outdoor enthusiasts (including myself) like to keep their feet on the ground. Thrill-seekers head for Dillingham Field in Mokuleia for skydiving or to the ridges above Sea Life Park for hang-gliding accompanied, I might add, by some useful instruction.

Hawaii is for walkers as well as lovers, even around the most popular attractions like Waikiki, a bonanza for people-watchers. Sunburn is your biggest worry in Hawaii, on beaches or anywhere else. Bring lots of sunblock for all sunny sea-level or misty volcano hikes. Needless to say, wear good shoes or hiking boots and bring along your favorite container of water.

I'm reluctant to recommend bicycling on Oahu. Most roads are just too narrow. Rent bicycles in Kailua-Kona and enjoy Alii Drive and the Waimea plateau on the Big Island which offer scenic 5- to 10-mile rides. The Hamakua Coast is too narrow, but bicycling is an excellent way to see the Big Island's Puna and Volcano areas as long as it's not raining torrentially.

East Kauai and its North Shore make an interesting bike ride except, once again, for narrow, busy roads. Lanai is a mountain-bikers' paradise, another excellent reason for staying at the marvelous Koele and Manele Bay resorts.

I'm always surprised at how few bones are broken on the downhill rides on Maui's Haleakala. I much prefer upcountry roads such as Route 37 and around Makawao and Haiku. Mountain-bikers should consider starting at Napili or Kapalua and bicycling past D.T. Fleming Beach Park around Honokohau Bay where Honoapiilani Highway ends and the rough road begins that is off-limits to rental cars. The scenery along this stretch is bizarre and dramatic, and the road's contortions are a fair match. Hardy or masochistic bikers will complete the trip by climbing 3-mile Waihee Ridge Trail to scenic Lanilili Peak.

Hawaii's beaches are unlike any others, anywhere. Their composition (coral sand, lava rock, and a variety of other granulated stuff) leaves out exoskeletons. The most scenic beaches are on the oldest, most eroded islands. That's why Kauai's beaches are so nice. Count on water temperature of about 68°–84°F.

Beach Trivia Quiz: Island with the best and most beaches: Oahu (over 50 miles of sandy coastline). Hawaii's longest beach? Polihale on Kauai (17 miles!). Where does sand bark like a dog? Barking Sands, of course, on Kauai. The only green beach? Big Island's Mahana. Emptiest beaches? Lanai. Least-known fantastic beach? Papohaku on Molokai's western end. Beach where you're most likely to meet native Hawaiians? Keamano Beach on Nihau.

Hawaii has more than a hundred beaches, all different and scenic in some way. Some, like Waikiki on Oahu, Poipu on Kauai, Kaanapali and Wailea's beaches on Maui, and Hapuna on the Big Island, are famous and very popular yet still very appealing and never too crowded. Oahu's North Shore, Haleiwa and Waianae beaches, Hanalei on Kauai, Makena on Maui, and Magic Sands on the Big Island have their own local cultures and regulars which add to their special flavor.

More than a few beaches are hidden, like Green-sand Beach on the southern tip of the Big Island; Goat Island and Lanikai on Oahu; the northwest and southwest beaches of Molokai; and beaches east of Po*ipu*, around Waimea, and between Wailea and the North Shore on Kauai. Lovers of secluded beaches should not leave Kauai without a trip off Kuhio Highway down Koolau Road to Moloaa Bay and Larsen's Beach.

On Maui, for example, Kapalua Bay is one of my favorite beaches; but nearby Mokuleia is secluded, pretty, and a marine conservation zone that should make snorkelers very happy. Black-sand beaches are found on the Big Island's volcanic shores of Puna and Kau, down a steep 20-minute climb from the end of Route 270 in Kohala to Pololu Valley beach, and on the volcanic shoreline west of Hana.

Camping on the Big Island at Hapuna Beach and on Kauai at Anini Park as well as on remote beaches on the northeast and southeast shores of Molokai are unsurpassed anywhere in America! Haena State Park near the head of Kalalau Trail along Kauai's incredible Na Pali is another favorite of campers.

Combine your interest in flowers and long walks through natural beauty in many of Hawaii's parks. Meander for hours through botanical gardens and enjoy waterfalls and exotic vegetation in Waimea Falls Park on Oahu, Hawaii Tropical Garden near Hilo on the Big Island and the National Tropical Botanical Garden on Kauai.

Golfers can get their fill of walking and sightseeing on every island. Give Ted Robinson credit for filling a beautiful plain with coconut palm trees, banyans, monkeypods, flowering bougainvillea, and, oh yes, 18 holes at scenic Ko Olinda golf course at Ewa Beach.

If you prefer undulating golf greens in a lovely deep valley, try Oahu's Makaha in Waianae. Pali is a magnificent municipal course in Kaneohe at the base of a *pali* on Oahu's Windward Coast. The setting for the Turtle Bay Hilton course along the water is gorgeous which, for some people, makes up for its toughness. In one day, you can combine golfing and horseback riding here on Turtle Bay's beautiful beach. Unbeatable!

You can play a hundred holes of superb golf between Keauhou-Kona and the Mauna Kea on the Big Island, and almost as many holes on the east coast of Mai between Kapalua-Kaanapali and Wailea-Makena. Golf courses at the Koele and Manele resorts lure golfers from all of the other islands. Princeville on Kauai, a golfing legend, is still hard to beat for both golf and superb views.

PRACTICAL TIPS

HOW MUCH WILL IT COST?

The variety of inexpensive or moderately priced accommodations and eating places on every island makes it easy to stay within budget in the Hawaiian Islands. Use this book to make your accommodations, dining, activity, and travel choices, and your entire trip, including airfare, can average less than $225 per day for one person for a seven-day trip. As of this writing, round-trip airfare to Hawaii from anywhere in the U.S. is still close to its lowest level in years. Consequently, for two people, the trip cost comes down to about $150 per person per day, including both airfares. For two persons, there is no extra cost for car rental and very little extra cost for accommodations. Of course, the total and per-diem average will be much lower for campers, hikers, cyclers, and travelers determined to maintain a strict ultra-budget itinerary.

CLIMATE

Hawaii has two seasons, winter and summer. The main differences are the amount of rain and (much less so) the temperatures, especially from place to place. The average temperature year-round is 75°F. Between the warmest weather in August and the coldest weather in January, the daytime temperature may vary 5 to 7 degrees. February is the most unpredictable month.

Temperatures depend on elevation. In summer, get above the 2,000-foot-level and it's definitely cooler; the temperature drops 3 degrees for every 1,000 feet of elevation. But it also rains more in the mountains, especially on the windward side.

The weather in the off-season (April through December 15, and especially April to mid-July and September to Christmas) may actually be better than the weather during high season. However, it can rain hard and long in winter. Even on the dry Kohala coast of the Big Island, it can rain on and off for weeks in January. In the Hilo area, more than 210 inches of rain fell in 1991. Usually it's possible to find at least partly clear skies somewhere on an island, even when it's raining somewhere else. Frequently, you'll see rainbows along with rain or mist.

Each island has a wet (windward) and a dry (leeward) side of the mountains. Trade winds blow on the northeast sides of mountains almost every day in summer, keeping the heat and humidity down, and frequently disappear in winter when you don't need them to moderate the temperature. When hot Kona winds take over from October to April, the temperature is cooler on the leeward side. As a result, notwithstanding occasional hurricanes, horrendous downpours, and bad Kona storms, nowhere in the world is the temperature more constant, moderate, and comfortable all year round.

HAWAII'S CLIMATE

Average daily high and low temperatures in degrees Fahrenheit, plus monthly precipitation in inches.

	Hawaii (Kailua-Kona)	Maui (Lahaina)	Oahu (Honolulu)	Lihue (Kauai)
Jan.	81/64	82/64	80/66	78/65
	2.73	3.49	3.55	5.89
Mar.	81/65	83/64	82/67	79/67
	1.80	1.79	2.20	4.17
May	82/68	85/67	85/70	81/70
	2.45	.61	1.13	3.15
July	84/69	88/69	88/ 74	83/ 73
	2.45	.17	.59	2.13
Sept.	85/70	89/70	89/74	85/74
	2.02	.34	.78	2.37
Nov.	83/67	86/67	84/70	81/70
	1.69	2.15	3.00	5.45

* Figures taken from the State of Hawaii Department of Land and Natural Resources, Commission on Water Resource Management

GETTING THERE

Most flights land at Honolulu International Airport. The flying time to Honolulu from Los Angeles is five to six hours. From Chicago, it's a nine-hour nonstop flight; one-stop flights from New York take about 11 hours in the air (a 13-hour trip). Return flights are slightly shorter.

Airline fares can be so confusing and changeable that the only sensible advice is to shop systematically through a travel agent or, better yet, through several travel agents to compare prices, since some tend to favor certain airlines. Prepare a detailed itinerary for arrivals and departures on the islands, rental cars, and either hotel or price preferences. Start by asking for the lowest airfare—without prepurchase requirements, packaged with car rentals—for the day of the week on which you prefer to leave the mainland.

If you plan to stay at any first-class hotels, look at what the packagers can offer, combining airfare, car rental, and hotels. One of the wonderful aspects of the islands is that you can select a convenient base on any island without having to drive excessively for sightseeing.

INTER-ISLAND TRAVEL

Inter-island flights between the major islands (Oahu, Maui, Kauai, and the Big Island) are so frequent that you have to wait only a few minutes to catch the next one. The Kahului Airport on Maui receives flights from Aloha Airlines, Hawaiian Air, Aloha Interisland Air, American, Delta, and United. Hawaiian Airlines has a one-stop (Honolulu) flight leaving Hilo on the Big Island for Lihue Airport, on Kauai, at 5:00 p.m., arriving on Kauai at 6:25 p.m. Aloha Airlines has flights at 5:15 p.m., 6:15 p.m., and 6:40 p.m. With one and two stops and change of planes, these flights take close to two hours. Flights from the other islands to Kauai are also available. Interisland airlines take you in about 30 minutes to Hilo on the east coast of the Big Island or to Kailua-Kona on the west. Flights to Hilo from Lanai are available on Hawaiian Airlines. Once the Big Island's main airport, General Lyman Field has yielded to Kailua-Kona's Keahole Airport, now the main landing facility on the island. Lyman in Hilo also has inter-island jet service.

Hawaiian Airlines will get you between all of the islands, including Lanai and Molokai, flying DC-9 jets and 50-passenger Dash-7 four-engine turboprops. On the mainland, call (800) 367-5320 for reservations. Aloha flies Boeing 737s. On the mainland, call (800) 367-5250.

The maximum cost of one-way flights between islands on both airlines has increased to $69.95. However, the cheaper fare on the first (5:30 a.m. or 6:30 a.m.) and last flights (6:50 p.m. or 7:55 p.m.) is $49.95.

The Maui-to-Molokai ferry service offered by Sea Link of Hawaii (Suite 230, 505 Front Street, Lahaina, HI 96761, 661-5318) on the *Maui Princess* has not attracted enough passengers to prove successful. See if the service is still operational. The $42 round-trip boat ride from Maui to Kaunakakai, Molokai, is well worth the price. The 118-foot, four-prop craft has an air-conditioned main cabin and an open deck above. You can leave Maui at 7:30 a.m. and arrive on Molokai at 8:45 a.m. The trip can be packaged with accommodations on Molokai. This is another way to get a look at humpback whales in the channel between the two islands.

CAR RENTALS

Only on Oahu can public transportation (TheBus) take you wherever you want to go (in fact, everywhere on the island) at the lowest fare in the hemisphere. On the Big Island, the MTA has cheap (but slow) bus service that won't take you to coastal Puna. MTA's Hele-On Bus will take you cross-island from Hilo to Kailua-Kona, and daily buses run as far north as Waimea but not to the tip of North Kohala at Hawi. On Lanai, you need a four-wheel-drive vehicle to see the Munro Trail and on some of the off-the-beaten track roads to the north and east of Lanai City. You won't need a four-wheel-drive on any other island unless you're deter-mined to *really* get off the beaten track, in which case you'll pay at least $85 per day.

For rental cars, the choices on the major islands are as great as your patience. First, if at all possible, package your car rental with your airfare and accommodations. Overnighter packages from Akamai Tours (971-3131 on Oahu), Roberts Hawaii (945-2444), Island Getaways (922-4400), or Hawaiian Overnighters (922-3444) give you a round-trip fare between any two islands, a compact car (and no mileage charge), and good-to-excellent accommodations for one night for about $90 plus tax per person. Additional nights and days of car rental and accommodations are low, especially for better hotels and resorts. The major airlines (and Hawaiian Airlines on their mainland service) are using rental cars as a bonus attraction, almost a giveaway, to get your airfare-hotel package business. In a fly-drive deal with an airline, which fluctuates too much these days to predict accurately, you shouldn't have to pay more than $25 per day or $135 per week (without insurance) for a compact car.

For quick reference, the national/international and statewide car rental agencies' mainland and Hawaii telephone numbers are:
American International: mainland, (800) 527-0202; Hawaii, (800) 527-0160
Avis: mainland, (800) 331-1212; Hawaii, (800) 645-6393
Budget: mainland, (800) 527-0700; Hawaii, (800) 527-0707
Dollar: mainland, (800) 367-7006
Hertz: mainland, (800) 654-3131; Hawaii, (800) 654-3001
National: mainland, (800) 227-7368; Hawaii, (800) 328-6321
Thrifty: mainland, (800) 331-4200; Hawaii, (800) 331-9191

Holiday: mainland, (800) 367-2631; Oahu, 836-1974
Tropical: mainland, (800) 367-5140; Oahu, 836-1176

The national and statewide car rental agencies will split their car rental rates around the neighboring islands, letting you rent from one company for three weeks with at least 15 percent savings. This arrangement eliminates bargaining with local companies island-by-island for possibly lower rates, and the savings are guaranteed. During peak season and holiday periods, it's wise to book a car in advance or you may be stuck without one. For the lowest rates, reserve a subcompact or compact with a stick shift and no air-conditioner; then, when you arrive at the booking desk, ask politely if you can get an upgrade at the same price. This request may actually work.

LODGING

C lean, comfortable, pleasant, well-located, and moderately priced accommodations are plentiful and easy to obtain on all the Hawaiian Islands except Lanai. For only one or two people to have a dream vacation in Hawaii and spend less than $75 per day on accommodations, B&B accommodations are the best bet. There are only a few motels (in Lihue on Kauai and Waimea on the Big Island), only two official youth hostels (both in Honolulu), and a few cabins in state parks scattered around the state, some of them in superb locations such as Wianapanapa State Park near Hana, Poli Poli Springs State Recreation Area in upcountry Maui, Hawaii Volcanoes National Park on the Big Island, and Kokee State Park on Kauai.

If you arrive in Oahu or on any other island without a reservation, the best source of hotel/condo information is the Hawaii Visitor's Bureau. Their free *Membership Accommodation Guide* is the most complete and up-to-date listing, including telephone numbers and addresses in all price ranges. When you look at accommodation prices, don't forget to add 9 percent room tax. Minimum-stay requirements of three days are common, especially "in season"—December 15 to April 15.

B&B rooms range in price from $35 to $125 single or double. Even though county and local governments are resisting the growing trend, B&Bs are springing up on all the major islands. If they are not officially approved, B&Bs may not advertise themselves. Other B&B operators, however, will tell you about them. Check local newspapers, supermarket bulletin boards, and shops. The most efficient way to find a wonderful variety of B&B bargains, hosts, and situations on all the islands is to contact: Bed & Breakfast Hawaii, (800) 733-1632, Box 449, Kapaa, Kauai,

HI 96746 (Kauai—822-7771, Maui—572-7692, Hawaii—959-9736); Bed and Breakfast Pacific Hawaii, 19 Kei Nani Place, Kailua, Oahu 96734 (262-6026 or 800-999-6026); Go Native Hawaii, 65 Halaulani Place, Hilo, HI 96721; and B&B Maui Style, P. O. Box 98, Puunene, HI 96784 (879-7865 or 800-848-5567).

Call Vickki Patterson at Affordable Paradise B&Bs, 362 Kailua Road, Kailua, HI 96734 (261-1693 or 800-925-9065) for a choice of more than 300 hosts throughout the islands.

CAMPING

Hawaii offers some of the world's best camping and hiking. Hike shorelines, mountains, volcanoes, deserts, and jungle terrain, sometimes a mix in one day, and end the day at campsites that are easily accessible, near beautiful beaches, and surrounded by spectacular landscapes. Most camping is either free or costs a pittance. Some parks even offer the comfort of housekeeping cabins with all amenities, which must be reserved well in advance of your trip. The climate couldn't be better for camping and hiking in two national parks, 16 state parks, and 36 county parks open all year. Permits and reservations are required for public camping facilities. Island-by-island, this book points out the best camping spots and hiking trails. The State of Hawaii offers an excellent pamphlet on camping, picnicking, hiking, overnight cabins, and group accommodations. Write: State of Hawaii, Department of Land and Natural Resources, Division of State Parks, P.O. Box 621, Honolulu, HI 96809 (808-548-7455/56). For more detailed camping and hiking information, see Robert Smith's book, *Hawaii's Best Hiking Trails*.

WHAT AND HOW TO PACK

Due to FAA pressure, airlines are strictly enforcing carry-on baggage regulations—you're allowed only three free bags, including one carry-on. Carry-ons must fit under your seat or in an overhead compartment. Be sure to tag each bag with your name and hotel destination. Carry cosmetic essentials and a change of clothes with you, especially some beachwear, in case luggage is temporarily misrouted and delayed. If you do intend to use commuter flights, it's important to know that only two normal-sized bags, together weighing up to 44 pounds, are free. A third bag or baggage over 44 pounds may be carried on board on a space-available basis only. Over 80 pounds, you may have to pay extra. Not so, however, for the big carriers. On flights from the mainland, your three bags can weigh 70 pounds each as long as the height, length, and width added together do not exceed 62 inches. Your carry-on bag should be no more than 9 inches on one side to fit under the seat.

Travel as light as possible. You'll want to pack jeans, shorts, loose-fitting shirts, and dresses (*aloha* shirts and *muumuus* await your shopping in Waikiki). Pack wrinkle-free and colorful clothing, dress shoes, walking and jogging shoes, and sandals. Hawaiians dress very casually, but bring one moderately dressy outfit for the rare nightlife or dining places that require it, if that's in your plan. Don't forget one very warm outfit, and strong but comfortable walking or hiking shoes for Haleakala on Maui or Mauna Kea, Mauna Loa, and Hawaii Volcanoes National Park on the Big Island. Pack a sweater or jacket for cool days or evenings and trips in the mountains, a poncho for windward Hawaii and other windward island destinations, and a small, flat, empty bag for beach trips and shopping. Don't forget sunblock/tanning lotion, your favorite moisturizer, a hat, sunglasses, and a bathing suit.

RECOMMENDED READING

There are a few books that you might consider taking with you to supplement this one. For hikers, *Hawaii's Best Hiking Trails* by Robert Smith (Berkeley, Calif.: Wilderness Press, 1985) is a readable, well-organized guide, with everything you need to know about preparing for Hawaii's hiking trails.

My *Shopper's Guide to Arts and Crafts in the Hawaiian Islands* (Santa Fe, NM: John Muir Publications, 1990) tells all about the artists working on each island. It also includes additional suggestions for sightseeing, accommodations, and dining.

The University of Hawaii Press has full-color topographic maps for only $2.50 for each island. These detailed maps show every town, point of interest, type of road and trail, stream and waterfall, ridge and peak, and beach and park. These maps can be found in local bookstores.

Note: The area code for all of the islands is 808.

1
HONOLULU

Declared a metropolis by King Kamehameha III, Honolulu is the nation's most exotic state capital. Since most visitors to Oahu head directly for Waikiki, it is also the most neglected. Indulge in Waikiki's famous beaches, shopping, nightlife and people-watching. Join the thousands who climb Diamond Head for the "big Pacific view." But don't miss Honolulu—so gentle, friendly, and easy to get around. (TheBus will take you anywhere, cheap.) The city lies between mountains (*mauka* means toward the mountains) and the sea (*makai* means toward the sea), a volcano (Diamond Head) and a large suburb to the west (*Ewa*). In Honolulu, these are the only directions you need to know. Honolulu consists of funky and sophisticated neighborhoods, magnificent views from great heights, unique museums like the Bishop, WW II graveyards on land and sea, and a diverse collection of unhurried people scattered over and between mountains and sea, incongruously divided by an eight-lane east-west freeway. From the city's waterfront, where sailors swaggered ashore in the eighteenth-century and inadvertently decimated the Hawaiian population, it's an easy walk through the downtown's historic Capitol District and Chinatown. Use a dining tour of Honolulu and Oahu to explore the island—from the art galleries and sundry herb and *lei* shops of Chinatown, to restaurant row along Ala Moana (a short taxi ride from Waikiki to Kaimuki); to misty Manoa Valley, perennially streaked with rainbows; and finally, toward and beyond Diamond Head. ◼

HONOLULU

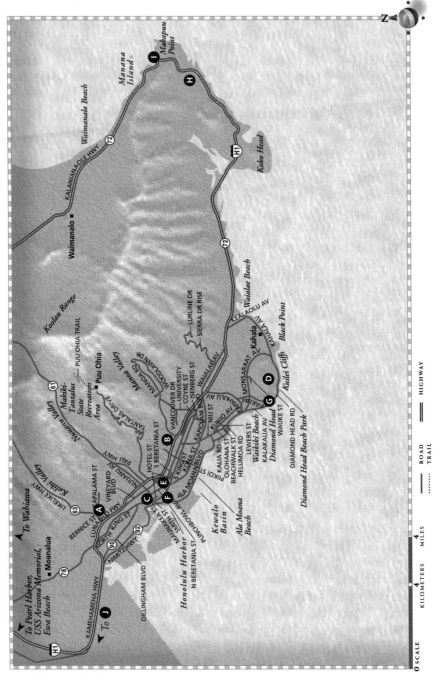

To Makapuu Point

Makapuu Point

Manana Island

Waimanalo Beach

Waimanalo

KALANIANAOLE HWY

Koko Head

72

H1

Waialae Beach

Koolau Range

PUU OHIA TRAIL

LURLINE DR

SIERRA DR RISE

KEALAOLU AV

MONSARRAT AV

Black Point

Makiki-
Tantalus
State
Recreation
Area

Puu Ohia

61

WOODLAWN DR

E MANOA RD

UNIVERSITY

COYNE ST

ISENBERG ST

WAIALAE AV

Kahala

KAHALA AV

Kuilei Cliffs

Nuuanu Valley

Kalihi Valley

LIKELIKE HWY

To Wahiawa

63

Moanalua

Manoa Valley

TANTALUS DRIVE

VANCOUVER DR

KAPIOLANI BLVD

NIU ST

KUHIO AV

KAPAHULU AV

KILAUEA AV

KAIMUKI AV

Diamond Head

D

G

To Pearl Harbor,
USS Arizona Memorial,
Ewa Beach

78

KAMEHAMEHA HWY

NIMITZ HWY

DILLINGHAM BLVD

NUUANU AV

PALI HWY

VINEYARD BLVD

BERNICE ST

LILIHA ST

APALAMA ST

HOTEL ST

S BERETANIA ST

S KING ST

KONA ST

ALA MOANA BLVD

PIIKOI ST

KALIA RD

OLOHANA ST

LEWERS ST

BEACHWALK ST

HELUMOA RD

KALAKAUA AV

Waikiki Beach

WAUKE ST

DIAMOND HEAD RD

Diamond Head Beach Park

A

B

C

E

F

North King St

PUNCHBOWL ST

MAUNAKEA ST

SMITH ST

MAUNAKEA ST

N BERETANIA ST

Honolulu Harbor

Kewalo Basin

Ala Moana Beach

To J

H1

90

92

H

I

N

Sightseeing Highlights

Ⓐ Bishop Museum

Ⓑ Contemporary Museum of Art

Ⓒ Chinatown

Ⓓ Diamond Head

Ⓔ Downtown Honolulu

Ⓕ Hawaiian Maritime Center

Ⓖ Kapiolani Beach Park

Ⓗ Koko Head and Koko Crater

Ⓘ Sea Life Park

Ⓙ USS *Arizona* Memorial

A PERFECT DAY IN HONOLULU

Start your day with a swim at Ala Moana Beach Park. After breakfast at Eggs 'n' Things, stroll through the gardens of "The Pink Lady," the Spanish-Moorish Royal Hawaiian Hotel. Bypass Waikiki's souvenir shops and head for the third floor of the Royal Hawaiian Shopping Center on Kalakaua to shop for authentic crafts at the Little Hawaiian Craft Shop. See marine life exhibits at the Waikiki Aquarium, then enjoy lunch on the beachside patio at the Hau Tree Lanai, in the New Otani Kaimana Beach Hotel. Continue up Kalakaua Avenue to the foot of Diamond Head. Plan on a half-hour walk up the 760-foot summit and plenty of time for the views. Back downtown, visit Bishop Museum, then browse through vintage Chinatown shops around Maunakea Street. Smell flowers at the lei stands on Beretania Street before sampling dinner choices in the food court of Maunakea Marketplace or treating yourself to a fine vegetable dish at the Buddhist Vegetarian Restaurant in Chinatown's Cultural Plaza.

GETTING AROUND OAHU

From the Airport: The Honolulu Airport is about 5 miles west of Waikiki. It's a 20-minute drive except during rush hour, when it can take 45 minutes. Many hotels have courtesy pickup, and their phones are near the baggage area. A taxi from the airport to Waikiki costs about $20 with tip depending on the distance and the number of bags. Call SIDA Taxis (836-0011) for the Honolulu area or Aloha State Taxi (847-3566) for elsewhere on the island. Better, use the Gray Line Airporter (834-1033) to Waikiki, Airport Motor Coach (926-4747), or Waikiki Airport Express (949-5249), all about $9 per person. Unfortunately, on the unbeatable TheBus, only a small carry-on bag (not a backpack) that you can hold in your lap is allowed. Buses 8 and 20 pass just outside the airport and can take you to Ala Moana Terminal to pick up connecting buses.

   TheBus: No matter where you go on Oahu, for a continuous trip in the same direction, TheBus costs only 60 cents (exact change only), free if you're under age 6 or over 65. Transfers are free for a bus on a different line in the same direction, so you can get on and off at will following this rule. You can do a complete circuit of the island, windward and leeward coasts, in about four hours on bus 52. Look for the bus painted yellow, brown, and orange, which has its main terminal at the Ala Moana Shopping Center on the Kona Street side of the ground-floor parking lot. At the information booth there (942-3702), you can pick up maps and schedules. These are TheBuses to some of the primary destinations from the Ala Moana Terminal:

Airport: 8 and 20
Waikiki Beach: 2, 4, 8, 14, and 20
Arizona Memorial/Pearl Harbor: 20, 50, 51, and 52
Wahiawa, downtown Honolulu, and Chinatown: 1 – 9, 11, and 12
Hanauma Bay: 1 and 57
Sea Life Park: 57
Polynesian Cultural Center: 52
Queen Emma's Palace: 4

   Driving: Avoid driving during rush hours (7:00 to 9:00 a.m. and 4:00 to 6:00 p.m.) anywhere near Honolulu or the Pali roads. Buy a copy of *Bryan's Sectional Maps, Oahu*, which is indispensable for finding towns, subdivisions, park and recreation areas, shopping centers, and all attractions.

   Car Rentals: Car rental prices may amaze you. For example, a Hertz subcompact (or even a compact if you are very nice) can be rented for $88 per week minus any discount such as AAA's 5 percent for members. If at all possible, on Oahu, rent a car. You'll need it. The expensive part of car rental is the insurance, so leave home with adequate coverage to save $9 per day in Hawaii. Car rental agencies vary in their policies on renting without credit cards. Dollar, for example, will rent with a cash deposit, while Tropical requires a credit card. If it makes a difference to you, ask when you make a reservation. Always make a reservation at least a day ahead of time through the company's 800 number for the lowest rates. If you're going to rent cars on other islands, ask for an interisland rate. Even if you spend less than a week on any one island, you can piece together stays on all of the islands to get a weekly or monthly rate.

Local Oahu car rental numbers are Avis (836-5531), Budget (836-1700), Dollar Rent-A-Car (926-4251), and Hertz (836-2511); all are at the airport. National (836-2655) is outside the airport. A phone call away, smaller firms offer slightly better deals. For older cars at bargain rates, call AAA Rents (524-8060) or Alpert's Used Cars (955-4370). Other small local firms include Aloha Funway Rentals (834-1016), Compact Rent-A-Car (833-0059), Five-O Rent-A-Car (836-1028), Holiday (836-1974), Thrifty (836-2388), Travelers Rent-A-Car (833-3355), Tropical (836-1041), and VIP Car Rental (946-1671).

Bikes and Mopeds: Most sightseeing in the Honolulu area is within easy reach of bicycles or mopeds. The main problem with biking on Oahu is heavy traffic on the coastal roads. Rent a mountain bike to get off the main roads. Bikes at Aloha Funway Rentals are $10 per day. Mopeds at Funway are $14 for 24 hours. For more cycling information, contact Hawaii Bicycling League, Honolulu. Guided bicycle tours of Oahu and other islands are available through Island Bicycle Adventures (569 Kapahulu Avenue, Honolulu, HI 96815, 732-7227), at costs of $90 to $120 per day including food and lodging.

SIGHTSEEING HIGHLIGHTS

★★★ **Bishop Museum**—This museum contains the most complete collection of historical displays on Hawaii and Polynesia in the world. The best exhibits are in the Hall of Hawaiian Natural History and in the Hawaiian Hall, which covers the Kamehameha I era to Queen Liliuokalani's forced abdication. The exhibit shows King Kamehameha IV's infatuation with the British monarchy. (If you visit the nearby Iolani Palace, you'll see the real thing. If you're in Honolulu Wednesday through Saturday, join a volunteer guide for a fascinating

45-minute tour of this one-of-a-kind opulent palace.) Food booths, craft displays, and entertainment are also offered at Bishop Museum. Don't miss the traveling exhibits in the Castle Memorial Building. To get there, take exit 20A off H1 to Highway 63. Quickly get into the right lane for a right turn on Bernice Street. Or, bus 2 lets you off 2 blocks from the museum on Kapalama Street. Admission is $7 for adults and $4.95 for children ages 6 to 17. Hours: Open Monday through Saturday and the first Sunday of every month (Family Sunday) 9:00 a.m. to 5:00 p.m. Address: 1525 Bernice Street. Phone: 847-3511. (2–5 hours)

★★★ **Diamond Head**—This extinct volcano rising 760 feet above the east end of Waikiki can be reached by car from Monsarrat Avenue; then you can hike a half-hour to the top. The crater got its name from British sailors in the early 1800s who found calcite crystals on the slopes and thought they were diamonds. Head to Kapiolani Park, then take Diamond Head Road and climb the kiawe-covered Kuilei Cliffs to the cliffside lighthouse. Beneath the cliffs are two parks you can walk down to: **Diamond Head Beach Park** and **Kuilei Cliffs Beach Park**, which has three turnouts. Stop at the second one.

Diamond Head Road descends between cliffside houses to Kahala Avenue and then climbs to the crater's east side. Pass through Fort Ruger (no longer operative) and down the crater's western slope on Monsarrat Avenue. At Diamond Head Road and 18th Street, take a left at a sign marked Civ-Alert USPFO and drive right into Diamond Head through a tunnel where the huge crater opens up to nothing more than the Hawaii National Guard Armory, the FAA's flight traffic control center, and many kiawe trees descended from a single seed planted by a priest 160 years ago. Your goal is the panoramic view from the crater's rim, reached by a 0.7-mile trail (one-way) up the northwest side of the crater. There are many lookout points along the way, as well as tunnels and bunkers, former gun emplacements, and towers. The observation point at the summit is an outstanding picnic spot. (1½ hours)

★★ **Chinatown**—On the eastern fringe of downtown between Nuuanu Avenue, North Beretania Street, and South King Street, this part of town is both modern and rundown (the whole district burned down in 1900). The pagoda of Wo Fat's at the corner of Hotel and Maunakea streets is a good starting point for a tour. The most interesting stores are on Maunakea Street between Hotel and King streets: little Chinese groceries, herb shops dispensing ancient medications like ground snakeskin and powdered monkey brain, jewelry shops, ceramic shops, acupuncture supplies, and import stores. Also note the art galleries on Nuuanu, Smith, and Maunakea streets. The island end of Maunakea Street is bounded by the Cultural Plaza, designed to exhibit Hawaii's multicultural makeup. Nearby is the People's Open Market, a cooperative of open-air stalls. (2–3 hours)

★★ **Downtown Honolulu**—King Kamehameha's statue in front of the **Aliiolani Hale** is a duplicate made to replace the original, which was lost at sea en route from Paris. It was found much later in a Port Stanley junkyard and erected in Kapaau not far from the king's birthplace. Aliiolani Hale (the Judiciary Building), at King and Mililani streets, was supposed to be a palace, but Kamehameha V, who commissioned it, died before its completion, and it was converted to a court building. Iolani Palace was completed in 1882 and used as a royal palace for only 17 years. To the left of Washington Place is **St. Andrews Cathedral**, built in 1867 of stone shipped from England. In front is the **Hawaii State Capitol**. Kawaiahao Church, at South King and Punchbowl streets, was built in 1841 out of coral quarried from local reefs. The **Mission Houses Museum** on King Street across from the church includes the oldest wooden structure in Hawaii, precut and shipped from Boston in 1819, as well as the first printing press west of the Rockies. It's open daily and charges $5 for adults, $3 for children ages 6 to 15. The gift shop has an excellent collection of Hawaiiana. The museum also offers a two-hour walking tour of Honolulu. (4–6 hours)

★★ **Koko Head and Koko Crater**—Travel along tree-shaded Kahala Avenue, past the Kahala Hilton to Kealaolu Avenue, then back to Kalanianaole Highway, through Henry J. Kaiser's 6,000-acre Hawaii Kai development to Koko Head Regional Park, scenic lookouts, and Koko Head Crater at 1,200 feet. On the crest of Koko Head is a side road that leads to a parking lot above picturesque Hanauma Bay, a volcanic crater opened to the ocean. Paths wind down the steep hillside to the coconut palm–fringed bay with tide pools, rocky headlands, and a pretty white sand beach. From one side of the lookout above Halona Blowhole, geysers shoot through the submerged lava tube. Halona Cove and Sandy Beach are especially nice places to have picnics. (1½ hours)

★★ **The Contemporary Museum of Art**—The Contemporary Museum of Art is housed in a beautiful historic structure on 3½ acres, the former Spalding Estate, and features extensive Japanese-style gardens. With a beautiful view of Honolulu, Diamond Head and the

Pacific, the rolling lawns and gardens are one of my favorite places of peace and relaxation. Except for David Hockney's work housed in its own pavillion, the Museum's six galleries change exhibits regularly. Tour the museum for free on Thursdays, and indulge in soup, a sandwich or a delicious meal (and homemade dessert) on the lawn at The Contemporary Café. Closed Mondays, admission charge. From Aala Moana Shopping Center, take Piikoi to Mott-Smith and then Makiki Heights drive (which connects with Round Top Drive that turns into Tantalus Drive). Address: 2411 Makiki Heights Dr., 526-1322.

★★ **Sea Life Park**—Opposite Makapuu Beach Park, this park is worth visiting if only to see the 300,000-gallon Hawaiian Reef Tank, a 3-story glass tank containing thousands of species of marine life. Also be sure to see the Ocean Science Theater's trained dolphins, sea lions, and penguins. Admission to the park is $14.95 for adults, $8.50 for children ages 7 to 12, and $4.50 for children ages 4 to 6. The **Pacific Whaling Museum** (free) just outside the entrance displays an outstanding collection of whaling artifacts. Rising above the coastal highway are the 1,200-foot Makapuu Cliffs. Sea Life Park is at the base of these cliffs. The Kalanianaole Highway brings you through Waimanalo, past Waimanalo Beach, the longest stretch of sand on Oahu (site of the Robin Masters estate and the home of Magnum P.I.), to the junction of Highway 61, where you turn left onto the Pali Highway. Hours: Open daily from 9:30 a.m. to 5:00 p.m. (until 10:00 p.m. on Thursday, Friday, and Sunday). Phone: 259-7933. (2–3 hours)

★★ **USS *Arizona* Memorial**—This memorial in Pearl Harbor is in a very special category as a sightseeing attraction. The hull of the USS *Arizona* is the tomb of 1,102 men who died in Japan's surprise attack on December 7, 1941. The shrine can be visited in two ways: on an excursion boat, which can't land at the memorial, and by land, which can be crowded but more informative. Catch a #4 shuttle bus from Waikiki (926-4747) or TheBus 50 directly to the site where a free shuttle boat ferries you out to the *Arizona* Memorial. Or drive from Waikiki's Kalakaua Avenue to Ala Moana Boulevard to Nimitz Highway (West 92) to H1 West to Highway 90 to USS *Arizona* Memorial Visitor Center. From the **Visitor Center** housing the museum and theater, free navy shuttle boats run across the harbor (7:45 a.m.–3:00 p.m.) to a concrete memorial built in 1962 above the aquatic graveyard. Next to the Memorial Visitor Center, the **Pacific Submarine Museum** and its *Bowfin* submarine are a memorial to 52 submarines and the thousands of men who died in them during World War II. Admission is $7 for adults, $1.50 for children ages 6 to 12. Hours: Open daily 8:00 a.m. to 4:30 p.m. (3–4 hours)

☆ **Hawaiian Maritime Center** consists of four attractions. The **Kalakaua Boathouse** features multimedia exhibits of the Hawaii Maritime Center. **Aloha Tower** on Pier 9, at 10 stories the tallest building in town when it was built in 1926, still commands excellent views of the harbor and city. The *Falls of Clyde* on Pier 7, built in Scotland in 1878, is the world's only full-rigged, four-masted ship. And the *Hokuke'a*, an authentic replica of an ancient Polynesian double-hulled sailing canoe, made a 5,000-mile round-trip to Tahiti in 1976. Admission is $7 for adults, $4 for children ages 6 to 17, under 6 free. Hours: Open daily 9:00 a.m. to 5:00 p.m. Phone: 536-6373. (1 hour)

☆ **Kapiolani Beach Park**—Named after King Kalakaua's wife, Queen Kapiolani, this park near the east end of Waikiki includes the world's largest saltwater swimming pool (**War Memorial Natatorium**), the **Waikiki Aquarium** (923-9741, $2.50 donation per adult), the **Honolulu Zoo** (971-7171, open daily 8:30 a.m. to 4:00 p.m., adults $3, children 12 and under free), and a rose garden at Monsarrat and Paki avenues. **Artists of Oahu/Sunday Exhibits**, along the fence at the Honolulu Zoo, bring together a large number of the island's professional and part-time artists and craftspeople on Wednesdays and weekends between 10:00 a.m. and 4:00 p.m. (1 hour)

FITNESS AND RECREATION

There are several walking tours to choose from in the Honolulu area. **Honolulu Time Walk** (943-0371) hosts a three-hour "Journey Through Old Waikiki." **Stories of Honolulu Walking Tours** (734-9245), sponsored by Kapiolani Community College, connects storytellers with places. A walking tour of historic Honolulu leaves from the **Mission Houses Museum** (553 S. King Street, 531-0481) Tuesday through Thursday at 9:30 a.m. The **Chinese Historical Society** (521-3045) offers two-hour tours of **Chinatown** at 10 a.m. Monday–Saturday (and **Foster Garden** plus river temples at 1 p.m. Monday–Friday).

Helicopter tours around the island range from $40 quickies over Waikiki to tours of Oahu for $200 or more per person. Contact **Hawaii Pacific Helicopters** (836-2071), **Kenai Air Hawaii** (836-2071), or **Royal Helicopters** (941-4683).

Nature-lovers shouldn't miss the tropical fauna of **Foster Botanical Garden** (522-7065) at the mouth of Nuuanu Valley (and the superb adjacent **Kuan Yin Temple**, 533-6361), both on Vineyard Boulevard. (Call the Friends of Honolulu Botanical Garden at 537-1708 to get information about weekend tours of all four of Honolulu's botanical gardens, including one inside the Koko Crater). Take a guided hike (only on alternate weekends) up **Kamehameha Valley** with the Moanalua Gardens Foundation (839-5334). Tropical **Lyon Arboretum** is set in lush Manoa Valley. Stroll (it may be muddy) through the rainforest to 100-foot Manoa Falls.

Puu Ohia, the highest peak of Tantalus, 6 miles from Honolulu, is the place from which to reach many of the area's best hiking trails, none of which are too difficult and all of which reveal magnificent natural beauty. **Puu Ohia Trail** starts at the top of Tantalas Drive (next to the locked gate of the Hawaiian Telephone Co.) and follows the ridge between Nuuanu and Manoa valleys. Contact the **Hawaiian Trail and Mountain Club** (247-3922), the **Nature Conservancy** (537-4508), the **Sierra Club** (538-6616), and the **Hawaii Nature Center** (955-0100) to find a group to hike with and to obtain trail maps, information, and directions to other trails.

Ted Robinson's **Ko Olina Resort Golf Course** in Ewa Beach (par 72, 6,867 yards), west of Honolulu, is beautiful and full of unforgettable water features (676-5300).

Check with the **Hawaii Bicycling League** (988-7175) for bike rides that fit your condition. **Island Triathalon & Bike** (569 Kapahulu Avenue, 732-7227) and **Blue Sky Sports Center** (1920 Ala Moana Boulevard, 947-0101) both rent mountain bikes and 10-speeds. A favorite route for bicyclists is through Kahala to Hanauma Bay, at Koko Head.

Tennis buffs should head for **Kapiolani Tennis Courts** (four courts, lighted) or the **Ilikai Hotel** (five courts, 7:00 a.m. to 5:00 p.m., 949-3811).

Greater Honolulu has one pretty beach at **Diamond Head Beach Park**, directly below the crater and backed by cliffs. Snorkeling and windsurfing are good but swimming isn't, and the park usually swarms with tourists and, on weekends, locals. Visit Diamond Head Beach Park and **Aloha Windsurfing** (926-1185) for gear and instruction. I love swimming in Hanauma Bay at **Koko Head Regional Park**, but it's essential to get there early in the morning before the crowds. Bodysurf at **Makapuu Beach** beyond Koko Head beaches, or at the Diamond Head end of **Prince** and **Kuhio beaches**. Board-surf at the

Waikiki Beach, Ala Moana Beach, Diamond Head Beach, and **Barbers Point**. Contact **Local Motion Surfboards** (944-8515) and **Waikiki Beach Services** (923-3111) for gear and instruction.

Hanauma Bay (early in the morning) and **Sans Souci Beach** are best for novice divers and snorkelers. More experienced divers will try **Manana ("Rabbit") Island, Makapuu Point**, and **Fantasy Reef** (off Waialae Beach at Kahala). In summer experienced snorkelers will find a friendly assortment of fish at **Black Point** and **Pupukea Bay Beach**. For diving excursions, gear, and instruction, contact **Dan's Dive Shop** (next to Little George's restaurant on Ala Moana Boulevard, 536-6181) or **Waikiki Diving** in two locations (420 Nahua and 1734 Kalakua, 922-7188). For snorkeling equipment rental, contact **Fort DeRussy Beach Services** (949-3469), **South Sea Aquatics** (538-3854), or **Blue Water Snorkel** (926-4485).

Look for free local tourist magazines to clip discount coupons for dinner cruises. Most depart from the Kewalo Basin Marina, near Fisherman's Wharf, about 6:30 p.m. and return at 8:30 p.m., for $35 to $50 per person. Pearl Harbor cruises, sunset cruises and Waikiki-Diamond Head cruises are offered by **Hawaiian Cruises Ltd.** (923-2061); sunset and dinner cruises can be arranged with **Windjammer Cruises** (521-0036).

For people like me who hate to get seasick, especially during a lunch cruise, take the ***Navatck I*** (848-6360 or 800-852-4183), a 140-foot, double-hulled catamaran designed using advanced SWATH technology and computer-controlled ballast to improve stability.

The waters offshore Oahu are full of ahi, ono, opakapaka, aku, mahi mahi, au, and marlin. The fishing charters moor at Kewalo Basin and include **Island Charters** (536-1555), **Coreene-C's Charters** (536-7472), and **Sport Fishing Hawaii** (536-6577). **Kono Fishing Charters** (536-7472) is gyro-stabilized for smooth riding in rough waters while pursuing elusive big game fish.

FOOD

Eggs 'n' Things (1911 B Kalakaua Avenue, 949-0820) has served my favorite pancake breakfasts with endless Kona coffee for decades, and now they fill crepes with fresh papaya. If your day starts near Aloha Tower and the harbor, have a giant muffin at **Heidi's Downtown Bistro** (Grosvenor Center, 536-5344).

Hee Hing Restaurant (Diamond Head Center, 449 Kapahulu Avenue, 735-5544) offers delightful dim sum lunches. You'll find

HONOLULU

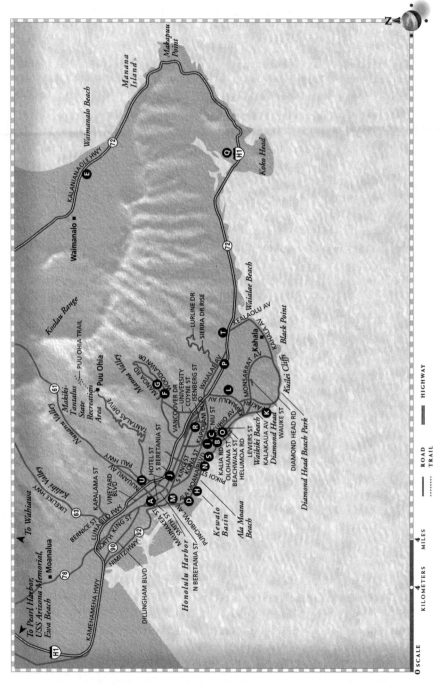

Z

Makapuu Point

Manana Island

Waimanalo Beach

KALANIANAOLE HWY

E

Waimanalo

Q   H1

Koko Head

72

Koolau Range

PUU OHIA TRAIL

Nuuanu Valley

Makiki-Tantalus State Recreation Area

Puu Ohia

61

LURLINE DR

SIERRA DR RISE

Waialae Beach

KEALAOLU AV

T

Black Point

Kahala

KAHALA AV

Kuilei Cliffs

MANOA RD

WOODLAWN DR

TANTALUS DRIVE

MANOA VALLEY

VANCOUVER DR

UNIVERSITY

COYNE ST

ISENBERG ST

KAPIOLANI BLVD

WAIALAE AV

MONSARRAT AV

F   G

P

L

Pali Hwy

Nuuanu Valley

PALI HWY

HOTEL ST

S BERETANIA ST

S KING ST

KONA ST

KALAKAUA AV

KAPIOLANI BLVD

NIU ST

R

I   C

B

N   S

KALIA RD

OHUA ST

OLOHANA ST

BEACHWALK ST

HELUMOA RD

LEVERS ST

Waikiki Beach

KALAKAUA AV

WAUKE ST

Diamond Head

DIAMOND HEAD RD

K

O

ALA WAI BLVD

PIIKOI ST

NUUANU AV

KAPALAMA ST

VINEYARD BLVD

Kalihi Valley

LIKELIKE HWY

To Wahiawa

63

BERNICE ST

LUNALILO FRWY

NORTH KING ST

N BERETANIA ST

SMITH ST

MAUNAKEA ST

A

U

M

J

D

H

ALA MOANA BLVD

PUNCHBOWL ST

Kewalo Basin

Ala Moana Beach

Diamond Head Beach Park

90

92

NIMITZ HWY

DILLINGHAM BLVD

Honolulu Harbor

KAMEHAMEHA HWY

78

To Pearl Harbor, USS Arizona Memorial, Moanalua

Ewa Beach

H1

To Pearl Harbor,
USS Arizona Memorial,
Moanalua

72

0 SCALE   4
          KILOMETERS   MILES
                  4

ROAD   HIGHWAY

TRAIL

Food

Ⓐ A Little Bit of Saigon

Ⓑ Bali-by-the-Sea

Ⓒ Cascada

Ⓓ The Chowder House

Ⓐ Buddhist Vegetarian Restaurant

Ⓔ Bueno Nalo

Ⓕ Cafe Brio

Ⓖ Cousin's

Ⓗ Crepe Fever

Ⓘ Eggs 'n' Things

Ⓙ The Garden Cafe

Ⓑ Golden Dragon

Ⓑ Harlequin

Ⓚ Hau Tree Lanai

Ⓛ Hee Hing Restaurant

Ⓜ Heidi's Downtown Bistro

Ⓑ Hilton Hawaiian Village Hotel

Ⓝ I Love Country Cafe

Ⓞ International Marketplace

Ⓛ Keo's Thai Cuisine

Ⓒ Kyoya Restaurant

Ⓞ La Mer

Ⓐ Legend Seafood Restaurant

Ⓡ Maple Garden

Ⓝ Makai Market Food Court

Ⓐ Maunakea Marketplace

Ⓚ Michel's at the Colony Surf

Ⓐ My Canh

Ⓟ On the Rise

Ⓛ Ono Hawaiian Food

Ⓞ Orchids

Ⓞ Parc Café

Ⓝ Qintero's Restaurant

Ⓠ Roy's Restaurant

Ⓐ Sea Fortunes

Ⓢ Takanawa

Ⓗ Ward Center

Ⓐ Wo Fat's

Ⓐ Won Kee Seafood Yen King

Ⓣ Yen Ying

Ⓗ Yum Yum Tree

Ⓤ Yung's Kitchen

Note: Items with the same letter are located in the same area of town everything imaginable at rock-bottom prices at **Yen King** (Kahala Mall, 4211 Waialae Avenue, 732-5505). **The Garden Cafe** at the Honolulu Academy of Arts (532-8734) is still one of my favorite lunch places, probably because of the combination of sculpture and tempting desserts. Get *lomilomi* takeout from **Ono Hawaiian Foods** (726 Kapahulu Avenue, 737-2275) for a picnic at Kapiolani Park. Pasta is the favorite at **Michel's at the Colony Surf** (2895 Kalakaua Avenue, 923-6552). The view is hard to beat alfresco at the **Hau Tree Lanai** (New Otani Kaimana Beach Hotel, 2863 Kalakaua Avenue, 923-1555). Enjoy a buffet or Sunday brunch at the **Parc Café** (Waikiki Parc Hotel, 2233 Helumoa Road, 921-7272). No trip to Manoa Valley to hike in the rainforests is complete without lunch at **Cafe Brio** (2756 Woodland Drive, Manoa Marketplace, 988-5555). For a quick and cheap picnic in Manoa Valley, try a plate lunch from **Cousin's** (2970 E. Manoa Road, 988-5592). The food court at the **International Marketplace** in Waikiki offers a wide variety of budget food: Mexican, Hawaiian, Korean, Chinese, Japanese, Thai, Italian, and American. Most meals are aroung $5 and filling.

A Pacific Rim–style lunch at the **Maunakea Marketplace** (1120 Maunakea Street) fits comfortably into tight budgets. If Asian fast food at the **Makai Market Food Court** at Ala Moana Shopping Center is not for you, at 451 Piikoi Street, behind Ala Moana, you'll find tasty vegetarian entrees at the **I Love Country Cafe** (526-3927). On the same street, **Qintero's** (1102 Piikoi, 593-1561) serves great Mexican combination plates. The only other Mexican food I'm ever tempted to eat on Oahu is at **Bueno Nalo** (259-7186), on Kam Highway in Waimanolo. Nearby **Ward Center** offers many excellent restaurants, but spend less for more and enjoy a gourmet vegetarian meal at **Crepe Fever** (521-9023). Then trash your diet at the **Yum Yum Tree** with a super slice of pie. At Ward Warehouse, you can get *mahimahi* in ginger sauce and the fixins for $10 at **The Chowder House** (521-56812). If you can squeeze it in, **Legend Seafood Restaurant** (North Bertania Street, 532-1868) will spoil you and hardly dent your pocket. My friends rave about **A Little Bit of Saigon** (1160 Maunakea Street, 528-3663) and I counter with the less sophisticated **My Canh** (164 North King Street, 599-1866).

The ultimate in fine Hawaii dining is **Roy's Restaurant** (Hawaii Kai Corporate Plaza, 6600 Kalanianaole Highway, 396-7697). **La Mer** (Halekulani Hotel) offers amazing fish dishes. (In the same hotel, I suggest breakfast or lunch on the terrace at **Orchids**, 923-2311.) The sushi at **Takanawa** (Hawaii Prince Hotel, 100 Holomoana Street, 956-

1111) is as good as any you'll find in Hawaii. There are several good restaurants at the **Hilton Hawaiian Village Hotel** (2005 Kalia Road). Try the wonderful crispy lemon chicken or Imperial Beggar's chicken at the elegant **Golden Dragon** (946-5336). For delicious Pacific Rim cuisine, dine at **Bali-by-the-Sea** (941-2254), **Cascada** (Royal Garden at Waikiki Hotel, 440 Olohana Street, 943-0202), **Harlequin** (Alana Waikiki Hotel, 1956 Ala Moana Boulevard, 941-7275), or **On the Rise** (3660 Wauakae Avenue, 737-1177). If you enjoy Thai food, definitely dine at **Keo's Thai Cuisine** (625 Kapahulu Avenue, 737-8240; 1486 S. King Street, 947-9988), and **Ward Centre**, (1200 Ala Moana Boulevard, 596-0020, reservations a must). Try the "Evil Jungle Prince" or my favorite, panang curry.

In 1986, **Wo Fat's** (115 Hotel Street, 537-6260) celebrated its 100th anniversary as Honolulu's premier Chinese restaurant. **Sea Fortune**, next door to Wo Fat's, at 111 King Street, is a dim sum dream. **Yung's Kitchen** at 1170 Nuuanu Avenue is practically next door to Pegge Hopper's gallery. It serves some of Hawaii's best Chinese dishes in a no-frills dining room, which closes at 11:30 p.m. **Won Kee Seafood Restaurant**, Chinese Cultural Plaza, 100 N. Beretania Street, will stretch your budget a bit with every imaginable seafood dish—fried, steamed, baked, marinated, or otherwise Won Kee'd—but the result is one of the very best in the state. **Kyoya Restaurant** (2057 Kalakaua Avenue, 947-3911) combines gracious friendliness, atmosphere, excellent food, and moderate prices. Try the **Buddhist Vegetarian Restaurant** in Chinatown's Cultural Plaza (100 North Bertania Street, 532-8218) for stir-fried noodles or 50 other culinary wonders. Szechuan food is the fare at **Maple Garden** (909 Isenberg Street, 941-6641).

LODGING

The **Outrigger** hotels (800-462-6262) are hard to beat for reasonable prices, cleanliness, location, and other values. My favorites consistently are the **Outrigger Reef** (2169 Kalia Road, 923-3111) and, next door, the **Outrigger Edgewater** (2168 Kalia Road, 922-6424). For a view of Kapiolani Park, choose the **Queen Kapiolani** (150 Kapahula Avenue, 922-1941 or 800-367-5004). For great ocean views and economy, choose the **Waikiki Terrace** (2045 Kalakaua Avenue, 955-6000 or 800-445-8811). My budget choices still are the **Outrigger Waikiki Surf East and West** (2200 Kuhio Avenue, 923-7671).

HONOLULU

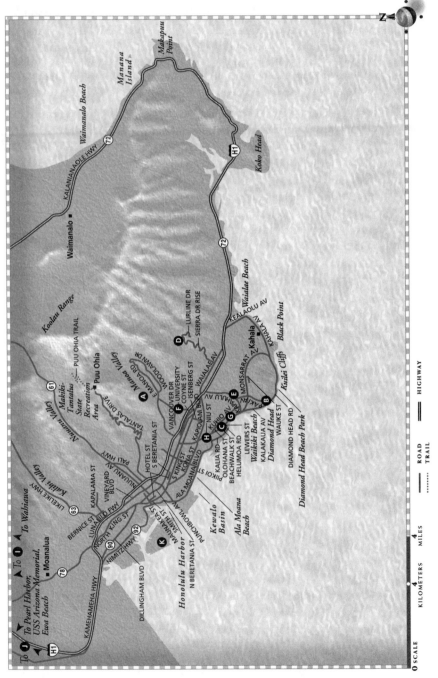

Lodging

- **A** B&B Manoa
- **B** Diamond Head Beach Hotel
- **C** Hawaiiana
- **C** Hawaiian Monarch
- **C** Niihau Apartment Hotel
- **C** Outrigger Edgewater
- **C** Outrigger Reef
- **C** Outrigger Waikiki Surf East and West
- **D** Paula Luv
- **E** Queen Kapiolani
- **C** Royal Garden at Waikiki
- **F** Victorian Manoa Valley Inn
- **G** Waikiki Beachcomber Hotel
- **C** Waikiki Joy
- **H** Waikiki Terrace

Camping

- **I** Kahe campground
- **J** Keaau campground
- **J** Keaiwa Heiau State Recreation Area
- **J** Luaualei campground
- **J** Nanakuli campground
- **K** Sand Island State Campground

Note: Items with the same letter are located in the same town or area

If you can't find what you're looking for through Outrigger Hotels, contact **Aston Hotels and Resorts** (800-922-7866) and ask about the **Hawaiian Monarch** (444 Niu Street, 949-3911 or 800-535-0085), with rooms from $65 to $84 off-season without kitchenettes, $80 to $98 in season. Look on Beach Walk, the quiet little street that runs from Kalakaua down to the beach, for more of the best accommodation bargains in Waikiki. You can get a small one-bedroom apartment for $60 to $75, without tub or free local calls but right near the beach, at the **Niihau Apartment Hotel** (247 Beach Walk, 922-1607). Other special favorites include: the upper floor suites of the **Waikiki Joy** (320 Lewers, 923-2300 or 800-922-7866); near the beach with kitchenettes, **Hawaiiana** (260 Beach Walk, 923-3811 or 800-367-5122); my moderate price all-around choices, **Royal Garden at Waikiki** (440 Olohana Street, 943-0202 or 800-367-5666) and **Waikiki Beachcomber Hotel** (2300 Kalakaua Avenue, 922-4646 or 800-622-4646); and, for peace and price, **Diamond Head Beach Hotel** (2947 Kalakaua Avenue, 922-1928 or 800-367-6046).

My favorite B&B belongs to charming **Paula Luv** (3843 Lurline Drive, Honolulu, HI 96816, 737-8011), folk dancer, instructor, and Pacific region traveler. Atop Wilhelmina Rise with a magnificent view of Diamond Head and Honolulu, a room and private bath with a huge breakfast is only $35 per night.

For a special treat in Manoa Valley, stay at the **Victorian Manoa Valley Inn** (2001 Vancouver Drive, 947-6019 or 800-634-5115), or the more modest **B&B Manoa** (988-6333).

CAMPING

Near Honolulu, camping is permitted at **Sand Island State Campground** in Honolulu Harbor. North of Honolulu, in the Koolau foothills, tent camping is available at **Keaiwa Heiau State Recreation Area**, surrounded by a forest with a network of trails. (Take Highway 90 west to Aiea, Aiea Heights Drive *mauka* to the park.) There's a five-day limit and no camping on Wednesdays or Thursdays. Throughout Oahu, camping is permitted at 15 county beach parks, Fridays through Wednesdays. On the leeward coast, you'll find other excellent campgrounds at Kahe, Keaau, Luaualei, and Nanakuli. For more information, contact the Department of Land and Natural Resources, Division of State Parks, 1151 Punchbowl Street, Room 310, Honolulu HI 96813, 548-7455.

NIGHTLIFE

For disco try the multilevel **Rascals** (2301 Kuhio Mall, 2nd floor, 922-5566) or the **Red Lion Dance Palace** (240 Lewers Street), where a disco-video system keeps the dance floor crowded. Both are open until 4:00 a.m. The **Blue Water Seafood** (2350 Kuhio Avenue, 926-2191), also has disco-videos. **Hawaiian Regent Hotel** (922-6611) has two dance floors and video dancing until 4:00 a.m. Other dance spots include **Hyatt Regency Waikiki** (922-9292), **Harry's Bar, Trappers,** and **Spats.**

Hear ukulele music from 9:00 p.m. to midnight on Sunday nights at **Buzz's Original Steak House** (2535 Coyne Street, 944-9781). Try low-key guitar music at the **Seafood Emporium** Wednesday through Sunday nights (2201 Kala Kaua, 922-5547) or at **Trader Vic's** (923-1581) daily. The **Jazz Cellar** (205 Lewers Street, 923-9952) has live rock and jazz until 4:00 a.m. **Garden Bar** and **La Mex** in the Royal Hawaiian Shopping Center (926-2000), **Sheraton Moana Hotel** (922-3111), and **Sheraton Princess Haiulani** (922-5811) also offer nightly entertainment.

Robert and Roland Cazimero (The Brothers Cazimero) and their hula dancers offer up a blend of traditional Hawaiian and contemporary music Tuesdays through Saturdays in the Monarch Room of the **Royal Hawaiian Hotel**, Waikiki (923-7311). Danny Kaleikini, hula dancers, and other musicians perform at the **Kahala Hilton Hotel** (734-2211). For an unforgettable experience, see the *imu* ceremony, torchlighting ritual, beachfront *hukilau* (communal net fishing), Polynesian review, arts and crafts display, and luau at **Paradise Cove Luau** (973-5828). Another outstanding cultural dance show is provided by dancers from Fiji, Samoa, New Zealand, and Tahiti at the **Ainahau Showroom**, Sheraton Princess Jaiulani Hotel, Waikiki (922-5811). The **Sea Life Park Hawaiian Revue** (259-7933), a Polynesian show, performs on Thursdays and Sundays at 8:30 p.m. The cost is included in park admission. **Kumu Kahua Theater Company** produces plays about Hawaii on the grounds of St. Andrews Cathedral (224 St. Emma Square, 599-1503). The **John F. Kennedy Theater**, University of Hawaii-Manoa (948-7655), produces Chinese opera, Kanuki, Noh plays, and also American musicals.

For up-to-date choices and information, consult the free *This Week in Oahu*, a valuable guidebook found at all hotels.

WINDWARD COAST

There are two quite different ways to reach the incoming tradewinds of Oahu's eastern coast. One is past Koko Head, where daredevil bodysurfers brave brutal Makapuu and Sandy Beach. Driving beneath hang-glider specks sweeping over Makapuu's 1,200-foot cliffs (pali), you'll skirt the caldera of an extinct volcano, emerald-blue Hanauma. You'll also see porpoises blissfully leap through leis at nearby Sea Life Park. My favorite route, however, is directly up the steep Pali Highway past spectacular vistas from Nuuanu Pali Lookout, and over the Koolau Mountains. Stretching due north from Makapuu to Kahuku, the Windward Coast embraces the famous Polynesian Cultural Center and its parent, The Mormon Temple, otherwise known as the "Taj Mahal of the Pacific." Where this highway audaciously breaks the pali, you hover breathlessly above Kailua's and Kaneohe's tame suburban tracts and fine swimming beaches, especially the little hidden gem, Lanikai. Views from these mysterious crenellated cliffs that parallel the coast look out over a scattering of Asian temples, remnants of Hawaiian fishponds (that used to number nearly 100 on Oahu), and tiny islands with quaint names like Chinaman's Hat and Rabbit Island, a sanctuary for seabirds that has never seen a stray bunny. In the distance, taro and anthurium sprout in the Waiahole and Waikane valleys, where Hawaiians tenaciously hold on to their precarious rural lifestyles. A third road, Kamehameha Highway, heads through soothing curves towards Kahana Bay Beach Park. Shaded by dense ironwoods, Kahana offers a perfect stopping place just before the road bends toward Laie, replicas of Polynesian villages, and the North Shore's monster surf beaches. ◼

WINDWARD COAST

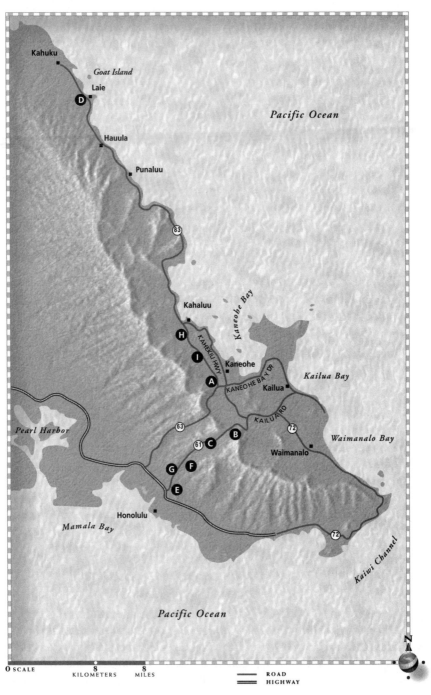

Sightseeing Highlights

Ⓐ Haiku Gardens

Ⓑ Nuuanu Pali Lookout

Ⓒ Pali Highway

Ⓓ Polynesian Cultural Center

Ⓔ Punchbowl Memorial

Ⓕ Queen Emma's Summer Palace

Ⓖ Royal Mausoleum

Ⓗ Senator Fong's Plantation and Gardens

Ⓘ Valley of the Temples Memorial Park

A PERFECT DAY ON THE WINDWARD COAST

Stop briefly at the Honolulu Memorial Park to see replicas of Japanese buildings in a picturesque setting next to Nuuanu Stream. Visit the Royal Mausoleum, then tour Queen Emma's Summer Palace. Turn on Nuuanu Pali Drive through the rainforest to the Pali Lookout over the windward coast. Afterwards, combine a stop at the lovely Haiku Gardens with a pleasant open-air lunch at the Haiku Charthouse. Continue to the Valley of the Temples, and visit the beautiful Byodo-In Temple at the back. Stay on Kahekili Highway (83) around Kaneohe Bay to scenic Kualoa Beach Park. Offshore is Chinaman's Hat, and inland is the spectacular Ko'olau wall. Drive past a series of picturesque bays and hamlets, green valleys and mostly empty beach parks, and Kahana Valley State Park to Sacred Falls State Park. At the end of a mile-long, uphill hike is another of my favorite picnic spots, especially nice after a swim in the pool under the falls. Bodysurfers should wait for nearby Pounders Beach, near the Mormon town of Laie and the Polynesian Cultural Center. Spend the afternoon there and then return at 7:30 p.m. for the Polynesian review.

SIGHTSEEING HIGHLIGHTS

★★★ **Nuuanu Pali Lookout**—This lookout offers spectacular sunset-watching as well as a magnificent morning view of windward Oahu in clear weather. Walk down to the old road for even better views. (1 hour)

★★★ **Pali Highway**—Highway 61 through Nuuanu Valley cuts across Oahu from Honolulu to the windward coast, passing a series of the region's outstanding sightseeing attractions. The off-ramp into Nuuanu Valley passes lush highlands and Queen Emma's Summer Palace, the royal retreat in the 1800s and now a museum (see page 51). Before the breathtaking overlook, turn onto Nuuanu Pali Drive, which winds back to the highway. (1–2 hours)

★★★ **Polynesian Cultural Center**—In 1963 the Church of Jesus Christ of the Latter Day Saints decided to package Polynesia into a highly successful theme park. The Polynesian Cultural Center, located in Laie, center of the Mormon church in Hawaii, is a unique educational experience worth its stiff price.

The core of the 42-acre PCC is its seven re-created villages: six Polynesian and one Melanesian—Hawaii, Samoa, Tonga, the Marquesas, Fiji, New Zealand, and Tahiti. Each village displays excellent craftsmanship in construction and handicrafts native to the particular cultural homeland. Guides native to each island explain the cultural background of the homeland and talk about the foods and handcrafts exhibited. Walk, take a shuttle tram, or tour the area by canoe over artesian-fed waterways.

"This Is Polynesia," the very exciting and moving 90-minute dinner show of music, dance, and historical drama begins at 7:30. An all-you-can-eat dinner is served at the center's Gateway Restaurant. At the end of the day, after the buffet dinner, a 70-foot by 130-foot-wide screen in a new theater shows a 40-minute adventure film about the Pacific region.

Packages ranging from $40 to $72 include assorted combinations of entertainment and meals in addition to admission to the seven Polynesian villages and craft and hula demonstrations. Book round-trip transportation for about $12 per adult. Better still, incorporate an all-afternoon and evening trip to the PCC with an all-morning excursion from Honolulu to Laie. Watch for special discounts that may be offered by tour operators or advertised in *This Week in Oahu*. Hours: Open Monday–Saturday from 12:30 to 9:00 p.m. Phone: 293-3333. (5–8 hours)

☆☆ **Punchbowl Memorial**—The National Memorial Cemetery of the Pacific is on the 112-acre floor of a long-extinct volcano. The almost perfectly round Punchbowl Crater was called Puowaina ("Hill of Sacrifice") by the ancient Hawaiians. Take a moment to reflect on the price of war: more than 30,000 service people are buried here, and over 26,000 are listed as missing in action. The lookout at the top of the crater offers a great view of Honolulu. To get there, take Punchbowl Avenue where it crosses King, go under the freeway, and watch for signs to Punchbowl Memorial. Take a right on Puowaina Street into the crater. Hours: Open daily 8:00 a.m. to 5:30 p.m. October through March, 8:00 a.m. to 6:30 p.m. March through September. Address: 2177 Puowaina Drive. Phone: 546-3190. (1 hour)

☆☆ **Senator Fong's Plantation and Gardens**—This lush 725-acre attraction in Eisenhower Valley contains the visitors center; Kennedy orchards and 75 varieties of edible trees and plants; Nixon Valley and its traditional ethnic gardens (Japanese, Chinese, Filipino, and Hawaiian); and Ford Plateau, a pine garden. Take the 3-mile, 40-minute guided mini-bus tour (10:30 a.m., 11:30 a.m., 1:00, and 2:00 p.m.). Admission is $6.50 for adults, $3 for children ages 5–12, under 5 free. Address: 47-285 Pulama Road, a mile from the junction of Highway 83 and Kahekili Highway. Phone: 239-6775. (2 hours)

☆ **Haiku Gardens**—Once a getaway for ancient Hawaiians, this 16-acre site was deeded to an Englishman in the mid-1800s by Hawaiian ali'i. Acres of exotic plants, streams, picturesque lily ponds and tropical fish ponds, bamboo groves, and huge banyan trees are the foreground for spectacular Koolau cliffs rising up from the dense foliage. On Saturdays, weddings take place in a thatched-roof hut tucked into the tropical vegetation. A Chart House restaurant (247-6671) now overlooks the *pali* cliffs and garden. Address: 46-316 Haiku Road. (1 hour)

☆ **Queen Emma's Summer Palace**—The wife of Kamehameha IV built her white frame house, now a museum, in the cool hills to escape the summer heat. This area was Honolulu's first suburb. Watch closely for the Pali Highway turnoff sign on the right so that you don't miss it. Be sure to see the Shinto shrine of Daijingu behind the palace. Admission is $4 for adults, $1 for children ages 12–18. Hours: Open daily 9:00 a.m. to 4:00 p.m. Address: 2913 Pali Highway. Phone: 595-3167. (½ hour)

✸ **Royal Mausoleum** contains the final resting place of every modern Hawaiian king and queen except King Kamehameha the Great and King William Lunalilo. Lydia Namahana Maioho, curator, and her son, William, will provide a memorable tour of this sacred place. (½ hour)

✸ **Valley of the Temples Memorial Park**—In Kaneohe, turn onto Kahekili Highway (83) to the entrance to this universal faith cemetery. Set in a classic Japanese garden with swans and peacocks, the center-piece of the park is the ornate Buddhist Byodo-In Temple ("Temple of Equality"), a replica of the famous 900-year-old Byodo-In Temple of Kyoto. From the pagoda (Meditation House) at the top of the hill is the best view of the grounds. Admission is $2 for adults, $1 for those under 12 and over 55. Address: 47-200 Kahekili Highway. Phone: 239-8811. (½ hour)

FITNESS AND RECREATION

In Kaneohe, stroll through the **Hoomaluhia Botanical Garden**, under the towering palis (233-7323). After leaving the Byodo-In Temple, continue on Kam Highway past Kaneohe to **Heeia State Park**, an ideal picnic site on a beautiful small peninsula overlooking Heeia Fishpond, one of the few left on the island and the largest. Just south of the village of Hauula, a clear pool at the base of an 80-foot waterfall awaits travelers determined to hike 2.2 miles up a rough trail (treacherous when muddy after rains) through dense vegetation for about an hour to **Sacred Falls**. In **Kahana Valley State Park**, a 5-mile trail past old Hawaiian farms winds deep into **Kahana Valley**.

A favorite route for bicyclists: drive out Highway 83 to Kaneohe Bay with a bike, then pedal north to Laie. **Kualoa Ranch** (237-8515) has horseback rides for $20 per hour, $30 for two hours.

Pali municipal golf course (par 72, 6,950 yards), in Kaneohe at the base of a huge cliff, is a beautiful and challenging course; get there early (296-7254).

For very pretty and superb beaches that rival those on other islands, spend some time in the **Kailua, Lanikai** (next to the more crowded Kailua Beach Park), and **Laie** areas. Visit **Waimanalo Beach** in Waimanalo. **Malaekahana Bay**, past the Mormon Temple and Laie, offers one of the few safe swimming beaches year-round. Board- and bodysurf at **Kalama Beach** (Kailua) between Kalaka Place and Kaiona Place. My secret snorkeling and diving spot is the reefs at secluded **Laie Beach** (between Laie and Laniloa Point), best suited for more experienced divers. **Kailua Beach Park** and **Windsurfing Hawaii** (261-3539) can set you up with gear and provide instruction. Large schools of delicious *akule* (big-eyed scad) visit Kahana Bay about 15 miles north of Kaneohe. Hawaiians living in the valley built shrines on bluffs surrounding the bay and the fishponds. **Kahana Bay County Park** has camping, picnic, and other facilities and good swimming and bodysurfing.

    Pounders Beach (appropriately named for its pounding surf) near the Polynesian Cultural Center is privately owned but open to the public and has no facilities. The mile-long beach in the armpit of **Laie Point**, reached by a stairway down the rocks through a right-of-way half-way up the peninsula, is one of the liveliest in Hawaii. Midway down the beach, look for an opening in the coral for extended, protected swimming and snorkeling. Shade trees make picnicking perfect on this beach.

    Malaekahana State Recreation Area is one of the island's prettiest parks. For campers, this beach should be the choice destination along the windward coast—it's insulated from the highway by shade trees. Don't miss wading over to **Mokuauia** ("Goat") **Island,** in water that's shallow on calm days, waist-high on others. The white sand beach on the leeward side of this bird refuge is a dream South Pacific getaway and wins the prize for seclusion.

FOOD

The **Windward Mall** in Kaneohe provides most of the inexpensive eating on this part of the island. The **Yummy Korea BBQ, Deli Express, Taco Shop, Cinnabon's** cinnamon rolls, **Harpo's** excellent deep-dish pizza, **Patti's Chinese Kitchen**, and **Little Tokyo** offer variety and filling portions.

    When you drive on the Kam Highway to Kahuku and see a bunch of people and parked cars, you're probably looking at the roadside stand of the **Amorient Aquafarm**, a 175-acre shrimp and fish farm. You can see the 1-acre ponds from the highway and the stand. Open 10:00 a.m. to 5:30 p.m. Sample the cooked shrimp tempura, cooked shrimp tails, or shrimp cocktail.

LODGING

The reef in front of Hauula's Halehaha Beach shelters a shoreline with condominium units known as **Pat's at Punaluu** (53-567 Kamehameha Highway, Hauula, 293-8111). The 30 to 40 units for rent in this building (others house permanent residents) start at $65. Pat's

WINDWARD COAST

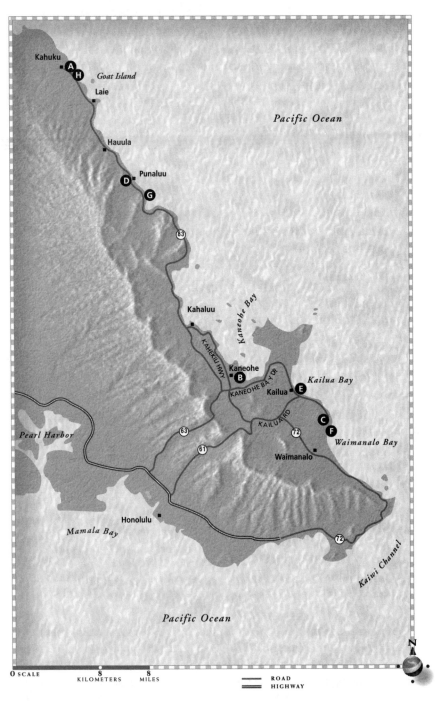

Food

- **Ⓐ** Amorient Aquafarm
- **Ⓑ** Cinnabon's
- **Ⓑ** Deli Express
- **Ⓑ** Harpo's
- **Ⓑ** Little Tokyo
- **Ⓑ** Patti's Chinese Kitchen
- **Ⓑ** Taco Shop
- **Ⓑ** The Windward Mall
- **Ⓑ** Yummy Korea BBQ

Lodging

- **Ⓒ** Akamai B&B
- **Ⓓ** Countryside Cabins
- **Ⓔ** Kailua Beachside Cottage
- **Ⓓ** Pat's at Punaluu
- **Ⓒ** Windward B&B

Camping

- **Ⓕ** Bellows Field Beach Park
- **Ⓖ** Kahana Bay Beach Park
- **Ⓗ** Malaekahana Bay State Recreation Area

Note: Items with the same letter are located in the same town or area

features a swimming pool, a sauna, a gym, and the popular Pat's at Punaluu restaurant (293-8502), where you can get breakfast, lunch, and dinner. About halfway between the Paniolo and Pat's, is Margaret Neal's **Countryside Cabins**, a tradition for budget travelers (53-224 Kamehameha Highway, Hauula, HI 96717, 237-8169). It is simply announced by an easily missed white sign that says "Cabins." Clean but rustic studios are $40 a night and $190 a week, in one of Oahu's prettiest coastal areas.

Wendy Judy's **Akamai B&B** (263-0227) offers two large studios, with a pool and near the beach, for $69 per night or $380 per week, with special rates for seniors. Minimum stay is three nights. If Judy's is full, she'll fix you up at one of the 26 other B&Bs.

Base yourself in Kailua at **Kailua Beachside Cottage** (262-4128) or the **Windward B&B** (235-1124). If you're looking for accommodations in Kailua, Kalaheo, and along the windward coast, call Grace Dowling at **Pacific Hawaii Bed & Breakfast** (262-6062, 263-4848, or 800-999-6026). Grace has a variety of really nice one- or two-bedroom cottages for $65 to $85 per night (with cooking facilities and no breakfasts), rooms with breakfast starting at $45 (share baths), and studios at $55 to $75. Grace also offers a B&B on Lanai (Lanai City) at $75, and a couple of units on Molokai, all of which are clean and pleasant with hospitable hosts. Or contact **Hawaiian Islands B&B** (800-258-7895) to find yourself the right B&B locations on the windward side.

CAMPING

Camping is available on weekends only at **Bellows Field Beach Park**, near the ironwoods that ring the beach. You'll need a permit, which can be obtained in person from the Department of Land and Natural Resources, Division of State Parks, 1151 Punchbowl Street, Room 310, Honolulu, HI 96813, 548-7455.

At beautiful **Malaekahana Bay State Recreation Area**, tent camping (county permit required) is idyllic; housekeeping cabins are also available. Or carry your gear over to Goat Island for unofficial camping. **Kahana Bay Beach Park** has a white sand beach that is excellent for camping (county permit required) and a 5-mile hiking trail into Kahana Valley State Park. Other excellent campgrounds are at Punaluu and Swanzy.

3
NORTH SHORE

The North Shore's first and only major hotel and resort, the Turtle Bay Hilton and Country Club, hardly prepares unsuspecting visitors for the huge tubes of surf that crash at Banzai Pipeline, Waimea Bay and Sunset Point—especially when winter swells are breaking like 30-foot jackhammers. Surfers stand around talking quietly, respectfully, about the "time when . . . ." The best place to see surfers riding tinderwood across the exploding waves is from above Waimea Bay. In Haleiwa, where the North Shore is more tame, Hawaiians, hippies, and a conglomeration of Japanese, Filipinos and others have shared a gradually changing community for the past forty years. Comfortably congenial boutiques, funky natural foods shops, and lots of good coffee share the scene with Matsumoto's one-of-a-kind "rainbow" shave-ice. Beyond Haleiwa and the picturesque plantation town of Waialua, the beautiful sands of Mokuleia are hidden *mauka* Farrington Highway. It's true that Prince Charles played polo matches here at the Mokuleia Polo Farm, and on Sundays country etiquette continues to blend with fierce competition in the shadows of Mount Kaala, Oahu's highest peak. The Waianae range extends down to the rugged, desolately beautiful Kaena Point, producing thermal currents that sustain soaring and diving in Hawaii's only glider area. ◼

NORTH SHORE

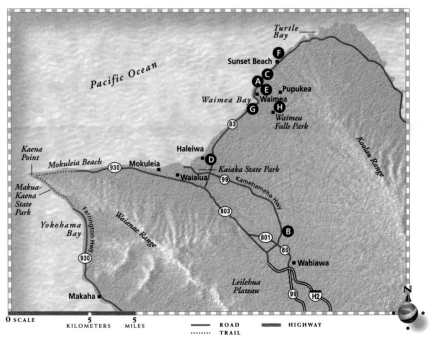

Sightseeing Highlights

- **A** Banzai Pipeline
- **B** Dole Pineapple Pavilion
- **C** Ehukai Beach
- **D** Haleiwa
- **E** Puu O Mahuka Heiau
- **F** Sunset Beach
- **G** Waimea Bay
- **H** Waimea Falls Park

A PERFECT DAY ON THE NORTH SHORE

S tart the day in Haleiwa at the Coffee Gallery, Café Haleiwa, or with the *kamaainas* at Rosy's Cantina. Haleiwa certainly was more charming when I first visited it in 1957, but it still has a lot of character. One of my favorite places in all of Hawaii is the 1,800-acre Waimea Falls Park and Valley, especially the Waimea Falls Arboretum and Botanical Gardens. Maybe you'll see *nene* geese in this paradise. I recommend having lunch at the Proud Peacock's terrace. But save dessert for the shaved ice at Matsumoto's. Head back to Waimea Falls Park for a memorable escorted walk on a full-moon night.

SIGHTSEEING HIGHLIGHTS

✰✰✰ **Waimea Falls Park**—The entrance to this privately owned 1,800-acre nature reserve is several miles inside a lush valley once inhabited by thousands of Hawaiians. Primarily a botanical garden, the park includes entertainment such as hula dancers, and divers who plunge 55 feet into the pool below the falls. You can swim at the base of the falls, walk on beautiful trails, or just stroll around the central meadow's **Waimea Arboretum and Botanical Gardens** with or without a free guided tour. You'll also see some Hawaiian wildlife—nene geese, "Kona nightingales" (wild donkeys), and wild boar. For visitors to the islands, admission is $14.95 for adults, $7.95 for children ages 7 to 12, and $2.25 for children ages 4 to 6. On weekends, the park can be quite crowded, but trails up the hillsides offer an escape. Ride the open-air tram to the top of the valley and walk down. Spend the whole day, if possible, and take a moonlit walk before dining at the Proud Peacock restaurant (closes at 9:00 p.m.). Hours: The park is open from 10:00 a.m. to 5:30 p.m. Phone: 638-8511. (5–8 hours)

✰✰ **Haleiwa**—Amazingly, Haleiwa (which means "House of the Frigate Bird") is among the only towns or villages along Oahu's coastline that preserves any of its original rural charm, today combined with boutiques, gift shops, and art galleries. The down-home country atmosphere is also preserved in neighboring **Waialua**, an old plantation town where R. Fujioka & Sons Ltd. has run a grocery store next to twin gas pumps for 50 years, and the local bank is now the Sugar Bar and Restaurant. (3–4 hours)

✰ **Dole Pineapple Pavilion**—Highway 930-803 from Mokuleia and

Highway 83 from Haleiwa rise through endless rows of pineapples up the 1,000-foot Leilehua Plateau toward Wahiawa, then split again into Kam Highway and Kaukonahua Highway (Highway 803/801). James Dole started his first cannery for pineapples in 1899, and, not far from Wahiawa, the Dole Pineapple Pavilion demonstrates the canning process for curious visitors. A little farther toward Wahiawa, Del Monte displays 20 kinds of bromeliads, the botanic name for pineapples. Hours: Canning demonstrations from 9:00 a.m. to 6:00 p.m. daily. (½ hour)

✸ **Puu O Mahuka Heiau**—Seated above Waimea Park, this spiritually significant and most famous temple of Oahu probably was the site of human sacrifices in the precolonization period. Puu O Mahuka means "Hill of Escape." The view of Waimea Bay is outstanding. (½ hour)

✸ **Sunset, Ehukai, Banzai Pipeline, and Waimea Bay**—Surfing beaches here, for experts only from November through February, are fairly safe for swimming at other times of year.

FITNESS AND RECREATION

In Haleiwa, call **Waimea Mountain Bikes** (638-5587) for a two-hour excursion in Waimea Valley. From Haleiwa you can bike north along the North Shore or west on Highway 930 to beautiful Mokuleia Beach.

Tennis buffs should head for the **Turtle Bay Hilton & Country Club** (293-8811). Sightseeing on horseback also begins here. The Turtle Bay Hilton has trails along the beautiful palm and ironwood groves of deserted beaches on the northwest Kahuku tip.

Mokuleia Beach was mostly deserted when I lived there more than 35 years ago, and remains so today. Board-surf at **Sunset Beach, Ehukai Beach Park, Banzai Pipeline, Pupukea Bay, Waimea Beach Park, Chun's Reef,** and **Haleiwa Beach Park**. Contact the Haleiwa **Surf Center** (637-5051) for gear and instruction. My favorite spot for snorkeling and diving is **Shark's Cove** (no sharks) at **Pukukea Bay.** More experienced divers will try **Haleiwa Beach**. In summer (not in winter), experienced snorkelers will find a friendly assortment of fish at **Sunset Beach** and **Waimea Beach**.

The least expensive, most thrilling and serene way to see the island from the air is in a glider. Drive past Haleiwa and Mokuleia to

Dillingham Air Force Base, where the **Honolulu Soaring Club** (677-3434) offers 20-minute one- or two-passenger piloted glider rides for $40 to $60 from 10:30 a.m. to 5:30 p.m. daily. Half-hour plane rides for only $30 and an hour for $50, in Cessna 172s or 206s, are available from **Surf Air Tours** (637-7003).

FOOD

Enjoy breakfast at the **Coffee Gallery** in the North Shore Center, or fill up with the surfing crowd at **Café Haleiwa** (66-460 Kamehameha Highway, 637-5561). This tiny place, across from the post office on the left as you enter Haleiwa, serves excellent and cheap breakfasts with names like "Surf Rat" and "Dawn Patrol," and outdoes the rest of the island for huge breakfasts. Sunday brunch (10:00 a.m.–3:00 p.m.) is the best way to start Sunday on the North Shore. Look for **Lappert's Ice Cream** (20% butterfat) everywhere, but in Haleiwa check out **Matsumoto's** (637-4827) for classic shaved ice and **Flavormania** at the Haleiwa Shopping Plaza for 40 or more flavors to satisfy any ice cream craving—maybe after a *Godfather* pizza at **Pizza Bob's** (637-3538). If you dare, try peanut butter or chocolate brownie ice cream at **Bubbies** (1010 University, near the Varsity Theater). The **Proud Peacock** in Waimea Falls Park is a very special place to have lunch or dinner. You'll dine surrounded by gardens, with peacocks roaming about.

LODGING

Haleiwa has no hotels. For a base in Haleiwa, Alice Tracy's 12 cottages, **Ke Iki Hale** (59-579 Ke Iki Road, Haleiwa, HI 96712, 638-8229), are outstanding but expensive. Ke Iki Beach is edged with coconut palms and ironwoods. At the front door of modest one- and two-bedroom cottages on the beach and duplex one-bedrooms behind them, white sand and calm swimming waters prevail in summer and high surf crashes on rocks in winter. Units cost from $105 to $135 for a one-bedroom with or without beachfront. The best deal is on weekly rates. In Mokoleia, condos like the **Mokuleia Beach Colony** (68-615 Farrington Highway, Waialua, HI 96791, 637-9311) offer very nice units facing the ocean with minimum stays of a week for $600, which is still a bargain compared to hotel rates. Contact **Backpackers Vacation Inn & Hostel** (638-7838) for all kinds of accommodations on the North Shore.

NORTH SHORE

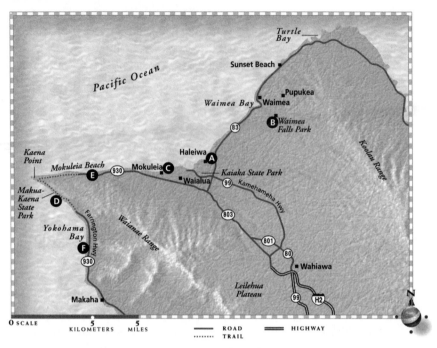

Food

Ⓐ Bubbies

Ⓐ Café Haleiwa

Ⓐ Coffee Gallery

Ⓐ Flavormania

Ⓐ Matsumoto's

Ⓐ Pizza Bob's

Ⓑ Proud Peacock

Lodging

Ⓐ Ke Iki Hale

Ⓒ Mokuleia Beach Colony

Camping

Ⓓ Kaena Point State Park

Ⓔ Mokuleia Beach

Ⓕ Makua Beach

Note: Items with the same letter are located in the same town or area

CAMPING

Mokuleia Beach has long unpopulated sections that are popular with unofficial campers. On the leeward coast, the long stretch of beach along Yokohama Bay is ideal for unofficial camping, especially on **Makua Beach**, the beginning of **Kaena Point State Park**.

SIDE TRIP: THE WAIANAE COAST

From 1895 to 1947, the now defunct Oahu Railroad passed through hot and dusty leeward Oahu, along the Waianae Mountains, looping around Kaena Point. Today Farrington Highway runs from Honolulu west and north to Kahe Point, passing few restaurants, shops, or hostelries. Most residents are locals. Highway 93 continues north to **Yokohama Bay**, where the pavement ends. From here you have to walk to **Kaena Point**, where, according to legend, souls await assignment to heaven or hell, finally exiting from Ghosts' Leap among the black lava rocks.

Makaha Beach is famous for its surfing competitions. Combine a snorkeling/diving trip to Makaha Beach with a two-tank dive trip with **Atlantis Reef Divers** (592-5801) or **Ocean Concepts Scuba** (677-7975 or 800-808-3483) on the famed wreck of the *Mahi* and at Makaha Caverns.

Follow Makaha Valley Road inland to the Sheraton Makaha Resort (P.O. Box 896, Waianae, HI 96792, 695-9511 or 800-325-3535). The Sheraton's 800 renovated bungalows and Polynesian-style buildings sit in an oasis of bougainvillea, hibiscus, and plumeria. Off-season rates of $90 a day for a double with a car are still possible. From the resort you can take a horseback ride up into the back reaches of Waianae's **Makaha Valley** (695-9511). And on at least one trip to Hawaii, every golfer has to try the beautiful **Sheraton Makaha Resort West Golf Course** (695-9544).

The **Kaala Room** at the resort serves elegant dinners in a somewhat formal atmosphere. The view down the valley to the ocean, especially during a legendary Waianae sunset, is one of the most unforgettable parts of the Makaha experience.

A safe beach and anchorage a little south, **Pokai Bay Beach Park**, backed by mountains, is a pretty place for a picnic lunch and a dip. In summer (not in winter), experienced snorkelers will find a friendly assortment of fish at **Nanakuli Beach Park** and **Kahe Beach Park**. For diving equipment rental on the Waianae Coast, contact the **Leeward Dive Center** (696-3414).

4

WEST MAUI

The state's first capital, Lahaina, is an old whaling port that has become the Valley Isle's main vacation attraction. Hawaiian royalty, starting with Kamehameha, loved it. Although he was from the Big Island, his favorite and sacred wives were from Maui. Even when Kamehameha moved his 21 wives to Honolulu, the capitol remained in Lahaina. Whalers poured in from the far reaches of the globe for R&R (and to spread venereal disease). Once ramshackle, Lahaina became a historic district in 1966. Hollywood couldn't have done a better job creating honky-tonk Front Street. Lahaina is for gourmands, art lovers, kids of all ages and people who don't fret and fuss about traffic jams in paradise. Gorged with galleries, shops, historic sites and many superb restaurants, it can be difficult to leave Lahaina—even with the luxury hotels and resorts, shopping, exquisite restaurants, a half dozen championship golf courses, and the wonderful beaches to the north, stretching from Kaanapali up to Kapalua and beyond. Passing through beach condo villages like Honokowai and Napili, there are plenty of places to watch whales breaching the waters between December and April. But a better way to see whale antics and the fascinating islands of Molokai and Lanai, clearly visible from Maui's shoreline, is to take a ferry or one of the many cruise ships from Lahaina's harbor. Snorkelers prefer to gravitate to the cliffs, reefs, and beaches past Kapalua. Against the earnest wishes of car rental agencies, the rough Kapalua Highway will take you around the southern end of West Maui and through the tiny town of Kahakuloa to Wailuku. ◼

WEST MAUI

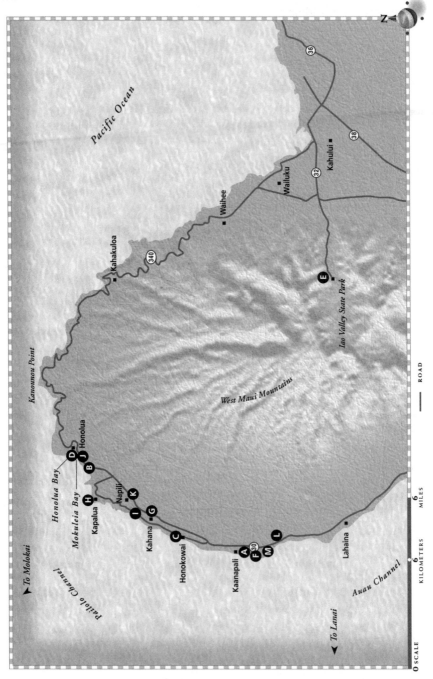

Sightseeing Highlights

West Maui

Ⓐ Black Rock

Ⓑ D.T. Fleming Beach Park

Ⓒ Honokowai

Ⓓ Honolua Bay

Ⓔ Iao Valley

Ⓕ Kaanapali Resort

Ⓖ Kahana

Ⓗ Kapalua

Ⓘ Maui Gold Coast

Ⓙ Mokuleia Bay

Ⓚ Napili

Ⓛ "Sugar Cane Train" (Lahaina-Kaanapali & Pacific Railroad)

Ⓜ Whaler's Village

LAHAINA

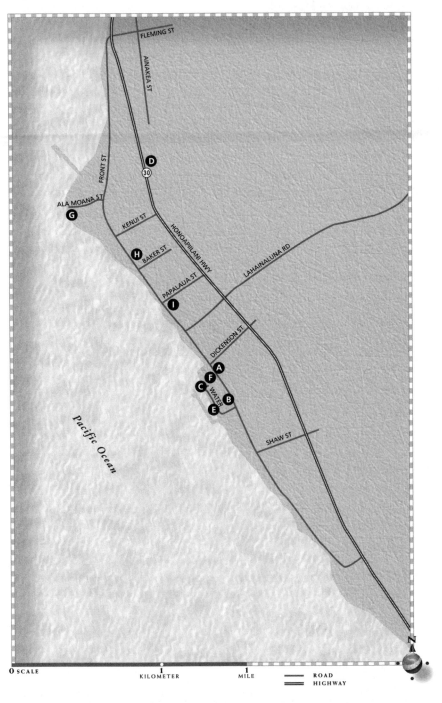

Pacific Ocean

FLEMING ST
AINAKEA ST
FRONT ST
30 **D**
ALA MOANA ST
G
KENUI ST
HONOAPIILANI HWY
BAKER ST
H
LAHAINALUNA RD
PAPALAUA ST
I
DICKENSON ST
A
F
C
WATER
B
E
SHAW ST

N

Sightseeing Highlights

Lahaina

Ⓐ Baldwin Home Museum

Ⓑ Banyan Tree

Ⓒ Brick Palace

Ⓓ The Cannery

Ⓔ *Carthaginian II*

Ⓑ Courthouse

Ⓐ Masters' Reading Room

Ⓑ Old Fort

Ⓕ Pioneer Inn

Ⓖ Lahaina Jodo Mission

Ⓗ Waiola Church

Ⓘ Wo Hing Society Hall

Note: Items with the same letter are located in the same area

A PERFECT DAY IN AND AROUND LAHAINA

Enjoy the town's best muffins at The Bakery or the pinnacle of pancakes at Gekko's on Front Street, where old and new come together. Begin your walking tour of historic Lahaina at the Lahaina Restoration Society, at Front and Dickenson streets. Relax over an early lunch at the Pioneer Inn and enjoy the brisk harbor scenery. Then drive north to Kapalua resort, where you'll find the clear blue water perfect for swimming. (Snorkelers should drive further on to picturesque Honolua Bay.) The terrace at the Plantation House Restaurant is the perfect spot for a drink at sunset. Return to Lahaina for dinner; I recommend Chef Mark Ellman's Chinese duck roasted in honey and saké at the famed Avalon Restaurant on Front Street. After dinner, stroll around town and visit The Gallery, South Sea Trading Post, and the Village Galleries.

GETTING AROUND MAUI

There's no public bus system on Maui, so you'll need a rental car to get around. Reserve one in advance, and ask whether the company has a pickup service at the airport. You'll find an abundance of local car rental companies here, more than on any other island, with cars for $25 to $35 per day, flat rate with unlimited mileage. Rent a car right at the airport or get a free ride to car rental offices nearby. In the airport are Alamo Rent-A-Car (877-3466), American International Rent-A-Car (877-7604), Andres Rent-A-Car (877-5378), Avis Rent-A-Car (877-5167), Budget Rent-A-Car (871-8811), Dollar Rent-A-Car (871-8811), Hertz Rent-A-Car (877-5167), Pacific Rent-A-Car (877-3065), Robert's Rent-A-Car (871-6226), and Trans-Maui Rent-A-Car (877-5222). Outside the airport, older model used cars can be rented at Rent-A-Wreck (800-367-5230), Uptown Service (244-0869), and Word of Mouth Rent-A-Used-Car (877-2436). Other car rental companies include Kamaaina (877-5460), Maui Car Rental and Leasing (877-2081), National Car Rental (877-5347), Sunshine Rent-A-Car (871-6222), Thrifty Car Rental (871-7596), and Tropical Rent-A-Car (877-0002).

Grayline (877-5507) has a shuttle service from Kahului to Lahaina-Kaanapali for about $11 per person. Trans-Hawaiian Services (877-7308) provides a shuttle service that stops running at 5:00 p.m.

SIGHTSEEING HIGHLIGHTS

★★★ **Lahaina**—Lahaina was the political center of the Hawaiian kingdom from about 1800 to 1945. Around 1820, the town became the main provisioning stop for whaling ships and the playground for thousands of seamen and quickly lost its innocence. About the same time, missionaries arrived for a classic confrontation between salvation and sin. In 1962, Lahaina was designated a National Historic Landmark. In the same year, the Lahaina Restoration Foundation was formed to restore the historic sites along Front Street. The rapidly growing collection of shops, galleries, restaurants, and other attractions draws millions of visitors annually and produces traffic jams and parking problems. Lahaina now stretches 2 miles, 4 blocks deep. The heart of the town is a ⅓-mile stretch between Shaw and Papalaua streets. Front Street, the main shopping and entertainment strip, runs between these streets.

The Cannery, a large air-conditioned shopping mall opened in 1987 in a former pineapple cannery, located on Highway 30 as you leave Lahaina, recently was joined by another 150,000 square feet of shopping mall extending between Front Street and Highway 30. Altogether, Lahaina shopping space far exceeds Ala Moana on Oahu and is approaching that of Waikiki. Where or when will it stop? Be sure to visit the Lahaina Print-sellers in the historic Seamen's Hospital on Front Street, and the Village Gallery, with branches at the Cannery and 120 Dickenson Street in Lahaina, and at the Embassy Suites in Kaanapali.

Lahaina's historic highlights lie within a few blocks of Front Street. Get your free copy of the *Lahaina Historical Guide* at the Lahaina Restoration Society located in the **Masters' Reading Room** at Front and Dickenson streets. Walk next door to Lahaina's oldest building, the **Baldwin Home Museum**, a New England-style residence with furnishings of medical missionary Dwight Baldwin, whose offspring became some of the largest landowners in the islands. Across Papelekane Street is Kamehameha I's **Brick Palace**, the first Western-style building in the islands. The massive banyan tree, planted behind the courthouse on April 24, 1873, by Sheriff William Owen Smith to commemorate the 50th anniversary of Lahaina's first Protestant mission, is the largest in the islands, covering about two-thirds of an acre. On the harbor side of the banyan tree are the coral stone ruins of the **Old Fort** constructed in the 1830s to protect missionaries' homes from whalers. Inside the courthouse visit the **Lahaina Art Society's exhibit**. Only a few steps away is the wraparound veranda of historic **Pioneer Inn**. Built in 1901, it provided the only accommodations in west Maui until the late 1950s.

Carthaginian II, anchored in the harbor directly opposite the Pioneer Inn, is a two-masted, square-rigged replica of the ship that went aground in 1920. It contains a museum exhibit on the whaling era. Admission is $3 for adults; accompanied children are admitted free. Hours: Open daily from 9:00 a.m. to 4:30 p.m.

It's not IMAX, but the 180-degree screen for the **Hawaii Experience Domed Theater** is well worth the admission price, and not just for the kids. Address: 824 Front Street. Phone: 661-8314.

Waiola Church, the first stone church in the islands (circa 1830), has been rebuilt several times, the latest in 1953, when the name was changed from "Wainee" in an attempt to change its luck. Waiola Cemetery behind the church dates back to 1823. Many Hawaiian chiefs and queens who became Christians are buried there.

Wo Hing Society Hall on Front Street, built in 1912 by Chinese laborers imported to the island, has a small museum and social hall.

Lahaina Jodo Mission at 12 Ala Moana Street, founded in 1921, contains the 12-foot bronze and copper giant Buddha cast in Japan and sent to Maui in 1968 for a centennial celebration of the first Japanese immigrants to Hawaii. (full day)

★★ **Kaanapali Resort**—Starting 4 miles north of Lahaina, this is the beginning of the west **Maui Gold Coast** that continues 10 miles to Kapalua ("Arms Embracing the Sea"). The 500-acre resort contains seven hotels (including the new Embassy Suites), five condominium complexes, two golf courses, a shopping center, and miles of sandy beaches. Beyond Kaanapali are the condominium "villages" of Honokowai, Kahana, Napili, and Kapalua. Highway 30 (the Hono a Piilani Highway) circles west Maui.

Visit the **Whale Center of the Pacific** on the third floor of Whalers Village Shopping Center to see a unique display of whaling artifacts and photos and a 30-minute whale video shown every half-hour. Hours: 9:30 a.m. to 9:30 p.m., closed 1:00 to 1:30 p.m. Phone: 661-5992.

The best place to swim and snorkel in the Kaanapali Resort is next to **Black Rock** (Pu'u Keka'a) at the Sheraton Hotel's beach. The great mid-eighteenth-century king-warrior, Kahekili, leaped from this ancient "leaping place" of souls into their ancestral spiritland. This event is reenacted nightly by divers from the hotel. (2–3 hours)

★ **"Sugar Cane Train" (Lahaina-Kaanapali & Pacific Railroad)**—An oil-fired narrow gauge steam locomotive (*Anaka or Myrtle*), refurbished to resemble a vintage sugarcane locomotive, carries you in an open passenger car on a 6-mile excursion past golf courses, cane fields, and ocean views. The train makes five 25-minute (one-way) trips daily between the Puukolii Boarding Platform (across from the Royal Lahaina) and the Lahaina Station, with a stop at the Kaanapali Station. A one-way ticket is $7.50, round-trip $11. (1 hour)

FITNESS AND RECREATION

Any golfer would enjoy glorious days on the more or less challenging **North** and **South courses** at Kaanapali (669-8044). My favorites, however, are **Kapalua Bay's** (669-8044) spectacular championship **Bay Course** (par 72; 6,761 yards), championship **Village Course** (par 71; 6,632 yards), and the **Plantation Course** (par 73; 6,547 yards), which are worth playing just for the scenery.

Beyond Kapalua, a hiking trail begins across from the church in **Kahakuloa** and climbs a few miles through a scenic valley. About a 15-minute drive from here, follow a side road to Maluhia Boy Scout Camp to find the start of the 3-mile **Waihee Ridge Trail** to Lanilili Peak. Everyone visits **Iao Valley**, west of Lahaina, at least once, but be sure to arrive as early as possible at this spectacular cleft in the West Maui Mountains. Stop at the **Hawaii Nature Center** (244-6500) near the Kepaniwai Heritage Gardens for hiking information.

Helicopter tours are very expensive and thrilling. If you can spend $100 to $300 (depending on the season) to see west Maui, Haleakala, Hana, the whole island, or Molokai, it's well worth it. Flightseeing excursions with **Papillon Helicopters** (669-4884 or 800-367-7095) depart from the Pineapple Hill Helipad near Kapalua, fly over the West Maui Mountains, and land in a wilderness spot for a champagne picnic.

Lahaina is a center for water sports activities—cruises, sailing, snorkeling, scuba diving, fishing, and whalewatching. Arrange for any of these activities at the **Lahaina Beach Center** (661-5959) or the **Lahaina Sea Sport Center** (667-2759).

For about $45, you can take either the *Kaulana*, a 70-foot motor-powered catamaran (667-2518) or the three-masted schooner *Spirit of Windjammer*, **Windjammer Cruises** (800-843-8113), with dinner and open bar. From Lahaina Harbor, the best sailing cruise is aboard one of **Trilogy Excursions'** (661-4743) multi-hull sailboats to Manele Bay on Lanai for a barbeque lunch and van tour of the island. Take a glorious sunset cruise or a snorkeling trip on a 40-foot catamaran offered by **Kamehameha Catamaran Sails** (661-4522).

Bear in mind when you sign up for fishing charters that most skippers sell the day's catch to keep costs down. Ask about your share of fillets. Deep-sea fishing runs about $65 a half day on a share basis and $125 to $150 for an eight-hour day at **Aerial Sportfishing** (667-9089), **Lahaina Charter Boats** (667-6672), **Finest Kind Sportfishing** (661-0338), and **Aloha Activity Center** (667-9564).

Whalewatching excursions run from January through April. You can combine your whalewatching with snorkeling around Lanai on **Seabird Cruises'** *Aikane III* (661-3643). Half-day trips should cost no more than $75 and with increasing competition may be as low as $45 off-season. Book a cruise through the **Pacific Whale Foundation** (879-6530). The price is $27.50 for adults, $15 for children 3 to 12. Check the **Whale Report Center** (661-8527) for the latest report on whale sightings.

Some of the easiest snorkeling to get to on Maui is at **Black Rock** (Pu'u Keka'a), in front of the Sheraton at the white sands of Kaanapali Beach. Park at the Whaler's Shopping Center to walk to the beach. (The Sheraton parking lot actually has a few spaces reserved for beach users.) In spring and summer, however, there is no place on Maui that I would rather be snorkeling and enjoying the beaches than at **Honolua Bay** and **Mokuleia Bay** north of Kapalua. Nearby is the white sand beach of equally uncrowded **D. T. Fleming Beach Park**. All of these beach areas have great bodysurfing for experts in winter. Snorkelers should contact **Maui Adventures** (661-3400) or **Snorkeling Hawaii** (661-8156) for two-hour cruises out of Lahaina at about $25 per person.

Half-day diving excursions with lunch or breakfast, to Molokai and Lanai or just offshore cost from $80 to $110. Contact **American Dive of Maui** (661-4885), **Central Pacific Divers** (661-8718 or 800-551-6767), **Dive Maui** (667-2080), **Hawaiian Reef Divers** (667-7647), **Lahaina Divers** (667-7496), **Scuba Schools of Maui** (661-8036), or **Kapalua Dive Company** (669-6200) for all your diving needs.

Surfing is best in the summer at Lahaina and Kaanapali. Check with **Lahaina Dive & Surf** (667-6001). Otherwise, for experienced surfers, **Honolua Bay** and near the Maalaea boat harbor, east of McGregor Point, are your best bets.

FOOD

Every meal in Lahaina is a delightful problem of choices. As soon as I arrive in town, I head for the wraparound veranda of the **Pioneer Inn** (658 Wharf Street, 661-3636) and sit for a while gazing at the harbor. The Inn has been restored along with its menu. Try a breakfast of fantastic coconut, banana, or macadamia nut pancakes, or a lunch of seafood chowder. There are a few better restaurants in Lahaina, but no better place to start the day. The patio of **Lahaina Coolers** (180 Dickenson Street, 661-7082) is another of my favorites for cappucino and breakfast. For pancake aficionados, **Gekko's** (658 Front Street, 661-0955) is one of the better places to have breakfast.

If you would rather not commit to a full Hawaiian luau meal but still want to sample it, the **Old Lahaina Café** (505 Front Street, 661-3303) is the best place in Hawaii to to have *Kalua* pig, *lomilomi* salmon, *kalbi* ribs, grilled fish, sweet potatoes, and the rest. For people-watching on the lanai or watching Venezuelan chef Reyna Pinero, tiny **Sunrise Café** (693-A Front Street, 661-3326) is full of pleasant plate lunch surprises. Don't miss the opportunity for lunch or dinner at the **Hula Grill** (Whaler's Village, 667-6636). Diners sit practically on Kaanapali Beach on the veranda of what seems like a Hawaiian beach home and enjoy the cuisine of fabled Peter Merriman (one of my favorites in Waimea on the Big Island). Take out an Italian picnic lunch for the beach from **Longhi's Pizzeria Deli** (888 Front Street). **Ricco's** (Whaler's Village, 661-4433) offers buffet platters and a variety of excellent subs that qualify as family budget meals.

Why travel to Hawaii to eat Mexican food? Here are three good answers between Lahaina and Napili for the whole family and, believe it or not, health-conscious travelers: **Chico's Cantina & Café** (Whaler's Village, 667-2777), **Maui Tacos** (Napili Plaza, 665-0222), and **Taco Jo's Cantina** (658 Front Street, 667-2917).

Traveling with kids? You'll find more than two dozen varieties of pizza at **BJ's Chicago Pizzeria** (730 Front Street, 661-0700) and **Scaroles Village Pizzeria** (505 Front Street, 661-8112). Real burgers are loaded with everything, even tofu, at **Cheeseburger in Paradise** (811 Front Street, 661-4855). You'll find smoked meats and BBQ at **Smokehouse BBQ** (1307 Front Street, 667-7005) and up in Whaler's Village at **Beach Barbeque** (661-8843), with everything from ribs and burgers to calzones. And, at last count, there were no less than two **Lappert's Ice Cream** emporiums on Front Street.

I hope you discovered the culinary joys of Roy's on Oahu; on Maui you won't want to miss the more casual but no less fantastic **Roy's Kahana Bar & Grill** (4405 Honoapilani Highway, 669-6999). New Zealand mussels may be fresher in Wellington but not tastier than those baked with a touch of garlic by Chef George Gomes. Gomes has his Peking duck canneloni with wild mushrooms, and Chef Mark Ellman serves Chinese duck roasted in honey and saké at the famed **Avalon Restaurant** in the courtyard of Mariners Alley (844 Front Street, 667-5559). Chef Ellman has to be looking over his shoulder at **David Paul's Lahaina Grill** (127 Lahainaluna Road, 667-5117), which is unsurpassed for creative dishes. It takes eclectic flavors and cooking styles and applies them to fresh local produce. Just down the street, a gourmet splurge dinner or lunch in the courtyard of charming **Gerard's**, located in the extraordinary Plantation Inn (174 Lahainaluna Road, 661-8939), is one of the outstanding dining experiences in Hawaii. Chef Gerard Reversade creatively changes his menus daily, and all of the beef, veal, duck, chicken, seafood, and other surprises are superbly prepared with the freshest ingredients and elegant sauces. Five miles south of Lahaina, about a ten-minute scenic

LAHAINA

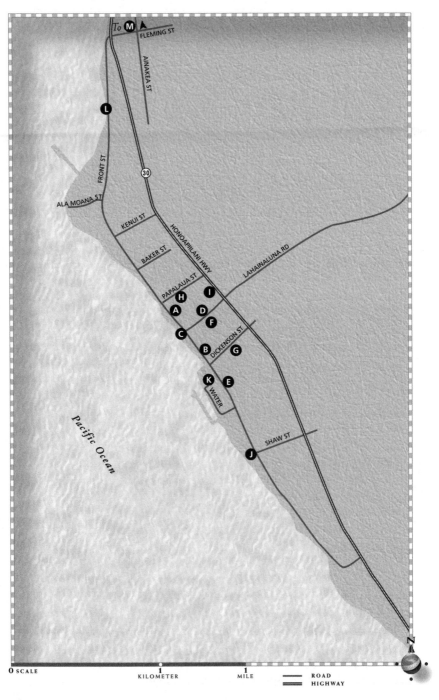

To **M** · FLEMING ST

AINAKEA ST

L

FRONT ST

30

ALA MOANA ST

KENUI ST

HONOAPIILANI HWY

BAKER ST

PAPALAUA ST

LAHAINALUNA RD

H · **I**

A · **D**

F

C

DICKENSON ST

B · **G**

K · **E**

WATER

SHAW ST

J

Pacific Ocean

N

0 SCALE

1
KILOMETER

1
MILE

ROAD

HIGHWAY

Food

A Avalon Restaurant

B BJ's Chicago Pizzeria

C Cheeseburger in Paradise

D David Paul's Lahaina Grill

E Gekko's

F Gerard's

G Lahaina Coolers

B Lappert's Ice Cream

H Longhi's Pizzeria Deli

I Maui Tacos

J Old Lahaina Café

K Pioneer Inn

J Scaroles Village Pizzeria

L Smokehouse BBQ

K Sunrise Cafe

E Taco Jo's Cantina

Lodging

M The Guest House

D Lahaina Inn

J Lahaina Shores Beach Resort

F Plantation Inn

Note: Items with the same letter are located in the same town or area

WEST MAUI

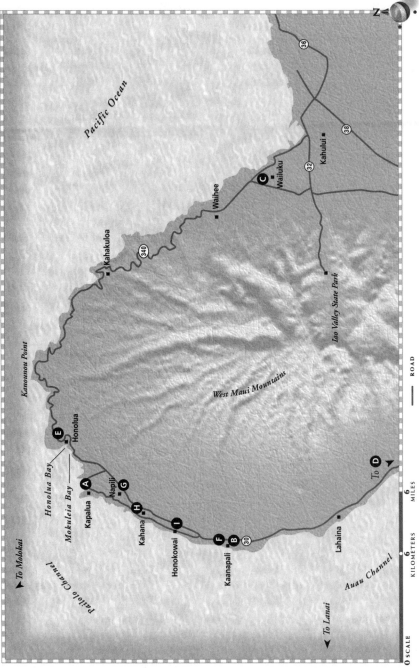

Food

- **A** The Bay Club
- **B** Beach Barbeque
- **C** Cafe Kup a Kuppa
- **D** Chez Paul
- **B** Chico's Cantina & Café
- **A** Haliimaile General Store
- **E** Honolua Store
- **B** Hula Grill
- **A** La Bretagne
- **F** Marriott's Moano Terrace
- **G** Maui Tacos
- **A** Plantation House Restaurant
- **B** Ricco's
- **H** Roy's Kahana Bar & Grill
- **C** Saeng's Thai Cuisine
- **C** Siam Thai
- **F** Swan Court
- **F** Westin Maui
- **C** Yori's

Lodging

- **G** Coconut Inn
- **I** Honokowai Palms
- **F** Kaanapali Alii
- **A** Kapalua Bay
- **A** Kapalua Bay Hotel & Villas
- **A** Kapalua Villas
- **I** Maui Sands
- **G** Napili Point
- **G** Napili Sunset
- **I** Paki Maui

Note: Items with the same letter are located in the same town or area

drive, **Chez Paul** (820-B Olowalu Village, 661-3843) has two seatings (6:30 p.m. and 8:30 p.m.) for excellent French cuisine.

Kapalua, of course, offers some of Maui's best dining. Both the views and the chef are marvelous at **The Bay Club** (Kapalua Resort, 669-8008)—especially good are the gourmet fish selections. **Haliimaile General Store** (900 Haiimaile Road, 572-2666), is an off-the-beaten-path plantation store converted into a gourmet dining treat. **La Bretagne** (661-8966) has fine French food in elegant yet comfortable surroundings. A drink on the terrace at sunset followed by fresh fish and great salad at the **Plantation House Restaurant** (Plantation Golf Course Clubhouse, Kapalua Resort, 669-6299) is the perfect way to end a day. Otherwise stop by for a delicious lunch. Surprisingly, some of the best dinner values can be found at dinner buffets at the big resorts, especially during summer months. Check out the seafood or regular buffet at the **Westin Maui** and the **Marriott's Moano Terrace** next door at Kaanapali. **Swan Court** (Hyatt Regency Maui, Kaanapali, 661-1234) is an ultra-elegant and romantic splurge.

Beyond Kapalua, when you're gazing at the fantastic surf in pic-turesque Honolua Bay and you get hungry for a snack, **Honolua Store** will provide a quick fix any day of the year.

On the other side of west Maui, in Wailuku, **Café Kup a Kuppa** (79 Church Street, 244-0500) will surprise you with its sophisticated and delicious lunch fare and coffees. Across from the Happy Valley Inn (309 N. Market Street, Wailuku), stop at **Yori's** for Japanese, American, or Hawaiian food. Try squid in coconut milk. **Saeng's Thai Cuisine** (2119 Vineyard Street, 244-1567) or **Siam Thai** (123 N. Market Street, 244-3817) are a toss-up for the best Thai food on the island.

LODGING

If you have a car, anywhere in the Lahaina, Kaanapali, Honokowai, and Napili Bay area can serve as a base for the day or the entire stay on Maui. The highest-priced accommodations are in Wailea, Kaanapali, and Kapalua; next is Kahana, with a resort atmosphere and mostly high-rise condos. Kihei and Honokowai's mix of older and newer, high- and low-rise condos are the largest "moderate" priced collection of vacation units on the island.

In Lahaina, the **Plantation Inn** is a Victorian-style hotel near the waterfront, with nine units ($99–$145 with breakfast, 174 Lahain-aluna Road, Lahaina, Maui, HI 96761, 667-9225 or 800-433-6815). The inn is one of a kind and right near the heart of town. **Lahaina**

Inn, a 13-room inn with turn-of-the-century charm and every modern convenience, is decorated with the utmost taste (127 Lahainaluna Road, Lahaina, Maui, HI 96761, 661-0577 or 800-669-3444). Rates are $89 to $99 standard single or double, including breakfast. **Lahaina Shores Beach Resort** was re-created from the ground up, and the Victorian architecture seems to fit old Lahaina ($115–$175, 475 Front Street, Lahaina, Maui, HI 96761, 661-4835 or 800-628-6699). **The Guest House** (1620 Ainakea Road, 661-8085 or 800-621-8942) B&B offers a good deal and a jacuzzi in every room.

Kaanapali Alii, in Kaanapali, is situated on beautiful grounds next to the beach ($175–$250, 50 Nohea Kai Drive, Kaanapali, Maui, HI 96761, 667-1400 or 800-642-MAUI).

A one-bedroom garden unit ($80) at the **Maui Sands** (3559 Lower Hono a Piilani, Lahaina, HI 96761, 669-9110 or 800-367-5037) is one of the best budget accommodations in Honokowai. You pay more for newer oceanside units, more luxurious furnishings, and lanais with views. The older **Honokowai Palms** (3666 Lower Hono a Piilani Highway, Lahaina 96761, 667-2712 or 800-669-MAUI) is across the street from the beach with one-bedroom oceanview units, or two-bedroom apartments without ocean view, for two at $75. **Paki Maui**, Honokawi, on the beach, has charming rooms, lush landscaping of the grounds, and lanais for outstanding views of Molokai ($119–$170, Aston Hotels & Resorts, 2255 Kuhio, Honolulu, HI 96815, 669-8325 or 800-535-0085).

The best value for the money in the Napili area is the **Coconut Inn** (181 Hui Road, Napili, HI 96761, 669-5712 or 800-367-8006). Forty-one units on two levels are tucked in a lovely garden setting, with pool and hot tub, away from the main road on a hill overlooking Napili. Comfortable studio units for two with kitchen and tub/shower cost $85 and include a delicious continental breakfast. Also try **Napili Sunset** (46 Hui Road, 669-8083 or 800-447-9229), right on Napili Bay, if their 88 units are available ($85 for a garden studio). **Napili Point** (115 rooms) is located next to the second-best beach on west Maui, with panoramic views from its lanais (5295 Honoapilani Highway, Napili, Maui, HI 96761, 669-9222 or 800-922-7866), and studios with garden views available for $85.

Beyond town, the beach at Kapalua is my favorite for swimming on Maui and, for golfers and others who want serenity rather than commercialism, **Kapalua Bay Hotel & Villas** (1 Bay Drive, Kapalua, Maui, HI 96761, 669-5656 or 800-669-4694) is one of the best choices. **Kapalua Bay** ($220–$400) contains only 200 units of stylish luxury (reminiscent of the Big Island's Mauna Kea) in 3-story buildings open to beautifully landscaped hills rolling to the ocean and one of the most perfect crescent beaches on Maui. **Kapalua Villas** ($155–$390) has luxurious rooms with wonderful views of the Pacific spread out over green sloping acreage to three beaches and several golf courses.

CAMPING

The best place for unofficial camping is at Honolua Bay, north of Kapalua.

NIGHTLIFE

The Old Lahaina Luau, the best luau on Maui, provides authentic Hawaiian food on the beach behind Whaler's Marketplace (505 Front Street, 667-1998). Catch the sunset there Tuesday through Saturday evenings at 5:30 p.m.; $46 for adults and $23 for children 12 and under. The Kaanapali Beach Hotel (which I suggest staying at for the aloha spirit) offers Aunti Aloha's Breakfast Luau (661-0011), where you'll start your day having a great deal of fun while drinking free mai tais and learning about what to do on Maui. Nightly from 6:30 to 7:30 p.m., see the hula show at the Kaanapali Beach Hotel's Tiki Terrace.

The Old Whaler's Grog Shop in the Pioneer Inn and the **Whale's Tale Restaurant** on Front Street are for drinking and fun. **Jazz at Blackie's Bar** (667-7979) is another local and tourist favorite just outside of Lahaina on the Kaanapali side. On Friday evenings, **"Art Night in Lahaina,"** from 7:00 to 9:00 p.m., galleries present artists, free entertainment, and refreshments. Strolling around Lahaina and people-watching between shopping, eating, and pub-crawling is entertainment enough. In addition, Lahaina's bars around Front Street and in the shopping complexes have all the music and activity you could want. The **Lahaina Broiler** hops until midnight. Disco at **Moose McGillicuddy's** nightly. On weekends, it's Hawaiian music at the **Banyan Inn** and dancing at **Longhi's**.

The $22 luau and cocktail or $36 dinner show ("Drums of the Pacific") at **Hyatt Regency** is one of the best in Kaanapali. Disco at the Hyatt's **Spats II** is one of the most popular on the island (open to 4:00 a.m.). Before or after, you can walk around the hotel's public areas to window-shop and view the displays of Oriental art. The disco at the Maui Marriott, the **Banana Moon**, is open until 1:30 a.m. and may be to your liking.

SIDE TRIP: MOLOKAI

A visit to Molokai will be a fascinating and totally different extension of your trip to Hawaii. It's a journey back in time. The southwest and northwest edges of dry west Molokai offer some of Hawaii's most picturesque and least-known beaches. Kayakers should discover Molokai's magnificent north shore, which rivals Kauai's Na Pali Coast, and mountain bikers will be pleasantly surprised by Molokai Ranch. (Bring your own bike on the ferry.)

The Halawa Valley, Kamakou Preserve, and Wailau hiking trails are as wild and off the beaten track as any you'll find in Hawaii. Arrange with Alex Pusa of Molokai Off-Road Tours to take you around the reserve areas and to the spectacular Waikolu Overlook. Snorkel at Halawa Bay (some of Hawaii's best snorkeling) or at Moomomi Beach on the north's shore's Pali coastline.

The town of Kaunakakai and its main street, Ala Malama, should be slow and antiquated as they have been for decades. Have breakfast in back of the Kanemetsu Bakery or up Farrington Road at Kualapuu Cookhouse. Buy some of the Bakery's fabled Molokai cheese and onion bread for a picnic lunch. Arrange in advance for a Rare Adventures/ Molokai Mule Ride down 1,600 feet to Kalaupapa, the former leper colony looked after many years ago by Father Damien and today by the National Park Service. Be sure to see Makanalua Peninsula and its historic leper settlement from Kalaupapa Lookout on the bluff next to Palaau State Park.

Kaunakakai Wharf is the best place to arrange a trip to southwest Lanai aboard Molokai Charters. Or talk to Walter Naki of Molokai Adventure Activities and he'll take care of your snorkeling, hiking, and anything else worth doing on the Molokai and Lanai.

From Maui, you can get to Molokai on one of the daily Island Air or Hawaiian Air flights; Air Molokai flies to the tiny airstrip at Kalaupapa. Somehow, however, arrival on even a small airplane powered unimpressively by propellers seems out of character. Instead, I suggest boarding Seal Link of Hawaii's 118-foot *Maui Princess* for a 90-minute excursion from Lahaina, either as a day trip, leaving at 5:45 a.m. (which really does not allow enough time to see Molokai), or on the more civilized 3:45 p.m. sailing, with the intention of staying at least overnight. Lodgings and even a bit of low-key nightlife at the Hotel Molokai or Pau Hana Inn or the unpretentious comfort at the Honomuni house B&B will fit perfectly with the island's relaxed, friendly atmosphere.

SIDE TRIP: LANAI

D on't get the idea that the old, isolated Lanai is fundamentally
changed because it now has two deluxe resorts—the Lodge at
Koele and Manele Bay—instead of just the rustic, clapboard, ten-room
Lanai Hotel. You'll still find only two paved roads on the island, and
Lanai City Service (now a Dollar Rent-a-Car affiliate) provides the
essential four-wheel drive vehicle at the airport when you arrive. Lanai
is a haven for hunters, and axis deer on the island still outnumber
humans (and consume more than their fair share of island vegetation).
And Lanai City, the quiet little plantation town at an altitude of 1,600
feet, remains in its own tranquil time warp. Its single-story buildings
are painted all colors of the rainbow and arranged in a grid around the
village green below the hotel.

I regard the tastefully-designed Lodge at Koele and its superb
dining as blessings of exceptional quality in a beautiful setting below
the Lanaihale mountains. I enjoy the benign juxtaposition of an old-
fashioned soda fountain, country stores and churches, and one of the
most sophisticated and lovely resorts in Hawaii. Likewise, while the
red lava cliffs overlooking Hulopo'e Bay were not originally designed
to have a resort hotel, at least this spectacular setting is minimally dis-
rupted by the hotel's contemporary architecture.

The island's pineapple fields are gone, but the rural and undevel-
oped wilderness-feel of the island remain. Just a mile out of Lanai City,
on Manele Road, you'll find fascinating Luahiwa petroglyphs, as good
as any you'll see at Puako on the Big Island.

Hulopo'e Beach, now adjacent to the Manele Bay hotel, remains
one of the best snorkeling beaches in Hawaii. Visit Kaumalapau harbor,
surrounded by 1,000-foot *pali* (cliffs), en route to Kaunolu, where King
Kamehameha I kept a summer home. In Kaunolu you will see stone
foundations of old homes and the remains of a small temple (*Heiau*).
Nearby, the king tested his warriors' courage by ordering them to jump
off a Kahekili's Leap, a ledge hovering 60 feet over the water.
Snorkeling in the cove beneath the cliff is delightful. Take the Trilogy
trimaran cruise from Lahaina to Manele Bay for snorkeling and an
optional raft excursion rather than a strenuous four-wheel drive trip to
Kaunolu Bay.

Four-wheel drive vehicles (or good hiking boots) are needed to
get to the best "secret" beaches on the island: Lopa, just south of
Keomuku Village, and the beachcomber's favorite, 8-mile-long
Shipwreck Beach on the wind-driven north coast between Polihua

and Kahokunui. Beachcombers can find no better beaches than these in Hawaii. Polihua Beach, a wide, white-sand strand with good swimming and outstanding fishing, is beyond the conglomeration of lava and multicolored boulders known as the Garden of the Gods. A profusion of tales about the origins of these lava formations make up for their murky history.

One of the best days in Hawaii starts with an exquisite breakfast at the Lodge at Koele (or a hearty one at the Lanai Hotel), then a drive up to the Munro Trail for a hike and a picnic lunch. The 7-mile trail is lined with Cook and Norfolk Island pine, eucalyptus, and koa. Steep, spectacular gulches are carved out of the east slope. If you're lucky enough to have a clear day, all of Hawaii's islands except Kauai are visible, and the view is unforgettable. Afterwards, sunset and dinner at Hulopo'e Court in the Manele Bay hotel is a perfect way to end the day.

Lanai Airport, several miles southwest of Lanai City, has a new terminal and extended runway for your flight on Hawaiian Air or Island Air to Lanaia. Daytrippers from Molokai or Maui will arrive by boat at Manele Bay, the much preferred way to visit Lanai unless you're coming for a stay at one of the hotels.

If you have extra time, drive around the West Maui
Mountains. Make sure you have a full gas tank. Four of Maui's
prettiest beaches are located on this route, all off Highway
30 north of Kapalua, each with different onshore scenery
and a sense of seclusion. Three of them are bounded by
cliffs: D. T. Fleming Park, under palm or ironwood trees, with
a view of Molokai; Oneloa Beach, past D. T. Fleming Park,
white sand in a cove backed by cliffs, with good swimming
and snorkeling; Honolua Bay, near Oneloa Beach, under
lovely trees near the water; and Pohakupule or Windmill
Beach, a white sand beach surrounded by cliffs. Farther
north, near Kahakuloa, the Kahakuloa Valley Trail passes
through one of Maui's untouched areas.

Driving from Kapalua to Wailuku takes about three
hours. Highway 30 changes to Highway 340 at Honokohau
Bay and becomes a rutted dirt road that your car rental
agency hates; they will not accept responsibility for car damage. (Check first to see if the road is passable or washed
out, which happens. Actually, you're following an old royal

KAPALUA TO WAILUKU ROUTE

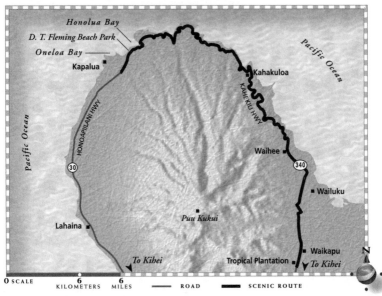

horse trail.) If you want to learn more about Maui's history, take a guided tour (40 minutes) through the Maui Tropical Plantation (244-7643) outside of Wailuku.

Pass picturesque Kahakuloa, cliffs, valleys, and lush fern gulches between razorbacked ridges that run from Puu Kukui's mile-high summit to the sea. After the road becomes paved again in the cane plantation town of Waihee, a side road leads up to Halekii Heiau, once football field-size temples, now rubble.

On the north end of the isthmus, in Kahului, the Alexander & Baldwin Sugar Museum (Hansen Road and Puunene Avenue, Kahului, 871-8058) will provide an informative addition to the history of sugarcane on Maui. And the Maui Art & Cultural Center (242-2787, Kahului) has several indoor and outdoor theater facilities where you can expect to see Hawaii's finest shows and a huge gallery for Maui and Pacific art. ◪

5

WAILEA COAST

Maui's sunniest weather, best beach, and its most peaceful resort can be found along the gorgeous beach-lined coast between Kihei and Makena. First, for about 6 miles, from Maalaena to Wailea along South Kihei Road, dry East Maui is an unsightly mix of shopping centers and condominiums (including a sprinkling of superior ones) redeemed again and again by miles of easy access to golden sand. The contrast with adjoining Wailea and Makena is striking, perhaps even disturbing. It's as though Hawaii's architects and landscape planners tried obsessively to make up in Wailea for 20 years of their blatant laxity in Kihei. Blessed with 1,400 uninterrupted acres of scrubland and beaches below the slopes of Haleakala, the resulting development includes no less than three masterful 18-hole golf courses and 14 tennis courts in Wailea and Makena. The hotels, resorts and condominiums of Wailea offer an unrivaled Mecca of sophisticated creature comforts and a variety of unforgettable dining experiences in beachfront settings among the best in the world. With fountains, Jacuzzis and even a river pool, spas and a wedding chapel, an abundance of art and sculpture, paintings and frescos worthy of a king's court, classes from sandcastle-building to zen, and beautifully landscaped grounds, until recently the only amenity Wailea lacked was a Moorish fantasy resort. That is, until the Kea Lani was built, designed by the same architect who created Las Hadas resort in Mexico. Complaints about lackluster nightlife in Wailea are answered by the fact that hip-hopping Lahaina is only 45 minutes away. More wishes, anyone? ∎

WAILEA COAST

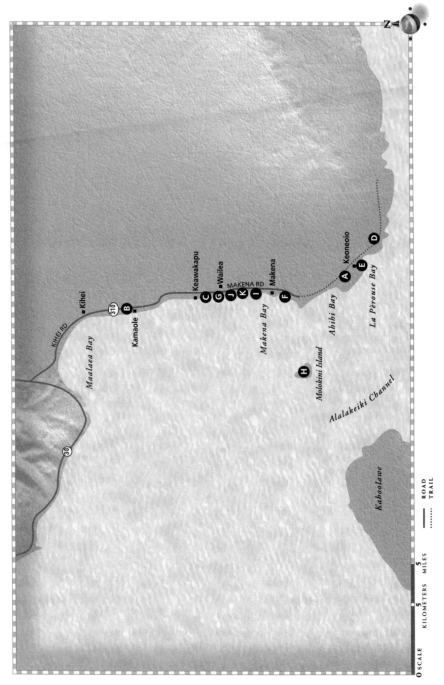

Kihei

Kamaole

Keawakapu

Wailea

MAKENA RD

Makena

Keoneoio

Maalaea Bay

Makena Bay

Abihi Bay

La Pèrouse Bay

Molokini Island

Alalakeiki Channel

Kahoolawe

KIHEI RD

310

30

A

B

C

D

E

F

G

I

J

K

H

——— ROAD
········· TRAIL

SCALE

5 MILES

5 KILOMETERS

Sightseeing Highlights

Ⓐ Ahihi-Kinau Natural Area Reserve

Ⓑ Kamaole Beach Park I

Ⓒ Keawakapu Beach

Ⓓ King's Highway

Ⓔ Magic Lagoon

Ⓕ Makena Beach

Ⓖ Mokapu Beach

Ⓗ Molokini Island

Ⓘ Polo Beach

Ⓙ Ulua Beach

Ⓚ Wailea Beach

A PERFECT DAY ON THE WAILEA COAST

The Wailea Resort and secluded Makena are complete contrasts to the more commercialized parts of Hawaii. Assemble a picnic in Kihei, then head for any of Wailea's five wonderful beaches (Keawakapu, Mokapu, Ulua, Wailea, and Polo) or to my favorite, splendid Makena Beach, a few miles south. If you visit the Ahihi-Kinau Natural Area Reserve, you'll need a four-wheel drive vehicle to get to the Cape Kinau edge of it. Follow the white paint trail across the lava to find snorkeling at Magic Lagoon and to see more remnants of the ancient King's Highway at La Perouse.

SIGHTSEEING HIGHLIGHTS

★★★ **Makena Beach**—Down winding Wailea Alanui Road, the Makena Surf condos and the Maui Prince Resort emerged from a vast arid acreage of kiawe trees to follow the same patterns as the Wailea Resort next door.

About 1.7 miles from Wailea Shopping Center on Makena Alanui Road, turn right to the white sands of Poolenalena Beach

Park; another 2.3 miles beyond Wailea, Makena Alanui Road (an easy-to-drive dirt track) leads to a turnoff to the right past Red Hill to Makena Beach (the turnoff on the Wailea side of Red Hill is to Black Sands Beach). This road continues to Ahini-Kinau Nature Reserve, 2,000 acres of land and ocean with wonderful tide pools and coral reefs. (2–3 hours)

★★★ **Molokini Island**—Hawaiian legend has it that Pele's dream-lover, Lohi-au, incurrred her terrible wrath by marrying a *mo'o* (dragon). The volatile fire goddess swiftly cut the mo'o in half: one-half became Puu Olai hill in Makena, and the other half became known as Molokini. Today, 5 azure miles from the white sands of Wailea and Makena, crescent-shaped Molokini Island surrounds the largest concentration of tropical fish in all of Hawaii. The 150-foot volcanic tuff cone (Maui's only one) opens to the north with a protective semicircle embracing more than 200 species of fish, many varieties of seaweed, reef coral, and a vast array of other sea creatures unwittingly enjoying the protections of Molokini Shoal Marine Life Conservation District.

Accessible only by boat, Molokini can be reached in 20 minutes on the *Kai Kanani* (879-7218), a sleek 46-foot sailing catamaran that departs from Makena. Arrangements for this wonderful morning snorkeling trip can be made at the Maui Prince/Ocean Activities desk (879-4485). The cruise includes continental breakfast, all snorkel gear, lunch, and sodas ($45).

Nonsnorkelers can arrange for a champagne sunset-dinner-sail that leaves from Maalaea Harbor on Mondays, Wednesdays, and Fridays (879-4485). Sail at 7:30 a.m. or noon on the 60-foot *Lavengro* out of Maalaea Harbor for Molokini Crater, with continental breakfast and a buffet lunch or on the *Trilogy* for a half-day excursion from Maalaea Harbor. (4 hours)

FITNESS AND RECREATION

Makena Beach, a favorite of hippies in the 1960s, is one of my favorite spots for swimming and beachcombing. Unless it's high tourist season, it's hard to beat the beautiful white sands of nearby **Wailea Beach**. But don't overlook **Kamaole Beach Park I**, with showers and restrooms, parking, and lots of excellent places to eat nearby.

Two of my favorite places for snorkeling and diving are **Mokapu Beach** (in front of Stouffer's Wailea Beach Resort) and **Ulua Beach** (between Stouffer's and the Intercontinental). **Makena** is a little harder to get to but worth the effort. Snorkel around the Puu Olai cinder cone. Harder to find but also worth the effort, is the **Ahihi-Kinau Natural Reserve Area** in La Perouse Bay. Some of the best snorkeling and scuba diving in all of Hawaii is in **Molokini Crater**, early in the morning, before the crowds. Contact the **Ocean Activities Center** (879-4485 or 800-869-6911). Combine morning snorkeling at Molokini and a cruise aboard a 60-foot schooner with **Maui Classic Charters** (879-8188), or ask about the 65-foot catamarans *Wailea Kea* and *Maka Kai* that will take you to the marine preserve of La Perouse Bay.

Golfers will delight in the **North** and **South courses** at **Makena** (879-3344), and the **Orange**, **Blue**, and **Gold courses** at **Wailea** (879-2966).

FOOD

For the best bargain breakfast with the best view of Wailea, have all-you-can-eat pancakes on the patio of the **Makena Golf Course Restaurant** (879-1154). Roy Dunn, owner of the Plantation House in Kapalua, has created a marvelous restaurant with terrific views and food at the **Sea Watch** in Wailea (100 Wailea Golf Club Drive, 875-8080). Maui onion soup (or any other dish) served outdoors in a bread bowl at **Café Kiowi** (Maui Prince Resort, Wailea, 874-1111) provides unsurpassed lunch fare at a reasonable price. Treat yourself to great fish entrées Hawaiian-style by master chef Roger Dikon at the **Prince Court** (Maui Prince Hotel, Wailea, 874-1111) or an exquisite Japanese dining and visual experience and worthy splurge at **Kincha** (Grand Wailea, 875-1234). **Raffles Restaurant** (Stouffer's Wailea Beach Resort, 879-4900) does indeed live up to its awards and reputation (despite some rumors to the contrary). For delicious splurge dinners, **Hakone's** Japanese food and environment at the Maui Prince Resort, Makena, are unsurpassed in the islands, as is **La Perouse** at the Maui Inter-Continental (879-1922) for continental dining in an Oriental decor.

Kihei is an unsightly boom strip along S. Kihei Road, but the public beaches and some of the local restaurants are great, especially for families on a budget feeding hungry kids. Try **Café Pastaria** (Lipoa Shopping Center, 879-9001) for a wonderful meal that you can take to the beach. **Alexander's** (1913 S. Kihei Road, 874-0788) serves grilled fish, chicken, and ribs, and **Kihei Café** (1945 S. Kihei Road, 879-2230) tempts with lots of sandwiches and other tasty choices, including great desserts; both eateries are across the street from Kalama Park.

KIHEI

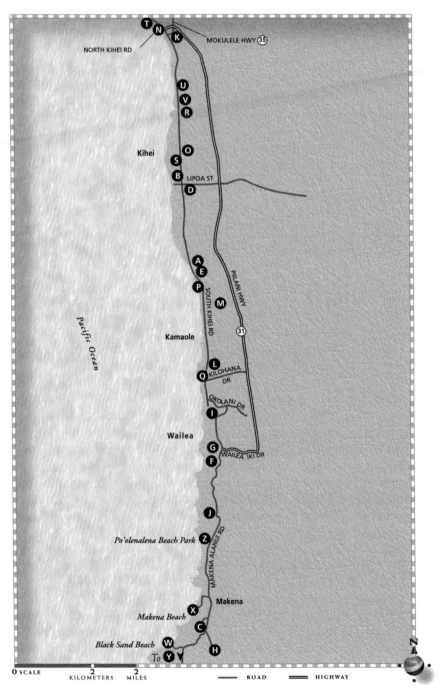

North Kihei Rd
Mokulele Hwy 35
Kihei
Lipoa St
Pacific Ocean
Piilani Hwy
South Kihei Rd
Kamaole
31
Kilohana Dr
Okolani Dr
Wailea
Wailea Iki Dr
Makena Alanui Rd
Po'olenalena Beach Park
Makena
Makena Beach
Black Sand Beach
To
N

0 SCALE 2 KILOMETERS 2 MILES   ROAD   HIGHWAY

Food

- Ⓐ Alexander's
- Ⓑ Azeka's Snack Shop
- Ⓒ Café Kiowi
- Ⓓ Café Pastaria
- Ⓒ Hakone's
- Ⓔ Kihei Café
- Ⓕ Kincha
- Ⓖ La Perouse
- Ⓗ Makena Golf Course Restaurant
- Ⓑ A Pacific Café Maui
- Ⓐ Paradise Fruit Stand
- Ⓒ Prince Court
- Ⓘ Raffles Restaurant
- Ⓙ Sea Watch
- Ⓚ Suda's Snack Shop

Lodging

- Ⓛ Hale Kamaole
- Ⓜ Kamaole Beach Royale Resort
- Ⓝ Kihei Kai
- Ⓞ Koa Resort
- Ⓟ Lihi Kai Cottages
- Ⓠ Mana-Kai Maui Condominium Hotel
- Ⓡ Maui Lu Resort
- Ⓢ Maui Sunset
- Ⓣ Nani Kai Hale
- Ⓤ Nona Lani Cottages
- Ⓥ Sunseeker Resort

Camping

- Ⓦ Black Sands Beach
- Ⓧ Makena Beach
- Ⓨ Oneloa Beach Park
- Ⓩ Po'olenalena Beach Park

Note: Items with the same letter are located in the same town or area

For quick and cheap snacks in Kihei, the top choices are **Suda's Snack Shop**, 61 S. Kihei Road, and a plate lunch at **Azeka's Snack Shop**, in Azeka's Place Shopping Center. Stop at **Paradise Fruit Stand** (1913 S. Kihei Road, in Kihei) for fresh fruit and delicious smoothies. Everyone who visits the Wailea side of Maui will have to eat at least once at Jean-Marie Josselin's **A Pacific Café Maui** (879-0069), located in the unlikely Azeka Shopping Center in Kihei. The decor is warm and the Pacific Rim cuisine superb.

LODGING

While Wailea and Makena were evolving as planned developments, condominiums were springing up like weeds west of Wailea along the Kihei Coast. Maalaea/Kihei became a 6-mile stretch of increasingly haphazard development, mostly high- and low-rise condos, cottage hostelries, and a few hotels, with shopping centers every few blocks in Kihei.

Kihei's advantages over other locations on Maui consist of a combination of less expensive accommodations, ample sunshine, and easy access to some very good beaches in Kihei and in Wailea and Makena.

The price is certainly right for accommodations in Kihei—$80–$160. Moderately priced condominiums are plentiful. Some of the beaches and beachfront parks are among the most attractive on Maui and in Hawaii, usually no farther than across the road from these accommodations. These hotel/condominiums are standouts at rates ranging from $80 to $105 in season and less off-season: **Maui Sunset** (1032 S. Kihei Road, Kihei, Maui, HI 96753, 879-0674 or 800-843-5880), **Hale Kamaole** (2737 S. Kihei Road, Kihei, Maui, HI 96753, 879-2698 or 800-367-2970), **Koa Resort** (811 S. Kihei Road, Kihei, Maui, HI 96753, 879-1161 or 800-877-1314), **Maui Lu Resort** (575 S. Kihei Road, Kihei, Maui, HI 96753, 800-922-7866), and **Nani Kai Hale** (73 N. Kihei Road, Kihei, Maui, HI 96753, 879-9120 or 800-367-6032). Some of these condominiums, like Nani Kai Hale, have minimum stay requirements of seven days in season. Ask about off-season discounts, rental car and airport pickup packages, and air-conditioning if it's important to you.

Additional moderately priced ($70–$90 for one-bedroom apartments for two persons in season) choices of condo/hotel accommodations, either on the beach or across from it, include **Kamaole Beach Royale Resort** (2385 S. Kihei Road, Kihei, Maui, HI 96753, 879-3131 or 800-421-3661), **Kihei Kai** (61 N. Kihei Road, Kihei, Maui, HI

96753, 879-2357 or 800-735-2357), **Mana-Kai Maui Condominium Hotel** (2960 S. Kihei Road, Kihei, Maui, HI 96753, 879-1561 or 800-525-2025), and the **Sunseeker Resort** (551 S. Kihei Road, Kihei, Maui, HI 96753, 879-1261).

In a category by themselves are Dave Kong's eight **Nona Lani Cottages** ($70–$85, 455 S Kihei Road, Kihei, Maui, HI 96753, 879-2497 or 800-733-2688), set back from the road in a landscaped setting, and the least expensive cottages in Kihei, Tad and Kimberley Fuller's **Lihi Kai Cottages** (2121 Iliili Road, Kihei, Maui, HI 96753, 879-2335 or 800-LIHIKAI), in an excellent location (except for traffic noise in some units) near Kalama Park. Nearby shopping at the Kamaole Shopping Center, Dolphin Shopping Center, Azeka's Place Shopping Center, and numerous other stores make this one of the most convenient and economical places to spend a few days.

CAMPING

The best places for unofficial camping are **Oneloa Beach Park, Po'olenalena Beach Park, Black Sand Beach**, and **Makena Beach** (all just a few miles from the Wailea Shopping Center).

6

HALEAKALA VOLCANO
AND UPCOUNTRY

According to legend, the sun rises and moves slowly, indeed cautiously, across the sky above Haleakala, "House of the Sun," fulfilling a promise to Maui, legendary Polynesian demigod, to lengthen the days so that his mother can dry her kapa cloth. The days can never be long enough once you poke through Pukalani, "Hole in the Heaven," at the entrance to Kula and Upcountry Maui. The raucous annual 4th of July Rodeo in nearby Makawao is about the only visible sign of Upcountry cowboys and the once-thriving cattle ranching. Now a whole new Hawaiian universe opens up, the rich volcanic soils grow succulently sweet Kula onions (not just Maui onions), acres of indescribably shaped and colored proteas, hidden botanical gardens, and thick, mist-shrouded pine forests. Five miles above Kehei and Wailea coasts, every imaginable vegetable and fruit grows abundantly—even grapes at Tedeschi's vineyard on Ulupalakua Ranch yield a surprisingly good sparkling Maui Brut. Above this flourishing green world, quite apart from any other in Hawaii, Haleakala Crater Road twists steeply up past a series of overlooks to National Park headquarters. Found only atop Haleakala, majestic symbol of this strange terrain, the silversword grows its dagger-shaped silvery leaves for 5 to 20 years, bursts forth in only one season with a gorgeous stalk of hundreds of purplish-red flowers, and then mysteriously ends its life, turning to a gray skeleton. Mark Twain might raise a bushy eyebrow to see space-age Science City, a speck on Haleakala's 21-mile crater rim. Otherwise, nothing much has changed since 1866 when he rolled boulders down the steep lava mountainside of "the sublimest landscape I ever witnessed." ◪

HALEAKALA VOLCANO AND UPCOUNTRY

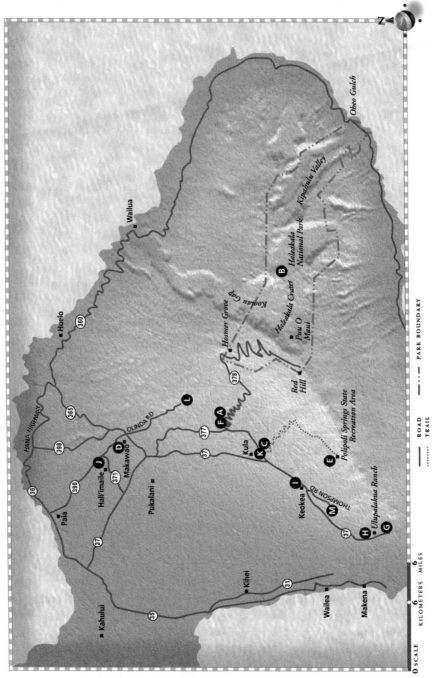

N

Oheo Gulch

Kipahulu Valley

Haleakala National Park

Wailua

Haleakala Crater

Kaupo Gap

Pa'u O Maui

Hosmer Grove

Huelo

360

Red Hill

378

Polipoli Springs State Recreation Area

B

HANA HIGHWAY

365

OLINDA RD

L

F A

378

377

Kula

K C

E

398

D

Makawao

37

Ulupalakua Ranch

390

J

Hali'imaile

I

M

THOMPSON RD

Pukalani

Keokea

H G

36

37

31

Paia

37

Kihei

31

Wailea

Kahului

35

Makena

0 SCALE   6 MILES
0   6
KILOMETERS

——— ROAD
·········· TRAIL
—··—··— PARK BOUNDARY

Sightseeing Highlights

Ⓐ Clouds Rest Protea Farm

Ⓑ Haleakala National Park

Ⓒ Kula Botanical Garden

Ⓓ Makawao

Ⓔ Polipoli Springs State
Recreation Area

Ⓕ Sunrise Market and
Protea Farm

Ⓖ Tedeschi Vineyards

Ⓗ Ulupalakua Ranch

Food

Ⓓ Casanova's

Ⓘ Grandma's Maui Coffee
House (Keokea)

Ⓙ Hali'imaili General Store

Ⓓ Kitada's

Ⓓ Makawao Steak House

Ⓓ Polli's Cantina

Lodging

Ⓚ Bloom Cottage

Ⓚ Elaine's Upcountry
Guest Rooms

Ⓚ Kula Cottage

Ⓚ Kula View B&B

Ⓛ McKay's Country
Cottage B&B

Ⓜ Silver Cloud Upcountry
Guest Ranch

Camping

Ⓑ Haleakala National Park

Ⓔ Polipoli Springs State
Recreation Area

Note: Items with the same letter are located in the same town or area

A PERFECT DAY AT HALEAKALA AND IN UPCOUNTRY

I don't care what anyone says: Sunrise is the best time to experience the summit of Haleakala. Stay at an Upcountry cottage and make sure that you leave with a thermos of coffee, snacks, and warm clothing. Believe me, at 10,000 feet it gets cold before dawn! From the Red Hill viewing shelter, return to the visitor's center and take Sliding Sands Trail to the crater floor. For an Upcountry lunch, I recommend a delicious vegetarian meal at Crossroads Caffé in Makawao. Afterwards window shop at The Mercantile, Collections, and other shops, and visit the Hui Noeau Visual Arts Center to see exhibits by the best local artists. Drive up the high road to Sunrise Farm and Clouds Rest Protea Farm to see dozens of varieties of these weirdly wonderful flowers, then visit Kula Botanical Garden. Drive into the 30,000-acre Ulupalakua Ranch to visit the tasting room of Tedeschi Vineyards. Dine that evening at the charming, rustic Hali'imaile General Store.

SIGHTSEEING HIGHLIGHTS

✩✩✩ **Haleakala**—This eerie pyramid of incredibly dense volcanic rock has a 3,000-foot-deep crater dwarfing nine cinder-cone mountains across its floor, including thousand-foot-high Puu O Maui. Frequently, misty clouds surround the 7-mile-long, 2-mile-wide crater, obscuring its 21 miles of rim from view. Before starting your drive (two hours from Lahaina, one hour from Kahului) to the summit of Haleakala, phone for a taped report on weather and travel conditions (871-5054). Start early because clouds begin rolling in by 9:00 or 10:00 a.m. *Dress warmly* (sweaters or parka), especially for sunrise and sunset excursions. Prepare to both freeze and fry. Bring insulated clothing, a blanket and mittens, rain gear and sun protection, including hats and sunscreen, lunch and plenty of liquids, as well as cameras, plenty of film, and binoculars.

From Kahului, go southeast on Highway 37 about 10 miles to Pukalani, then turn east (left) on Highway 377. After 6 miles of climbing through cane and then pineapple fields, turn east again onto Highway 378, which snakes 12 miles to park headquarters (open 7:30 a.m. to 4:00 p.m.) through pastures and rocky wastelands at higher elevations. It's more than 10 miles from park headquarters to the summit. Drive carefully on the many switchbacks.

At **Halemauu Trail** (8,000 feet), walk a mile to the crater rim, where you can see the trail zigzagging down the crater wall, or wait until you reach the **Leleiwi Overlook** for the same view closer to the road. At **Kalahaku Overlook** you'll see silverswords, the Hawaii state flowers that take 5 to 20 years to bloom once (sometime from May through October) and then die.

Two visitor's shelters await at the summit: the **Haleakala Visitor's Center** on the rim with exhibits and hourly talks explaining the region's geology and legends, and the glass-enclosed **Puu Ulaula Visitor's Center** where you'll see unforgettable sunrises or sunsets, is an easy ¼-mile hike past the stone shelters and sleeping platforms used by Hawaiians who came up to quarry iron-hard stone for tools.

After spending all the time you want on the summit, go down inside the crater. **Sliding Sands Trail**, the main crater trail, starts near the Visitor's Center. (You can return to the road via Halemauu Trail, hitching back to the summit.) As you descend Sliding Sands Trail, through cinders and ash, you can see the contrasting lush forests of the **Koolau Gap**. It's about 4 miles to the crater floor. On the drive down, stop a mile past the park entrance at **Hosmer Grove** (7,030 feet) for a walk on the nature trail through cedar, spruce, juniper, pines, and trees imported from Australia, India, and Japan. (4–8 hours)

★★★ **Upcountry**—This area encircles Haleakala from Haiku and the cowboy town of Makawao to Kula, **Polipoli Springs State Recreation Area** south of Kula, and out Highway 37 to the Ulupalakua Ranch and the Tedeschi Winery, part of a 37,000-acre ranch.

In **Makawao**, the unofficial capital of Upcountry, behind Old West wooden storefronts you'll find espresso, bagels and cream cheese, more and more boutiques, and galleries favoring local artists down Baldwin Avenue. After spending many months visiting art galleries and artists throughout the islands, my heart is still with the **Hui Noeau Visual Art Center** (2841 Baldwin Avenue, 572-6560), which shows Upcountry and other Maui artists in a 75-year-old plantation house. Stop at the **Maui Crafts Guide** (579-9679) at the intersection of Hana Highway and Baldwin Avenue for an excellent sampling of Maui craft artistry.

The rich volcanic soil of **Kula** makes it Maui's flower and vegetable garden spot. The special experience of Upcountry touring should include a visit to one of Kula's small protea or vegetable farms. Kula is famous for its protea, one of the most amazing and beautiful varieties of flowers, with huge blossoms in 1,400 varieties. These botanical wonders are grown by Upcountry farmers like John Hiroshima at

Sunrise Market and Protea Farm, on Highway 378, 3 miles past the Haleakala National Park turnoff. Phone: 876-0200.

Just before Highway 37 joins Highway 377, native koas, kukul trees, Norfolk Island pine, bamboo orchids, proteas, and native and imported flora grow in the **Kula Botanical Gardens**. This is a perfect spot for a picnic lunch. The gardens display more than 700 types of plants. Besides proteas, orchids, bird of paradise and other exotic blooms, check out Taboo Garden, filled with poisonous plants. Admission is $2.50. Hours: Open 9:00 a.m. to 4:00 p.m. Phone: 878-1715.

To visit the **Tedeschi Winery**, turn left on Highway 37 through the town of Keokea (take the right-hand fork in the road, which has no sign) and pass the **Ulupalakua Ranch**. Allow at least a half-hour before the 5:00 p.m. closing time. Phone: 878-6058. (full day for Upcountry touring)

FITNESS AND RECREATION

If you love to hike, you're in for a treat at Haleakala National Park. Inquire at the visitor's center for maps and information about the park's 32 miles of trails. Miles of well-marked hiking trails traverse Polipoli Springs State Recreation Area, including the 2-mile Redwood Trail.

Highway 377 leads to the Polipoli Springs State Recreation Area and the **Kula Forest Reserve**. After a rugged but beautiful drive through towering trees on Waipoli Road off Highway 377, definitely requiring a four-wheel-drive vehicle, a 4-mile hike leads to spectacular views from the 6,000-foot level on slopes over Ulupalakua. One of Ken Schmitt's **Hike Maui** (879-5270) trips includes Polipoli, solving the transportation problem. If you want to see and learn about Maui's mountain and coastal terrain, there is no better way than to join Ken and explore Haleakala, the West Maui Mountains, Oheo Gulch, and other places. **Hawaiian Trail and Mountain Club** (734-5515) offers information on all of the hiking trails in the islands.

Walkers and hikers will miss out on some the best scenery on Maui unless they tour on horseback. For horse treks around Haleakala, call **Charley's Trail Rides and Pack Trips** (248-8209). Stay at **Thompson Ranch** (878-1910) and ride around the western side of the mountain, or trek up the mountain toward Thompson Ranch and the Tedeschi Vineyards from **Makena Stables** (879-0224).

The most famous bike tour in Hawaii is **Cruiser Bob's Downhill Bicycle Tour** (579-8444 or 800-654-7717) from the top of 10,000-foot Haleakala to Paia. If you can rise to leave at 2 a.m. for sunrise atop Haleakala, you'll be back at sea level by noon.

You can enjoy great scenery and fun golf at the Upcountry **Pukalani Country Club** (par 72, 6,692 yards; 572-1314, Pukalani).

For surfing, **Ho'okipa Beach** near Paia is your best bet. Most of your best windsurfing rental and school facilities are in Kahului. Contact **Hawaiian Sailboard Techniques** (871-5423) or **Hi Tech Surf Equipment** (877-2111), both at 444 Hana Highway.

Papillon Helicopters (669-4884 or 800-367-7095) has a flight that will get you to Haleakala for sunrise, followed by a visit to Hana.

FOOD

In Upcountry, follow Haleakala Highway and the Hali'imaile sign to the Hali'imaili General Store (900 Hali'imali Road, 572-2666). Joe and Beverley Gannon serve beef, pork, and seafood dishes, not to mention an unforgettable Sunday brunch that has made their restaurant the best kept culinary secret in Maui. In Makawao, a big, sophisticated Italian eating surprise is **Casanova's**, (1188 Makawao Avenue, 572-0220); $10 to $14 for a meal à la carte. **Polli's Cantina** (1202 Makawao Avenue, 572-7808) is an excellent vegetarian Mexican restaurant with full dinners for $8 to $12. Until you get to Lihue on Kauai, you won't find better or less expensive saimin than at **Kitada's** (572-7241), on Baldwin Avenue across from the **Makawao Steak House** (572-8711).

In Keokea, on the way to Ulupalakua and Tedeschi Winery, stop at **Grandma's Maui Coffee House** (878-2140) for a cappuccino and bakery products or lunch.

For dining options in Paia, see Chapter 7, "Hana."

LODGING

Don't leave Maui without staying a few nights in Upcountry! You'll never forget it, and you'll keep coming back. The B&Bs in Kula and nearby Olinda reinforce this get-away-from-it-all experience.

Surrounded by two acres of lush greenery, Susan Kauai's **Kula View B&B** provides a very comfortable guest room on the upper level with its own private entrance, surrounding deck area, and beautiful views of the ocean and West Maui mountains. Single or double occupancy at $75 per night includes Kona coffee, fruit, and home-baked muffins. An excellent base for Haleakala trips, Susan can provide a warm blanket and some extra warm clothes for a sunrise visit to

Haleakala. For reservations write to Susan Kauai at P.O. Box 322, Kula, Maui, HI 96790, or call 878-6734.

Another outstanding Upcountry B&B, with marvelous views and surroundings, is Stewart and Shaun **McKay's Country Cottage B&B** (536 Olinda Road, Makawao, Maui, HI 96768, 572-1453). At the top of Olinda Road, 4,000 feet up the slopes of Haleakala, the McKay's "manor house" sits in the midst of a 12-acre protea flower farm. Located 5 miles above Makawao, beautiful, winding Olinda Road is one of the loveliest drives in Hawaii. McKay cottage sleeps four and rents for $95 for two and $18 each additional person with breakfast.

In the midst of a pineapple farm, **Elaine's Upcountry Guest Rooms** (Elaine and Murray Gildersleeve, 2112 Naalae Road, Kula, Maui, HI 96790, 878-6623) has three attractively furnished guest bedrooms with private baths in the main house and a cottage. Rent charming **Bloom Cottage** from Lynne and Herb Horner (229 Kula Highway, 878-1425) or **Kula Cottage** from the Gilberts (206 Puakea Place, 871-6230). The **Silver Cloud Upcountry Guest Ranch** (Old Thompson Road, 878-6101) affords my favorite view of Wailea and the offshore islands.

CAMPING

Haleakala National Park has three multibunk cabins (Kaalaoa, Paliku, and Hokua Cabins) on the crater floor assigned by lottery, as well as tent camping. Write or call Haleakala National Park, P.O. Box 369, Makawao, Maui, HI 96768, 572-9306.

The best camping available in Upcountry is at **Polipoli Springs State Recreation Area** south of Kula. Stay overnight or for several days at the park's three-bedroom cabin ($10 per night for one person, less for each additional person), which has to be reserved well in advance with the Division of Parks (54 High Street, Wailuku, HI 96793, 244-4354).

NIGHTLIFE

Upcountry has only one nightlife spot worth mentioning, and only on weekends—the Casanova Restaurant, a nightclub and dance hall, located in the center of Makawao.

A lmost always described as "heavenly," Hana certainly deserves the appellation. Hidden behind the windward side of Haleakala, remote Hana is part rain forest, part green meadows and, at its essence for those who really know and cherish it, the quintessential spirit of aloha. The legendary Hana Highway supposedly assures this isolation and, indeed, its 617 curves help to explain why the 56 miles from Paia seem so much longer. The real reason, however, may be that Hana doesn't offer typical day-trippers much sightseeing to rave about. Besides the spectacular scenery along the highway itself, the tortuous and twisting six or seven hour round-trip leads mainly to sublime tranquillity. Along the way are rain forests, waterfalls, taro patches, ancient lava flows, traditional Hawaiian houses and churches, peaceful detours and unexpected panoramas, one-lane bridges, and banana groves encircled by eucalyptus. Most visitors miss or ignore the ancient 3-mile trail from Waianapanapa State Park to Hana along the lava and low sea cliffs. Here the island's most fascinating legends cluster around a cave, a water-filled lava tube, where Maui's chiefs and their enemies launched countless vicious attacks. Visitors are drawn beyond Hana to the Seven Sacred Pools where a hiking trail leads to several falls in Haleakala National Park. From the final resting place of Charles Lindbergh, where the ocean view may be best of all, the narrow dirt road reaches around East Maui to Ulupalakua Ranch. ◪

HANA HIGHWAY

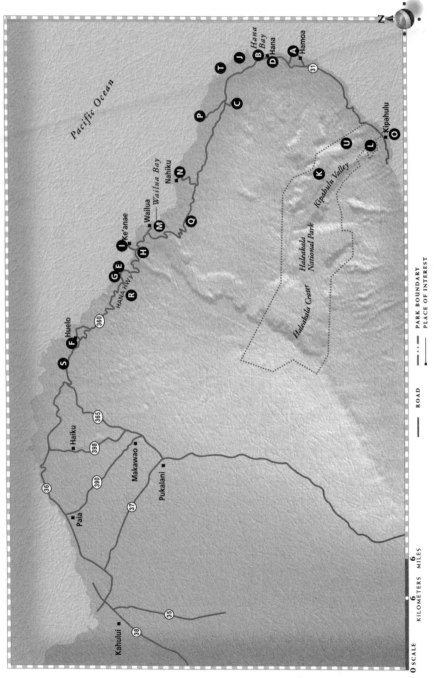

Pacific Ocean

Hana Bay

Hamoa

Hana

Kipahulu

Wailua Bay

Nahiku

Kipahulu Valley

Wailua

Ke'anae

HANA HWY.

Haleakala
National Park

Huelo

Haleakala Crater

Haiku

Makawao

Pukalani

Paia

Kahului

PARK BOUNDARY
PLACE OF INTEREST

ROAD

SCALE

KILOMETERS   MILES

Sightseeing Highlights

(A) Hamoa Beach

(B) Hana Cultural Center

(C) Hana Gardenland Nursery

(D) Hana Ranch

(D) Hasegawa's General Store

(D) Helani Gardens

(E) Honomanu Bay

(F) Huelo

(F) Kaulanapueo Church

(G) Kaumahina State Wayside Park

(H) Keanae Arboretum

(I) Keanae Peninsula

(J) King's Trail

(K) Kipahulu Valley

(L) Makahiku Falls

(M) Miracle Church of Wailua

(N) Nahiku

(O) Ohe'o Gulch

(P) Pi'ilanihale Heiau

(Q) Puaa Kaa State Park

(R) Puohokamoa Falls

(B) Red Sand Beach

(S) Twin Falls

(M) Uncle Harry's Roadside Stand

(T) Waianapanapa State Park

(M) Wailua

(M) Wailua Lookout

(U) Waimoku Falls

Note: Items with the same letter are located in the same town or area

A PERFECT DAY ON HANA ROAD AND IN HANA

Pick up breakfast and a box lunch in Paia at Peach's and Crumble Café and Bakery. Stop a few miles past Kailua Village for a delightful walk up the Waikamoi Ridge Trail. Several other trails of varying difficulty along streams at Puohokamoa and Hailuaena lead to waterfalls. From Kaumahina State Wayside Park descend into Honomanu Valley. Visit Keanae Arboretum and Keanae Peninsula. Stop at Uncle Harry's Fruit Stand at the half-way mark. Past the Wailua Village turnoff, stop at the Wailua Wayside Lookout to see Waikani Falls. When you finally come to Kalo Road, visit Hana Gardenland Café and enjoy lunch in a nursery that could pass for a botanical garden. After lunch follow a nature trail to lava caves in Waianapanapa State Park and coastal footpaths, remnants of the ancient King's Highway, that lead to Hana. On the far side of town, take Haneoo Road to beautiful Hamoa Beach for a swim or just beachcombing. Ten miles further on at Oheo, "Seven Sacred Pools" are formed by Pipiwai Stream filling hollowed out lava basins. Trek up to the Makahiku Falls overlook or perhaps Waimoku Falls a few miles higher. You can continue on past Oheo to Lindbergh's Grave at Hoomau Church, but I suggest returning to Hana for a splurge dinner in the lovely dining room at the Hana-Maui.

SIGHTSEEING HIGHLIGHTS

★★★ **The Hana Highway**—Acclaimed as one of the most beautiful drives in Hawaii, paved in 1962, the "highway" still has one-lane bridges and hairpin turns that haven't been straightened a bit. It's only 52 miles, but allow at least three hours to zigzag at 10 to 25 miles per hour through the 600 bumpy, twisting turns and over 50 one-lane bridges to Hana. Don't try a round-trip in one day, but make reservations for the night and return via Hana Road tomorrow. Day-trippers outnumber the local population, so start early to beat the traffic.

Stop for breakfast in quaint and weatherbeaten **Paia**, a former sugar town that once had a population of more than 10,000. To visit **Twin Falls** and its idyllic swimming holes, drive about 15 minutes down the jeep trail to the double waterfall and first pool, then walk down to the others.

Pause at **Huelo**'s New England-style **Kaulanapueo Church** (b. 1853) en route to the turnout for the nature trail through bamboo and trees on Waikamoi Ridge. Campers already may have found **Kaumahina State Wayside** and its rainforest campground overlooking the sea and another pool at nearby **Puohokamoa Falls**. Tucked in the rugged coastline is the black sand beach at **Honomanu Bay**. **Keanae Arboretum**'s tropical gardens cover the spectrum of Hawaiian plant life: rainforest, plants, flowers, and vegetables. Circle **Keanae Peninsula** to the dead end for views of old Hawaii's farms growing taro and a splendid view of Haleakala.

Other side roads bring you to the fishing village of **Wailua** and **Wailua Lookout, Puaa Kaa State Park**, and nearby waterfalls. A few miles away is another picturesque fishing village, **Nahiku**. The **Miracle Church of Wailua** on Wailua Road at the 18-mile marker is so named because a storm left Wailua Bay strewn with the coral that enabled parishioners to build the church. Just before the airport and **Hana Gardenland Nursery** is the turnoff to **Pi'ilanihale Heiau**, reputed to be Hawaii's largest traditional temple. Stop at beautiful **Waianapanapa State Park**. Garden lovers should visit wonderful **Helani Gardens**, featuring a tremendous variety of groomed and wild trees and plants. Admission is $2 for adults, $1 for children ages 6 to 16. Hours: Open only 2:00 p.m. to 4:00 p.m. Phone: 248-8274. Please call for an appointment. (4–6 hours for Hana Highway tour)

✰✰✰ **Red Sand Beach**—Red Sand Beach, tucked into the side of Hana's Ka'uki Hill, is truly beautiful but dangerous to reach. Follow the tricky footpath from the parking area at the end of Uakea Road, behind the Hana School and Hana Community Center, around the hill and down to the cove. (2 hours)

✰✰✰ **Waianapanapa State Park**—This park has something for everyone. Explore its black sand beach on Pailoa Bay, where you can swim and snorkel on a calm day, walk the rocky lava-strewn **King's Trail** past blowholes and magnificent coastal scenery, and see **Waianapanapa Caves**, a lava tube. (2–3 hours)

✰✰ **Hana Cultural Center**—Hale O Waiwai 'O Hana ("Hana's House of Treasures") on Uakea Road, is a one-room wooden building featuring displays of artifacts from the area and handicrafts of local residents. Hours: Open 10:30 a.m. to 5:00 p.m. Monday through Saturday, 10:00 a.m. to noon on Sunday. Phone: 248-8622. (½ hour)

✰✰ **Hasegawa's General Store**—This charmingly cluttered store is one of Hawaii's famous institutions. Rebuilt after a disastrous fire in 1990, it still packs in an amazing assortment of goods. (½ hour)

⋆⋆ Keanae Arboretum—This arboretum above Keanae Peninsula provides insight into the cultivation of taro, traditionally Hawaii's most important food crop. The arboretum also shows banana and sugarcane cultivation, and grows native and non-native plants and trees. An unmarked 1-mile trail, a little tough and often muddy, can be hiked from the end of the taro patches.

Follow the King's Trail of ancient Hawaiians who used to travel the southern shore to Hana down to Ahini-Kinau Nature Reserve and La Perouse Bay. See firsthand what the final phase of the struggle to preserve Hawaii's cultural and natural environment is all about. Catch glimpses of scarce wildlife: axis deer, wild turkeys, ring-necked pheasants, chukar, California valley quail, and Hawaii owl. In winter, pause on a grassy knoll and watch humpback whales perform in choppy channels between nearby islands. Walks or trail rides later in the day will almost always include a magical Maui sunset lighting up the ocean and the islands of Lanai, Kahoolawe, and Molokini. (½–1 hour)

⋆⋆ Ohe'o Gulch/Kipahulu Valley—South of Hana, private lands and roads conceal many *heiau* that Hawaiians must have built in tropical terrain reminiscent of temples proliferating in Guatemalan jungles. A terrible winding road through gorgeous terrain brings too many tourists to large parking lots near the Seven Sacred Pools that are neither "sacred" nor "seven." Water cascades down Ohe'o Gulch through a few dozen pools to the ocean along a path of rocky ledges perfect for picnics and swimming. About a mile beyond Ohe'o Gulch is Kipahulu, one of Hawaii's most precious and beautiful valleys.

The trip from Kipahulu to Kaupo or Ulupalakua Ranch should only be attempted with four-wheel drive or on foot. The pavement ends shortly beyond Kipahulu and turns into a one-lane gravel road that skirts rocky cliffs and dips steeply into gulches. (In winter, watch out for flash floods.) The tin-roofed semi-ghost town of Kaupo is the start of Kaupo Gap Trail.

⋆⋆ Pi'ilanihale Heiau—By arrangement with the Hotel Hana-Maui (248-8211), visit the otherwise inaccessible fifteenth-century Pi'ilanihale, probably Hawaii's largest traditional temple (340 ft. x 415 ft. terraced stone platform, 50-foot-high walls). If you're a guest of the Hana-Maui, ask them to pack a picnic lunch for excursions to any of these locations. (1 hour)

⋆⋆ Uncle Harry's Roadside Stand—Sadly, "Uncle" Harry Mitchell is no longer around, but his *aloha* spirit still is. Operated by his family, this stand (adjacent to the Wailua exit from the Hana Road) sells Hawaiian food, snacks, and souvenirs with a rare warmth and knowledge of old Hawaii. (15 minutes)

FITNESS AND RECREATION

Take your time and hike the scenic ancient **King's Trail** from Waianapanapa State Park to Hana, along the coast. The 3-mile trail passes over volcanic rock (requiring very sturdy shoes) in a forest of *hala* trees. At **Ohe'o Gulch** ("Seven Sacred Pools"), hike up the gulch to **Makahiku Falls**, or, for the more physically fit, the 1½ miles through an exotic bamboo forest to **Waimoku Falls**.

Hana Ranch offers trail rides on horseback (including breakfast or dinner) along Hana's scenic coastline or to hidden waterfalls, or four-wheel-drive ranch safari tours through unspoiled countryside to see their modern ranching system (248-7238). Horseback riding on the Hana-Kaupo Coast can be arranged through **Ohe'o Riding Stables** (248-7722), **Hauoli Lio Stables** (248-8435), **Charley's Trail Rides and Pack Trips** (248-8209), the **Hotel Hana-Maui** (248-8211), and **Adventures on Horseback** (242-7445). Horseback riding will cost up to $150 for a one-day trip including lunch.

For beach-lounging, snorkeling, and surfing, head for **Hamoa Beach**, between Hana and Seven Sacred Pools. The tricky walk down to **Red Sand Beach** is worth it.

FOOD

At the north end of Hana Highway, in Paia, pick up some delicious espresso and breakfast (and maybe even a box lunch) at **Picnics** (30 Baldwin Avene, Paia, 579-8021). Another suggestion for your coffee, baked goods, and box lunch as early as 6:30 a.m. is at **Peach's and Crumble Café and Bakery** (2 Baldwin Avenue, Paia, 579-8612). **Little Vegan Restaurant** (115 Baldwin Avenue, Paia, 579-9144) will amaze you with its vegetarian specials. **Mama's Fish House** (between Paia and Ho'okipa Beach Park, at 700 Poho Place, 579-9672) serves fresh ono with Hana ginger and Maui onions, a perfect house salad, chilled papaya coconut soup, Mama's homemade bread, and luscious desserts. It's more expensive than you think, but worth it. Nearby **Paia Fish Market** (101 Hana Highway, 579-8030) obviously doesn't aim to win prizes for decor, but the fresh fish meals are inexpensive and tasty

HANA HIGHWAY

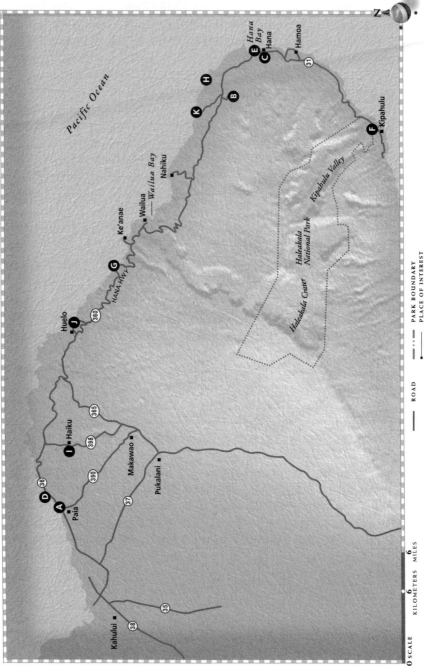

Food

- **A** Bangkok Cuisine
- **A** Dillons's Restaurant
- **B** Hana Gardenland Café
- **C** Hana-Maui
- **C** Hana Ranch Restaurant
- **A** Paia Fish Market
- **A** Peach's and Crumble Café and Bakery
- **A** Picnics
- **A** Little Vegan Restaurant
- **D** Mama's Fish House
- **E** Tutu's

Camping

- **F** Ohe'o Gulch
- **G** Kaumahina State Wayside Park
- **H** Waianapanapa State Park

Lodging

- **C** Aloha Cottages
- **B** Ekena
- **I** Golden Bamboo Ranch
- **I** Haikuleana B&B
- **C** Hana Kai-Maui Resort
- **B** Hana Plantation Houses
- **C** Heavenly Hana Inn
- **C** Hotel Hana-Maui
- **J** Huelo Point Flower Farm
- **K** Kaia Ranch
- **C** The Red Barn
- **I** Tea House Cottage

Note: Items with the same letter are located in the same town or area

lunches. Be daring and try the raw fish Thai-style (marinated with lime juice, lemon grass, chili pepper, kaffir lime leaves, onion and spices) at **Bangkok Cuisine** (120 Hana Highway, Paia, 579-8979). **Dillon's Restaurant** (89 Hana Highway, Paia, 579-9113) is a home away from home for hungry travelers with a taste for artistic cooking and drinks.

When you get to Hana, the best place to start the day with a cappuccino or to have lunch is the **Hana Gardenland Café** (Kalo Road and Hana Highway, 248-7340) inside the Hana Gardenland Nursery. Another special place, also well hidden, is **Tutu's** at Hana Bay—that's right, a stand right on Hana Beach Park where you can enjoy homemade papaya bread and other dishes at the picnic tables. **Hana-Maui** (Hotel Hana-Maui, 248-8211) serves expensive prix fixe meals in a beautiful setting. On the hill across from the post office, the **Hana Ranch Restaurant** serves inexpensive breakfasts and lunches from the take-out window; inside, an all you can eat buffet lunch offers an excellent variety of meat, chicken, fish, vegetable, and salad servings from 11:00 a.m. to 3:00 p.m or dinner (Friday and Saturday only).

LODGING

For an early morning start to Hana and a base near Paia, stay in Haiku at the **Haikuleana B&B** (575-2890), or at a cottage on the ample grounds of the **Golden Bamboo Ranch** (572-7824, or 800-334-1238), or at Ann DeWeese's **Tea House Cottage B&B** (572-5610). On the road from Paia to Hana, the **Huelo Point Flower Farm** (572-1850) rents a cottage with glass walls on three sides over-looking the oceanfront. Down the Ulaino Road, the **Kaia Ranch** (248-7725) fruit and flower farm rents private units. (Further down this road is the beautiful oceanside Kahanu Gardens and the 50-foot, fifteenth-century Piilanihale Heiau.)

Traveling on a tight budget? Reserve one of the 12 fully fur-nished, not fancy but perfectly adequate housekeeping cabins (sleeps up to six, $15–$30 per night depending on the number of persons) next to **Waianapanapa State Park** (Department of Land and Natural Resources, State Division of Parks, 54 High Street, Wailuku, HI 96793, 244-4354).

On the way into Hana, behind a Japanese gate on the left guarded by two stone lions, is the charming **Heavenly Hana Inn** (Box 146, Hana, Maui, HI 96713, 248-8442, $85–$110). Around a common area designed in Japanese motif are four two-bedroom garden suites, one in each corner of the building, with private bath and kitchenette, and screened-in lanai. Other comfortable alternatives managed by the inn include a beach cottage on Hana Bay and **"The Red Barn,"** which is not a barn at all but a very roomy and homey cottage, next to Hasegawa's.

Hana Plantation Houses (P.O. Box 489, Hana, Maui, HI 96713, 923-0772 or 800-228-4262) has a wide variety of attractive units: the Lani Makaalae Studio ($80), very private with its own entrance to a tropical bath garden and jacuzzi tub/shower built into a deck under plumeria trees; Lani Too ($100), a two-bedroom cottage in Japanese-Balinese style; and three other units on a beautifully landscaped five-acre site.

The 19 private oceanview studios and one-bedroom apartments of the **Hana Kai-Maui Resort** condominiums (1533 Uakea Road, P.O. Box 38, Hana, HI 96713, 248-8426 or 800-346-2772) are only a few steps from a stony ocean beach. The lanais with lovely ocean views more than compensate for the plain rooms and lack of air-conditioning.

My heart sank when Rosewood Hotels sold the **Hotel Hana-Maui** (248-8211 or 800-782-9488) to Sheraton, but not to worry: the gracious style and aloha spirit remain unchanged, and no television sets have made their way into this heavenly resort. In its garden setting, low-rise bungalows framed by orchids and plumeria reflect the Hawaii of a half century ago combined with plenty of contemporary pampering and activity choices. Three meals are included in the extravagant price. The hotel shuttles its guests over to lovely Hamoa Beach, west of Hana town. Completely different, much less expensive, but a superbly located and furnished option in Hana is **Ekena** (248-7047). Situated on 9 acres with incredible views, Ekena is within walking distance of the Hana Gardenland Cafe.

Above the Hana-Maui, Fusae Nakamora's **Aloha Cottages'** (73 Keawa Place, P.O. Box 205, Hana, Maui, HI 96713, 248-8420; $60–$85) six simple, cozy two-bedroom units seem to have grown up together with surrounding papaya and banana trees.

The cabins at state parks and private cabins in Hana are the most economical and enjoyable way for adventuresome people to spend a vacation on Maui, with a base either in Hana or on Haleakala. For your vacation pleasure, Stan and Suzanne Collins of **Hana Bay Vacation Rentals** (P.O. Box 318, Hana, Maui, HI 96713, 248-7727 or 800-657-7970) have gathered many home, cabin, and apartment choices in secluded shoreline or hillside locations.

CAMPING

Camping is available at **Kaumahina State Wayside Park**, en route to Hana; **Waianapanapa State Park**, on the outskirts of Hana; and **Ohe'o Gulch**, south of Hana on the bluffs over the sea.

8
HILO

S eedy in appearance and the miraculous survivor of two tsunamis (tidal waves), Hilo nonetheless possesses a turn-of-the-century charm that is easy for some people to enjoy and hard for anyone to forget. Besides the few blocks of historic restoration around Keawe Avenue and the Lyman Mission House and Museum, don't look for tourist attractions or architectural splendor. Hilo offers small but memorable rewards, especially to visitors who rise early and don't demand too much: a lovely landscaped Japanese garden and teahouse, an early morning fish auction or a rainbow dazzling over a falls. Shops and restaurants in Hilo are too good to miss and, in some instances, too hard to find. The town has become one of the main havens and getaways in Hawaii for artists and craftspeople. An inexpensive base for sidetrips up the Hamakua Coast and into Puna, Hilo is only about 30 miles from the far end of Puna where lava flows destroyed Kalapana in 1990. Do search out the orchid and anthurium gardens in and around Hilo, especially the Hawaiian Tropical Botanical Gardens—the Gardens and its cliffside setting are too lovely to miss. If you arrive in Hilo from Honokaa, return to the Kona Coast or Kamuela over Route 20, the spectacular Saddle Road, between Mauna Loa and Mauna Kea. ◪

HILO

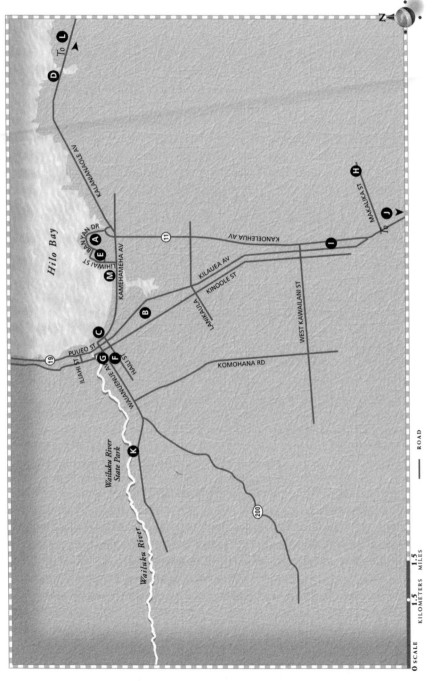

ROAD

SCALE
0   1.5
     KILOMETERS
0   1.5
     MILES

Sightseeing Highlights

Ⓐ Banyan Drive

Ⓑ Dan Deluz's Woods

Ⓒ Downtown Hilo Walking Tour

Ⓓ Hilo Tropical Gardens

Ⓔ Liliuokalani Gardens

Ⓕ Lyman Mission House and Museum

Ⓖ Naha Stone

Ⓗ Nani Mau Gardens

Ⓘ Orchids of Hawaii

Ⓙ Panaewa Rainforest Zoo

Ⓚ Rainbow Falls

Ⓛ Richardson's Beach

Ⓜ Suisan Fish Market

A PERFECT DAY IN HILO

Rent a car at General Lyman Airport. Highway 11 passes the airport and heads downtown to Banyan Drive, which loops around Waiakea Peninsula. Check into the friendly, small Dolphin Bay Hotel north of downtown and, with some directions from John Alexander (and probably some fruit from his garden), you'll be off to Rainbow Falls. With a little luck, rainbows arch over the Wailuku River from sunlight passing through the mist. Back on tree-lined Banyan Drive, the Liliuokalani Gardens invite a stroll through the Japanese garden and over the footbridge. Make your way up Haili Street to the Lyman Museum and Mission House. On the way, at Kinoole Street, stop at the Hawaii Visitors Bureau for all of the information you'll need about Hilo and the Big Island. Explore the Lyman Museum while you're waiting for a tour of the Mission House. Afterwards, you're near several excellent choices for lunch. Try the Lehua Grill or Café Pesto on Kamehameha Avenue before driving out Highway 11 to the Nani Mau Gardens for at least an hour or two of exploring the tropics. The nearby Panaewa Rainforest Zoo closes at 4:00 pm. See if you have time even for a brief visit. It's free. Otherwise return to downtown Hilo for a Japanese dinner at Restaurant Fuji or perhaps a French creole splurge at Roussel's.

GETTING AROUND THE BIG ISLAND

It's a $12 cab fare for the 9-mile ride from the airport into Hilo, and there's no bus service. Once in Hilo, you can use the Hele-On Bus system to get anywhere you want to in the Hilo Bay area or north-south to various botanical gardens for only 75 cents, but it's time-consuming. Within Hilo, the Banyan Shuttle Bus makes two round-trips (one in the morning and one in the midafternoon), stopping at most of the visitor's attractions.

The intra-island buses, Mass Transportation Agency (MTA; 935-8241), are among the best transportation values in the United States and a great way to meet interesting people. It's only four hours by bus from Hilo to Kailua-Kona, but traveling by bus eliminates seeing the island's byways. The Hele-On Bus provides cross-island service Monday through Friday from Hilo to Kailua-Kona via Hawaii Volcanoes National Park, $6 for the cross-island run. The twice-daily round-the-island trip costs $7. You can hail the bus from anywhere along the roadside. There are daily buses from Hilo north to Honokaa and Waimea.

To explore outside of Hilo, Kailua-Kona, and Hawaii Volcanoes National Park, your best bet is car rental. When renting a car, aim for a flat weekly rental rate with unlimited mileage. The daily rate should be around $17.95 (winter) and $14.95 (summer), returning the car back in Hilo seven days later. Pick your car up at or near the airport when you arrive. If you want a car in Hilo, package it with a night at the Hilo Hotel for maximum economy. Otherwise, your best choices are: Phillips's U-Drive (935-1936), Robert's Hawaii Rent-A-Car (935-2858); United Car Services (935-2115), Tropical Rent-A-Car (935-3385), American International Rent-A-Car (935-1108), National Rent-A-Car (935-0891), Dollar Rent-A-Car (jeeps, too; 961-6059), Avis (935-1290), Hertz (935-2896), and Budget Rent-A-Car (jeeps, too; 935-6878).

Tour bus companies offer standardized rates. Jack's Tours, Inc. (961-6666) offers a circle island tour for $40. Gray Line Hawaii (935-2835), Hawaii Resorts Transportation (885-7484), and other companies provide round-the-island, half-day, and full-day tours. Ask about van tours of Mauna Kea ($50). Tours are available to each major sightseeing attraction on the island, including, in the Hilo area, Nani Maui Gardens and the Hawaii Tropical Botanical Gardens (on Onomea Bay).

SIGHTSEEING HIGHLIGHTS

★★ **Banyan Drive**—A drive along the waterfront is hard to miss, since the banyan-shaded thoroughfare passes Hilo's prime hotels. Each tree has been named for a celebrated American, like Babe Ruth, Amelia Earhart, or Cecil B. DeMille, as shown on plaques in front of the trees. (½ hour)

★★ **Dan Deluz's Woods**—This is one shop in Hilo that qualifies as an attraction not be be missed, a museum of wood craft in dozens of types of wood. If you miss this shop, see the other one in Waimea (885-5856). Address: 760 Kilauea Avenue. Phone: 935-5587.

★★ **Historic Downtown Hilo Walking Tour**—To explore Hilo's historic sites, take a self-guided walking tour in the area between Kinoole Street, Furneaux Lane, Kamehameha Avenue, and Waianuenue Avenue. The heart of historic Hilo covers a 24-block area with over 200 buildings of historical interest, including many in Pacific art deco style. The walking tour starts at **Kalakaua Park**, named in honor of King David Kalakaua. The first destination, across Kalakaua Street, is the old police station, which houses the **East Hawaii Cultural Center**'s Old Police Station Gallery.

Kalakaua Park, with a bronze statue of Hawaii's last king, is next to the Hilo Hotel; go down Kalakaua Street, then right to Haili Street, with three (out of the original five) churches, then down Kilauea Avenue, past the **Taishoji Soto Mission** started by Zen Buddhists (1913), to Furneaux Lane. Turn left on Kamehameha Avenue to see some interesting architecture: Renaissance Revival (**Hafa Building**); Mediterranean (the **Vana Building**); and even art deco (the **S. H. Kress Building**). Turn up Waianuenue Avenue to Keawe Street, and make a left to see several wooden buildings typical of early twentieth-century Hilo, which have been remodeled. (3–4 hours)

★★ **Lyman Mission House and Museum**—In a restored Mission House that was built in 1839, you'll see handsome handmade koa mantels and doors, ohia wood furniture from the 1850s, portraits, and family china. The museum was established by members of the Lyman family in 1932, 100 years after their arrival as missionaries in Hilo. The Mission House, listed in the State and National Registers of Historic Places, was built in 1839 and later restored to its original appearance and furnishings. Watch for special events at the museum on local history and culture, folklore, and the arts. The museum's Hawaiian and ethnic exhibits, volcanic and mineral exhibit, large Pacific shell collection, and Oriental exhibits are well worth the visit. Admission fee is $3.50 for adults, $2.50 for children ages 12 to 18, $1.50 for children ages 6 to 11. Hours: Open daily except Sunday, 10:00 a.m. to 4:00 p.m. Address: 276 Haili Street. Phone: 935-5021. (1–2 hours)

✮✮ **Nani Mau Gardens**—Seeing a nursery with commercially grown orchids and anthuriums, the city's chief crop (although the anthurium capital actually is nearby Pahoa in the Puna District), is a must for visitors. Three miles south of Hilo, 1½ miles off Highway 11, these 20 acres grow all the varieties of trees (coffee, macadamia, and fruit), plants (orchids, ginger, and hibiscus), and unusual Hawaiian herbs and flowers that make the island famous. Also visit the Japanese garden, miniature lake, and herb garden. With a change of ownership, the admission charge has jumped to $6 but is still worth it. (An alternative is to wait and see the Hawaii Tropical Botanical Gardens on the way north to the Hamakua Coast.) Arrive early before the loads of tour buses. Hours: Open daily from 8:00 a.m. to 5:00 p.m. Address: 421 Makalika Street. Phone: 959-3541. (1–2 hours)

✮✮ **Panaewa Rainforest Zoo**—A few miles south of Hilo, across Highway 11 from Nani Mau Gardens, this rare zoo features rainforest creatures in a natural setting. Admission free. Hours: Open daily 9:00 a.m. to 4:30 p.m. Phone: 959-7224. (1 hour)

✮✮ **Rainbow Falls**—Rainbow Drive, off Waianuenue Avenue, at Wailuku River State Park, offers memorable views around 9:00 to 10:00 a.m. when rainbows rise in the morning mist. Up the road a couple of miles are the **Boiling Pots**, water bubbling up from lava beds. Watch for the signs. (1–2 hours)

✮ **Hilo Tropical Gardens**—Kauai may be the "Garden Isle," but more than 2,500 species of plants and flowers flourish in the Big Island's landscape, 95 percent found only in Hawaii. At the eastern end of town on

Highway 12, about 2 miles from the airport, Hilo Tropical Gardens display enough native Hawaiian shrubs, trees, tropical flowers, and other plants in its gardens to satisfy most visitors. Admission $1. Adddress: 1477 Kalanianaole Avenue. Phone: 935-4957. (1 hour)

✿ **Liliuokalani Gardens**—Located on Waiakea Peninsula at the north end of Banyan Drive, this garden boasts 30 acres of colorful flowers and greenery including a Japanese garden with pagodas, lanterns, ponds, bridge, and ceremonial teahouse. This is one of the largest such gardens outside of Japan. The **Nihon Japanese Cultural Center** (123 Lihiwai Street, 989-1133) overlooks Liliuokalani Gardens and contains many authentic Japanese treasures, an art gallery, tearoom, and restaurant. Check on special events. The gardens are always open, and admission is free. (½ hour)

✿ **Naha Stone**—Standing in front of the County Library on Waianuenue Avenue, this is the bigger of two stones (the other is the Pinao Stone) that in ancient days stood before the temple of Pinao near the library site. The Naha Stone was used by Hawaiians to prove the legitimacy of heirs to the Naha lineage. He who could move the stone would become king. The one who overturned it would conquer all the islands. According to legend, Kamehameha the Great overturned the stone while still a young boy. (Yes, it weighs about a ton!)

✿ **Orchids of Hawaii**—You still need to see a nursery operation where tropical cut flowers, orchid sprays, and leis are packed for shipping. Drive south on Highway 11, take a right at Palai and a left on Kilauea Avenue to Orchids of Hawaii. Admission free. Address: 2801 Kilauea Avenue. (1 hour)

✿ **Richardson's Beach**—On Hilo Bay's south shore is Hilo's best beach for views of the bay and the best beach in the area for swimming, snorkeling, surfing, and fishing. **Richardson Ocean Center**, an oceanographic museum, is located next to the beach ¼ mile beyond the end of Kalanianaole Avenue. Admission is free. Hours: Open from 9:00 a.m. to 5:00 p.m. Phone: 935-3830. (1–2 hours)

✿ **Suisan Fish Market**—Stop by the corner of Banyan Drive and Lihiwai Street to see shop owners bidding in many languages for the day's fish catch. Arrive by 8:00 a.m., when the fish auction starts. Address: 85 Lihiwai Street. (1 hour)

FITNESS AND RECREATION

Most coastal roads are ideal for bicycling. The **Saddle Road**, roads to **Waimea**, and **Hilo to Hawaii Volcanoes National Park** are hard pedaling. Rent bicycles in Hilo at **Ciao Activities** (969-1717).

Consider *flightseeing*—a thrilling helicopter tour, second to none in Hawaii. Take off from Hilo's General Lyman Field (which is cheaper for volcano flights) or a helicopter pad near the Waikaloa Resort along Highway 19 and fly over Mauna Loa, volcano scenery, Puna and Kau, Kealakekua Bay and the City of Refuge, Kailua-Kona and the Keauhou-Kona Coast, Waimea and North Kohala, Waipio and the Hamakua Coast. A two-hour round-the-island Kilauea Tour costs about $300 per person. Contact **Kenai Air Hawaii** (329-7424 or 800-622-3144) or **Papillion Helicopters** (885-5995 or 800-562-5641).

FOOD

Everyone who visits Hilo will want to have breakfast at **Bears Coffee** (106 Keawe Street, 935-0708). It's where you'll meet some of the most interesting residents of Hilo, who linger at sidewalk tables as long as possible. There's still only one place for pancakes in Hilo (or the Big Island) 24-hours-a-day—**Ken's House of Pancakes** (1730 Kamehameha Avenue, where it intersects with Banyan Drive, 935-8711). Open 24 hours, it offers pancakes, burgers, and classic roadside meals from chicken to steak all day, and late-night eats from midnight to 6:00 a.m.

Cafe 100 (969 Kilauea Street, 935-8683), on your way out of town across from Kapiolani School, is a drive-in that belongs at the top of the lunch bargain list with its teriyaki steak, mahi mahi, chicken and steak dishes, and chili. Just follow the crowds of locals. Closed Sunday. You love Thai food? **Soontaree's** (Hilo Shopping Center, 934-SIAM) may be the best Thai restaurant that you have ever eaten in, certainly on the Big Island. You want the freshest fish in Hawaii? **The Seaside** (1790 Kalanianaole Avenue, 935-8825) takes your fish out of their own fish ponds. Try the rainbow trout.

For a long time, **Roussel's** (60 Keawe Street, 935-5111), classic French New Orleans creole cooking, was an oddity in Hilo and the only restaurant worth talking about. Enjoy Chef Oliver's lunch menu with the same superb dishes at lower prices. Try the blackened fish. I ate at **Café Pesto's** (882-1071) first location, in the nondescript Kawaihae Shopping Center, several years ago when it touted great pizzas and good pastas. They still serve some of the best and most unusual pizzas in Hawaii, and the menu is exponentially better, only they have a new location in the Hata Building (969-6640). One of the other unlikely bistro restaurants is the older **Lehua's Bay City Bar & Grill** (11 Waianuenue Avenue, one block from Keawe, 935-8055), serving imaginative sauces and seasonings combined with fresh local ingredients. Prices are very reasonable, and the menu includes char-broiled beef and chicken burgers as well as exotic dishes. Another Hilo surprise is **Pescatore** (235 Keawe Street, 969-9090) for Italian favorites with a gourmet touch. **Queen's Court** (935-9361) in the Hilo Hawaiian Hotel is my first choice for salad bar.

Hilo is the best place on the Big Island and arguably in Hawaii for excellent Japanese cuisine and atmosphere at reasonable prices. **K.K. Tei Restaurant** (1550 Kamehameha Avenue, 961-3791) out toward the airport is a good example. **Restaurant Fuji**, in the Hilo Hotel (142 Kinoole Street, 961-3733), offers authentic and reasonably priced Japanese food, with outstanding hibachi-grilled food and a tempura bar, in comfortable indoor and outdoor settings. The Nihon Cultural Center's **Nihon Restaurant** (123 Lihiwai Street, 969-1133), open 11:00 a.m. to 2:00 p.m., and 5:00 p.m. to 8:30 p.m., has full-course dinners at moderate prices and also an excellent sushi bar.

Ting-Hao Mandarin Restaurant (Puainako town center, off Highway 11 beyond the airport, 959-6288) serves every style of Chinese food, not just Mandarin. Chef Cheng's huge menu, the restaurant's low prices, generous portions, ample daily specials, variety of vegetarian dishes, and friendliness earn every hungry visitor's loyalty and gratitude. Presumably you won't be bothered by formica-topped tables and fluorescent lighting. This restaurant captures Hilo and the Big Island at its best. **Sun Sun Lau's Chop Sui House** (1055 Kinoole, 935-2808) is consistently selected as one of the Big Island's top Chinese restaurants, with amazingly reasonable gourmet food. **Leung's Chop Suey House** (530 East Lanikaula Street, 935-4066, at the intersection of Kanoelehua Avenue about a mile past Banyan Drive) is in an unappealing industrial area, but it serves some of the best eat-in or take-out Cantonese food in town until 8:30 p.m.

LODGING

Hilo is finally fulfilling its promise as a tourist destination, with accommodations options to suit every budget. A lush garden setting full of fruit trees in a quiet neighborhood makes the 18-unit **Dolphin Bay Hotel** (333 Ilahi Street, Hilo, HI 96720, 935-1460)

HILO

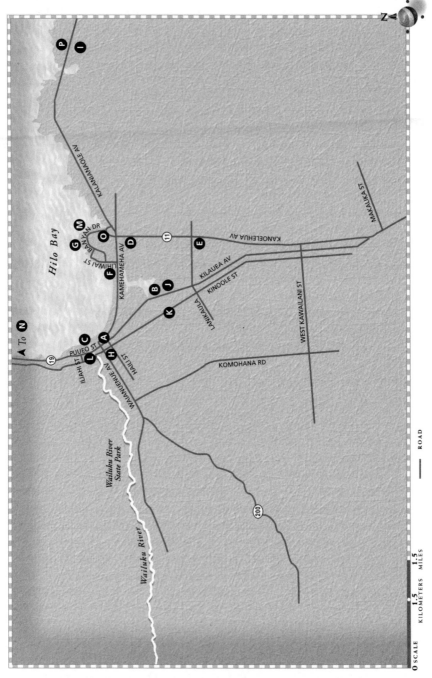

Food

Ⓐ Bears Coffee

Ⓑ Cafe 100

Ⓒ Cafe Pesto's

Ⓓ Ken's House of Pancakes

Ⓓ K.K. Tei Restaurant

Ⓐ Lehua's Bay City Bar & Grill

Ⓔ Leung's Chop Suey House

Ⓕ Nihon Restaurant

Ⓐ Pescatore

Ⓖ Queen's Court

Ⓗ Restaurant Fuji

Ⓒ Roussel's

Ⓘ The Seaside

Ⓙ Soontaree's

Ⓚ Sun Sun Lau's Chop Sui House

Ⓓ Ting-Hao Mandarin Restaurant

Lodging

Ⓛ Dolphin Bay Hotel

Ⓜ Hawaii Naniloa Hotel

Ⓝ Hale Kai

Ⓗ Hilo Hotel

Ⓞ Hilo Hukilau Hotel

Ⓟ Seaside Studio

Ⓛ Wild Ginger Inn B&B

Note: Items with the same letter are located in the same area everyone's favorite little hotel on the Big Island. The hotel has large, nicely furnished studios, one- and two-bedroom apartments, full kitchens, and tub-shower combinations. For a budget price, you can have a roman bath in your one-bedroom apartment with a kitchen, but no TV, air conditioning, or phones.

Robert and Sandra Woodward took over the Old Lanikai Hotel across from the Dolphin Bay and transformed it into **Wild Ginger Inn B&B** (100 Puueo Street, Hilo, HI 96720, 935-5566 or 800-882-1887), a serene alternative to more expensive hotels in Hilo. The $45 single and double (nonsmoking) rooms include continental breakfast.

Hilo's bed-and-breakfast accommodations compare favorably with any place on the island. Patty Oliver's **Seaside Studio** (961-6178) is especially attractive for families and large groups. Patty's three-bedroom oceanfront house with a private beach, tide pools, and private lanai, rents for $55 for one or two people. Surfers should contact Evonne Bjornen to stay at **Hale Kai** (111 Honalii Pali, Hilo, HI 96720, 935-6330), overlooking one of the best surfing spots on the island, Honalii Surfing Beach. Rates are about $70, including a delicious, hearty breakfast.

The **Hilo Hukilau Hotel** (126 Banyan Way, 96720, 935-0821 or 800-367-7000) has single or double rooms, standard to deluxe, for $55 to $70. Located bayfront at the far end of Banyan Drive, they're on a side street fronting on Reed's Bay. The 139 rooms are small and plain, but lanais overlook lush gardens. The **Hilo Hotel**, (142 Kinoole Street, 96720, 961-3733) across from Kalakaua Park is as basic (and clean), with or without kitchens, as you'll find in Hawaii. Rooms have telephones. Ask for the standard ($49 per day) or deluxe ($62–$68) room with car. Otherwise, single or double standard and deluxe rooms cost $38 and $49 for one or two persons. The renovated **Hawaii Naniloa Hotel** (93 Banyan Drive, 969-3333 or 800-367-5360), with excellent views of Hilo Bay and Mauna Kea, spa and health club, is one of the best accommodation deals on the island. Referred to locally as the "Queen of Banyan Drive," this high-rise hotel is right on the water, with beautiful grounds and a very attractive swimming pool area, spacious lobby, and large comfortably furnished rooms.

NIGHTLIFE

Downtown Hilo shuts down by 9:00 p.m, and few bars stay open past 10:00 p.m. The hot spot for dancing is upstairs at **Apple Annie's**, 100 Kanoelehua Avenue. Rock 'n' rollers who don't want to dance should head for **J.D.'s Banyan Broiler** on Banyan Drive after

10:00 p.m. until 2:00 a.m. For a bar where you're likely to meet interesting locals, try **Rosey's Boathouse**. There's no place to dance, but an excellent guitar combo provides light background music, perfect for good conversation.

Lively Hawaiian entertainment on Friday and Saturday nights continues until 2:00 a.m. at **Lehua's Bay City Bar & Grill** (11 Waianuenue Avenue, one block from Keawe, 935-8055).

Much of Hilo's nightlife centers around the hotels. For a lively evening out, the **Springwater Café and Bar**, Waiakea Villas Hotel, has a light menu, drinks, and entertainment from pop to Hawaiian, Wednesday through Saturday until 2:00 a.m. The **Ho'omalimali Bar** of the Hawaii Naniloa Hotel has a disco that stays open on Friday and Saturday nights until 3:00 a.m.

Like the spectacular road to Hana on Maui, Saddle Road is not the driving nightmare that you've heard about, and driving it opens up incomparable vistas. Check your gas beforehand since there are no gas stations for 87 miles.

About 2 miles past Rainbow Falls, Saddle Road splits off to the left. Alternatively, most visitors simply turn inland at the **Highway 200** sign off Highway 19 just north of Hilo. On the way up the mountain, you'll pass **Kaumana Caves**, a lava tube worth exploring. The caves contain a fern grotto. If you intend to explore the caves, bring a flashlight.

Saddle Road first passes through thick rainforest, then fern and *ohia lehua* forest until the 3,000-foot level, when the landscape changes dramatically to a vast lava flow. Midway up from either the Kona or Hilo side is the turnoff for the **Mauna Kea Summit Road,** paved until the **Ellison Onizuka Center for International Astronomy** (329-3441) at the 9,200-foot level. From this base camp for scientists and astronomers, a gravel road winds across and up the steep mountain another 7 miles, nearly to the 14,000-foot level. (4–5 hours)

At Mauna Kea's summit, location of the world's foremost collection of optical and infrared telescopes, the **W. M. Keck Observatory**'s instruments will be on line by the time you read this book. At that time, the road to the summit will be paved, too. The best way to see Mauna Kea's observatory complex, view a magnificent sunset (with visibility that can range for 100 miles), and see the clear night sky full of stars through a portable telescope is with Monte Wright's **Paradise Safaris** (322-2366, $80 per person) or **Waipio Valley Shuttle/Mauna Kea Summit Tours** (775-7121). A five- to six-hour customized van tour by the owners of Waipio Shuttle, they will pick you up and drop you off in the Honokaa-Waimea area.

Five miles west of the Mauna Kea Observatory Road (20 miles from Highway 190), at 6,500 feet in the midst of rolling grasslands, seven fully furnished cabins (with hot showers as well as cooking utensils) in **Mauna Kea State Park** (Pohakuloa) can be rented from the State Department of Natural Resources (961-7200).

Among the four **Hawaiian Eyes-Big Island Bicycle Tours** (P.O. Box 1500, Honokaa, HI 96727, 885-8806), as of this writing, **Mauna Kea Iki** makes a 2½ hour, 10-mile descent down a 3,000-foot slope of Mauna Kea ($48). A Saddle Road trip covers 27 miles and a 4,000-foot descent from 9:00 a.m. to 3:00 p.m. (including lunch, $90).

At the 12,000-foot level, a trail leads ¼ mile from the jeep road to the **Keanakakoi** ("Cave of the Adzes"), where ancient Hawaiians mined stones for their adzes. Almost at the top is **Lake Waiau** (13,020 feet), the highest lake in the United States, 400 feet across and 15 feet down to an impervious bottom in a porous mountain.

It's about a two-hour drive from Hilo's tropical nurseries to the frigid lunar landscapes of Mauna Kea and Mauna

SADDLE ROAD TO MAUNA KEA SUMMIT

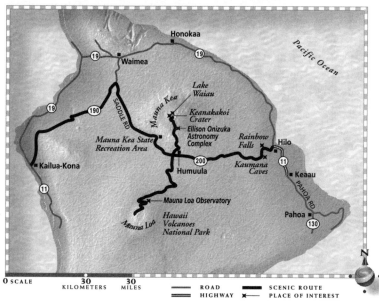

Loa where the endangered silversword plant and the *nene* goose, the state bird, thrive in rarified isolation. Waimea is 55 miles from Hilo via Saddle Road, descending 3,000 feet in 15 miles from Saddle Road through the gamebird grasslands of the Pohakuloa Area of Mauna Kea State Park. Kailua is 87 miles from Hilo on Saddle Road, a two- to three-hour drive if you're in a hurry.

You can drive to the 9,400-foot level of Mauna Kea in an ordinary passenger car, though car rental agencies will refuse to rent if you say that you're going to drive on the rough Saddle Road. Twenty-seven miles from Hilo, a 9-mile spur road leads to the Mauna Kea trailhead at Kilohana (9,620 feet) and a 17-mile road up Mauna Loa. At Humuula Junction, the **Mauna Kea Road** heads north and the **Mauna Loa Road** south. On the Mauna Loa Road, if your car is tuned for high altitudes you can drive 8 miles to a locked chain across the road (weekdays), 9 miles below the observatory, or the full 17 miles on weekends past fantastic black, silvery, brown, and reddish lava shapes. If you intend to get out of your car and walk around at altitudes above 4,000 feet, bring one or two layers of warm clothing (sweaters, jackets, or pullovers). At higher altitudes, temperatures can drop suddenly to the 40s and near freezing at the summits. ◼

9

HAMAKUA COAST

Many visitors to the Big Island miss this former sugarcane coast with its beautiful gorges and valleys, tiny one-street villages tucked in tropical landscapes, scenic parks, and little-known forest reserves. The 50 miles along Route 19 from Hilo to Waipio, and magnificent Waipio itself, are worlds apart from the rest of Hawaii and the resorts of the Kohala coast. Now that the Hamakua Sugar Company has shut its doors, who knows what will befall the thousands of acres of shimmering green landscape and the peaceable people who depended on sugarcane for a living and life itself. For those who love the Hamakua Coast, it's painfully difficult to dissociate the 4 miles leading to the dense growth of Akala State Park, the 12 miles of winding road leading down to Laupahoehoe Point, and the few miles up the side of Mauna Kea to Kalopa State Park from the visual embrace of sugar cane. But these scenic forest areas and their lacy cascades carved out of mountainsides and black lava-crusted shorelines remain as beautiful as ever. Honokaa, an old-fashioned plantation town, will likely have to join the twenty-first century after its seemingly effortless evasion of the twentieth. Between Honokaa and nearby Kukuihaele en route to Waipio, art and crafts undoubtedly will continue to flourish along with B&Bs and their exceptional gracious hospitality. ◨

HAMAKUA COAST

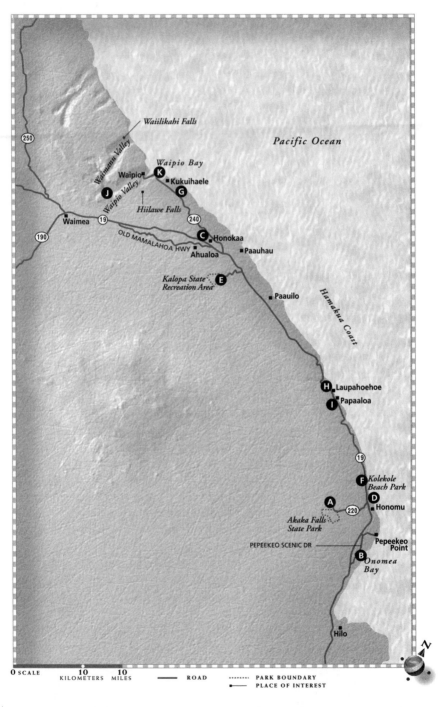

Waiilikahi Falls

Pacific Ocean

Waimanu Valley

Waipio Bay

Waipio ■ **K**

J ■ **Kukuihaele**

Waipio Valley **G**

Hiilawe Falls

■ Waimea (19) OLD MAMALAHOA HWY (240)

(250)

(190)

C ■ Honokaa

■ Ahualoa ■ Paauhau

Kalopa State Recreation Area **E**

■ Paauilo

Hamakua Coast

H ■ Laupahoehoe

I ■ Papaaloa

(19)

F *Kolekole Beach Park*

A **D** ■ Honomu

(220)

Akaka Falls State Park

PEPEEKEO SCENIC DR ■ Pepeekeo Point

B *Onomea Bay*

■ Hilo

N

0 SCALE   10   10
KILOMETERS   MILES   ——— ROAD   ········ PARK BOUNDARY

■—— PLACE OF INTEREST

Sightseeing Highlights

A Akaka Falls State Park

B Hawaii Tropical Botanical Garden

C Honokaa

D Honomu

E Kalopa State Recreation Area

F Kolekole Beach Park

G Kukuihaele

H Laupahoehoe Point

I Papa'Aloa

J Waipio Valley

K Waipio Valley Lookout

A PERFECT DAY ON THE HAMAKUA COAST

A long the 50 miles from Hilo to Waipio, take side roads to enchanting attractions. About 7 miles from Hilo, take the 4-mile Pepeekeo Scenic Drive across wooden bridges along the Old Mamalohoa Highway and Onomea Bay. Stop at the Hawaii Tropical Botanical Garden. Drive on, turning onto Highway 220 at Honomu, where you can climb about 4 miles to beautiful Akaka Falls. Return to Highway 19 and drive another 12 miles to Laupahoehoe Point for breathtaking views. About 13 miles further on Highway 19, visit Kalopa State Park. Drive on to downtown Honokaa. Of course, you'll want to visit the Hawaiian Macadamia Plantation but, if your time is limited, have lunch at the Honokaa Club, your last chance to eat before Waipio Valley. Drive on to Kukuiliaele where you can visit the Waipio Valley Artworks. Arrange ahead of time to check in at Jackie's Waipio Wayside B&B and ask her to prepare a supper for you before you board the Waipio Valley Shuttle for a 90-minute tour of Waipio Valley.

SIGHTSEEING HIGHLIGHTS

★★★ **Hamakua Coast: Hilo to Waipio**—The lush Hamakua Coast, from Hilo to Waipio Valley, is an attraction in itself. One of the most unique drives in Hawaii, it rewards with gorgeous views up the gulches and down to the lava shore.

After touring the Hawaii Tropical Botanical Garden, at Honomu, follow steep Highway 220 past sugarcane fields for another 3 miles to **Akaka Falls State Park**. Besides several stunning falls, the 65-acre park in the junglelike gulch contains tropical plants from all over the world.

The stream from Akaka Falls runs 4 miles toward the ocean and empties at **Kolekole Beach Park** under the first bridge on Highway 19 north of Honomu, a popular local picnic area with camping facilities. A much better spot for picnics or just a rest stop is **Laupahoehoe Point**, a beautiful peninsula just 11 miles from Honakaa. **Papa'Aloa**, just south of Laupahoehoe, is a picturesque village thick with tropical growth and palm trees.

One of the least visited natural areas on the Big Island, 100-acre **Kalopa State Recreation Area** is easily accessible, 2 miles south of Honokaa and another 2 miles up a good secondary road. The park provides a rare opportunity to explore one or more of the lush gulches along the Hamakua Coast; camping and cabins are also available. A series of well-marked nature trails identify a tremendous variety of flora. **Honokaa** and **Waipio Valley** complete your tour of the Hamakua Coast. (2 hours)

★★★ **Hawaii Tropical Botanical Garden**—Five miles north of Hilo near the start of the 4-mile scenic road along Onomea Bay, this garden consists of 27 acres running the gamut of Hawaii's flora, with waterfalls, streams, and a lily pond. It is one of the most beautiful botanical gardens in the Hawaiian Islands. Bring mosquito repellent to fully enjoy the tropical environment.

Visitors are taken down to the valley in a shuttle van from the HTBG's parking lot and registration area about ½ mile from the garden's entrance along Turtle Bay and 1 mile from the turnoff on Highway 19 which says Scenic Route 4 Miles Long. The last minibus departs for the garden at 4:30 p.m. Adults are charged a $12 tax-deductible admission fee, and children under 16 are admitted free. Phone: 964-5233. (2 hours)

★★★ **Waipio Valley**—At the Waipio Valley Lookout (at the end of Highway 240 just beyond Kukuihaele), a ribbon of sparkling white surf disappears around the headland as you gaze down on Waipio Valley. A mile wide at the sea, it is 6 miles deep in rich green, checkered with taro patches, bounded by 2,000-foot-high cliffs, and constantly watered from the *pali* at the rear of the valley. Hawaii's highest waterfall, **Hiilawe Waterfall**, cascades 1,300 feet to the valley floor. Kamehameha the Great came many times to the valley, where many great kings were buried, to renew his spiritual power.

You can hike down to the valley (see "Fitness and Recreation," below), ride a horse or a mule, or be driven in a four-wheel drive or van. **Waipio Ranch**, operated by Sherri Hannum and Wayne Teves, has horseback rides into Waipio Valley which can be arranged 24 hours in advance through Joe Matthieu at Waipio Woodworks (775-0958). A half-day tour costs $55, full-day $100, including a four-wheel-drive ride down and back up the valley to Kukuihaele. **Hawaiiana Resorts Transportation** (885-7484, Hilo) can also put you on horseback for $65. An alternative to horses is provided by Peter Tobin: **Waipio Valley Wagon Tours** (775-9518) is a two-hour trip by mule wagon, Wednesday through Monday, for $45 per person (half price for children under 12).

If you prefer wheels, let Les Baker and the **Waipio Valley Shuttle's Land Rover** (775-7121) drive you down from the lookout, 900 feet above the *pali* coast. The round-trip cost is $40 for adults, $20 for children, for a 90-minute tour or $60 to $100 for a half- to a full-day jeep and hiking tour into the valley, including a light lunch. (This same company offers the state-authorized four-wheel-drive tour of Mauna Kea, a six-hour trip for $65 per person.) Contact **Gray Line Hawaii** (935-2835, Hilo) or Hawaii Resorts Transportation about van tours of Waipio. (4–8 hours)

★ **Honokaa**—Forty miles north of Hilo, on Highway 240, Honokaa is the second-largest city on the Big Island. Honokaa only has 2,500 residents, and it still feels like the 1920s. However, a real estate and population boom is in the making as the Hamakua Sugar Company seeks solvency by selling off a large part of its holdings for development. Main street Honokaa consists of false-front buildings and local stores with a smattering of shops catering to tourists. One of the world's largest macadamia nut growing areas, Honokaa is 9 miles from Waipio Valley and 16 miles from Waimea. From the center of town, take

Lehua Street down a steep hill toward the sea to the **Hawaiian Holiday Macadamia Nut Factory**, open daily 9:00 a.m. to 6:00 p.m. The macadamia nut industry in Hawaii, currently another depressed agricultural business, actually started in Honokaa. On the way down the hill is **Kamaiina Woods**, a factory and gift shop (with an outlet in Waimea's Opelo Plaza) for handcrafted items from koa, milo, and other local woods. Open daily 10:00 a.m. to 5:00 p.m. (1 hour)

✯ **Honomu**—Drive 10 miles north of Hilo on Highway 19 to the turnoff on your left for Highway 220 to Honomu. The **Honomu Plantation Store** is worth a visit just to see photographs of plantation life along the Hamakua Coast at the turn of the century. You can buy some snack items for a picnic, coffee, and delicious pastry at the bakery next door. (20 minutes)

FITNESS AND RECREATION

Akaka Falls State Park north of Hilo offers easy paths for hiking through dense growth to Akaka Falls. Two miles south of Honokaa and another 2 miles up another road, **Kalopa State Park** has many easy marked trails through the rainforest. Be sure to walk the **Kalopa Gulch Trail**; hike through groves of acacia, koa, kopiko, pilo, and hapuu along the **Native Forest Nature Trail**.

The jeep trail running through Waipio Valley to the twin 1,000-foot waterfalls is my favorite "hike" in this region. Drive up to the Pololu Lookout at the end of Highway 27, north of Waipo and, starting early in the morning, hike all the way to Waipio, then hitch-hike back.

Waimanu Valley is for the adventuresome with hiking experience and stamina. Continue from Waipio Valley for 9 miles on the **Waimanu Valley Trail**. The trail climbs up steep cliffs to the adjoining and even wilder valley, through a series of 14 gulches. The trail shelter is nine gulches from Waipio Valley, two-thirds of the way to Waimanu. About half the size of Waipio Valley, Waimanu is very similar. **Waiilikahi Falls** about 1½ miles along the northwest *pali* of the valley, and the large pool of water for swimming below it is worth making your own trail there. There's water in the valley (boil or treat it, though) and numerous beachfront campsites, or you can return that night to Waipio.

FOOD

On the way up to Akaka Falls, **Ishigo's Inn and General Store** (963-6128) in Honomu Village, has munchies and a remodeled B&B. The **Hotel Honokaa Club & Restaurant** (Highway 240, 775-0678) serves a mix of Japanese and American food, breakfast, lunch, and excellent seafood and steak dinners at moderate prices. Otherwise, drive to Kamuela for the best dinner choices (see the next chapter for dining in Kamuela).

LODGING

My favorite places to stay are the Big Island's B&Bs. Each one offers a totally different get-away-from-it-all-environment. Try **Ishigo's Inn B&B** (963-6128) in Honomu Village on the road to Akaka Falls State Park. Wake up to fresh pastries from Ishigo's bakery downstairs and then head up the hill to the park.

Waipio Wayside (P.O. Box 840, Honokaa, HI 96727, 775-0275 or 800-833-8849), Jackie Horne's renovated and very charming sugar plantation home, between Honokaa and Waipio, is bordered by a white picket fence that is unmistakable from the road. This lovely bed-and-breakfast retreat has five tastefully redecorated rooms for rent—from one with shared bath at $55 to the Bird's-Eye Room, an $85 suite opening onto the deck and garden. The gourmet breakfasts are superb.

At the 2,500-foot elevation on Mauna Kea, in Ahualoa 3 miles from Honokaa toward Kamuela, the rustic **Log House B&B Inn** (P.O. Box 1495, Honokaa, HI 96727, 775-9990) has five nicely furnished bedrooms, two with private baths, a living room with fireplace and a library upstairs, all for $55 with an excellent breakfast. To get to the Log House, turn left at Tex Drive-In and then right on Mamalahoa Highway. Mamalahoa Highway winds up the mountainside 11 miles through Ahualoa to rejoin Highway 19, about 6 miles from Waimea Center, after crossing beautiful rolling pastureland. In Ahualoa, off twisting tree-lined roads to hidden-away places, where usually no one drives unless they know someone living there, is another of the Big Island's finest B&Bs: Michael Cowan's **Mountain Meadow Ranch B&B** (775-9376, $55 per couple), with two lovely bedrooms for rent on the private first floor, with their own sauna and bathroom, and a patio leading to a pretty garden in the woods.

The **Hamakua Hideaway** (Box 5104, Kukuihaele, HI 96727,

HAMAKUA COAST

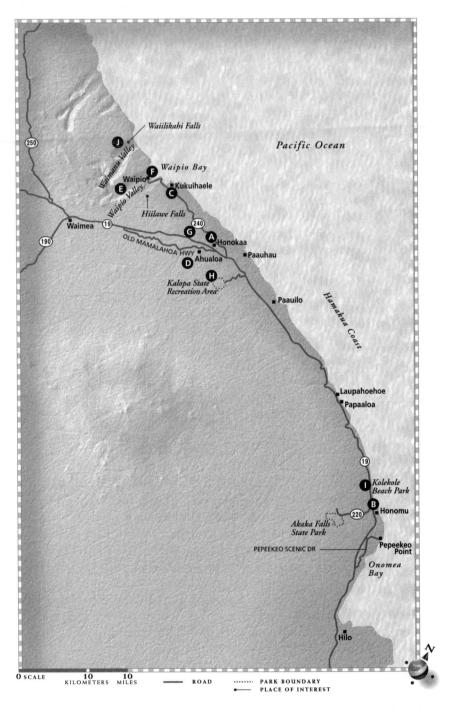

Waiilikahi Falls

J

Waimanu Valley

Pacific Ocean

Waipio Bay

F

Waipio ■

E

Waipio Valley

■ Kukuihaele

C

Hiilawe Falls

■ Waimea

19

OLD MAMALAHOA HWY

240

G

A

■ Honokaa

190

■ Ahualoa

D

■ Paauhau

H

Kalopa State Recreation Area

■ Paauilo

Hamakua Coast

■ Laupahoehoe
■ Papaaloa

19

I *Kolekole Beach Park*

B

220

■ Honomu

Akaka Falls State Park

PEPEEKEO SCENIC DR

■ Pepeekeo Point

Onomea Bay

■ Hilo

N

O SCALE | 10 KILOMETERS | 10 MILES ——— ROAD ········ PARK BOUNDARY ■—— PLACE OF INTEREST

Food

Ⓐ Hotel Honokaa Club & Restaurant

Ⓑ Ishigo's Inn and General Store

Lodging

Ⓒ Hale Kakui

Ⓒ Hamakua Hideaway

Ⓑ Ishigo's Inn B&B

Ⓓ Log House B&B Inn

Ⓓ Mountain Meadow Ranch B&B

Ⓔ Waipio Hotel

Ⓕ Waipio Treehouse

Ⓖ Waipio Wayside

Camping

Ⓗ Kalopa State Recreation Area

Ⓘ Kolekole Beach Park

Ⓙ Waiilikahi Falls

Note: Items with the same letter are located in the same town or area

775-7425), three houses down from the Waipio Woodworks, is a B&B, less than 1 mile from the Waipio Lookout, at $60 per night. Christan Hunt's two units—the treehouse suite, nestled in a huge 100-year-old mango tree ($60 per night or $350 per week), and the cliff house (with fireplace, $75 per night, lower rates for a longer stay), on a cliff over-looking Maui, are rustic, secluded, and an excellent value. Guided jeep trips leave from in front of the Woodworks a few doors away. The **Waipio Treehouse** (775-7160) is either hugely overpriced or a bargain depending on how much it means to you to tell friends you lived in a tree overlooking Waipio with a hot tub down below.

Bill and Sarah McCowatt have planted a 2-acre organic orchard with over 30 species of tropical fruits from around the world (that their guests are free to pick). This is just one of the reasons to stay at **Hale Kakui** (P.O. Box 5044, Kukuihaele, HI 96727, 775-7130 or 800-444-7130) guest cottages, located on about 4 (beautifully landscaped) acres overlooking Waipio Valley with a fabulous ocean view. Studio, two-bedroom, and three-bedroom units, fully equipped with full baths and kitchenettes, range from $75 to $150 per night. Breakfast is sup-plied on the first day only. Located about a mile toward Waipio from the village of Kukuihaele, and 8 miles from Honokaa, there is no bet-ter combination of units, site, location, and view on the big island.

As the next best thing to camping, for $15 per person per night you can stay at octogenarian taro farmer Tom Araki's five-room **Waipio Hotel** (no water, electricity, or refrigerator, two kitchens equipped with Coleman stoves and kerosene lamps), with reservations (no deposits) arranged by mail at least a month in advance to Tom Araki, 25 Malana Place, Hilo, HI 96720, or contact Waipio Valley Shuttle, or call 775-0368 or 935-7466 (Hilo). Bring your own food from the Last Chance Store next to the shuttle's office. It's 2 miles from the lookout to the hotel in the valley. Bring plenty of mosquito repellent for the hike or ride. The nearby river has fresh prawns, and the road to the beach is lined with fruit trees.

CAMPING

Kolekole Beach Park has camping facilities (county permit required). In addition to tent camping with a state permit, several cabins are available at **Kalopa State Recreation Area** (961-7200). You'll find beachfront campsites at **Waiilikahi Falls** in Waimanu Valley.

10

KAMUELA AND NORTH KOHALA

Waimea (Kamuela) is one of Big Island's most delightful surprises. There are four very unique ways to arrive in Waimea, and each is a totally different part of the Waimea experience. Try them all: ten miles up the plateau from the Kona-Kohala coast and its resorts; ten miles winding up the hill from Honaaka and Waipio, and then directly through the meadows, with magnificent Mauna Kea on your left; 25 miles winding from Kailua-Kona on Route 190 along the base of Mauna Loa and through Parker Ranch; or, instead of driving up the long hill from Hapuna Beach, drive north through Kawaihae around North Kohala on the Akoni Pule Highway to Hawi, and come back to Waimea on the beautiful 20-mile Kohala Mountain Road, past sloping grassland and stands of eucalyptus and Norfolk pine, and down the mountain. Waimea actually spreads out in the saddle between the Kohala Mountains and Mauna Kea. In any case, visitors should pass through North Kohala's Hawi and Kapaau en route to the Pololu Valley Lookout. More so than in most parts of Hawaii, time moves very slowly in North Kohala. In Waimea, Parker Ranch and its visitors' center, historic homes, and churches offer more of a sense of Hawaii's history than you'll find on other islands. Many people are even more impressed with the town's unique restaurants, some of the best in Hawaii, and the small tourist-oriented shopping malls in the restored Hale Kea. ◪

KAMUELA AND NORTH KOHALA

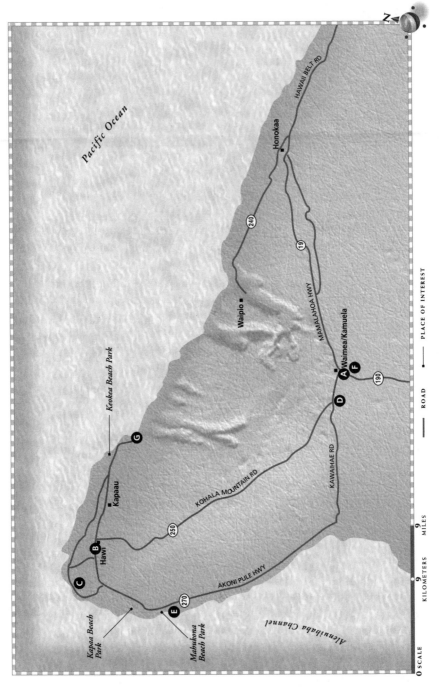

Sightseeing Highlights

Ⓐ Cook's Discoveries

Ⓑ Hawi

Ⓒ Kamehameha Akahi Aina Hanau

Ⓓ Kamuela Museum

Ⓔ Lapakahi State Historical Site

Ⓒ Mookini Heiau National Historic Site

Ⓕ Parker Ranch Visitor Center and Museum

Ⓖ Pololu Valley Lookout

Ⓕ Puuopelu

Note: Items with the same letter are located in the same or town area

A PERFECT DAY IN KAMUELA AND NORTH KOHALA

Spend your morning at the Parker Ranch Visitor Center and Museum and the mid-nineteenth century Parker Ranch homestead, Puuopelu. Let either Chef Ann Sutherland or Peter Merriman prepare an unforgettable lunch for you. Head up beautiful Highway 250 to Hawi, the gateway to another era. After a stroll through sleepy Kapaau, drive out to the Pololu Valley Lookout. Backtrack to Highway 271 to loop past King Kamehameha's birthplace and the temple Mookini Heiau. Follow Highway 270 down the Kawaihae Coast, stopping at Lapakahi State Historical Park. Dine in Kamuela, and spend the night at Waimea Garden Cottage or one of the B&Bs that Barbara Campbell can find for you in the area.

SIGHTSEEING HIGHLIGHTS

★★★ **Kamuela**—Kamuela offers the best of both worlds as a touring base: great hiking or horseback riding in the cooler mountains, some of Hawaii's most beautiful beaches only minutes away, and relatively low-priced accommodations. (Also known as Waimea, the name of another town on Kauai, Kamuela is used as the post office address to avoid confusion.)

Besides the restaurants and Parker Ranch, the main local attraction is the reconstructed Spencer House on Highway 19 that now is **Cook's Discoveries** (885-3633), filled with everything Hawaiian in craft, art, food, and other items (long overdue on the Big Island).

✩✩✩ **North Kohala**—This region was the home of Kamehameha the Great, from which he launched a conquest of all the islands. The shoreline of North Kohala is etched with historical sites and beach parks that tourists rarely visit. At the end of coastal Highway 270 (Akoni Pule Highway), which passes through Hawi and Kapaa, is the steep *pali* overlooking **Pololu Valley**, a major taro valley of old Hawaii, accessible by a trail from the lookout. (4 hours, including driving Highway 250)

Lapakahi State Historical Park (A.D. 1300), a 600-year-old, partially restored Hawaiian fishing village, stands on isolated, rugged terrain about 12 miles from Kawaihae. Canoe sheds, a fishing shrine, a demonstration of Hawaiian salt-making, game exhibits, numerous house sites, stone tools and utensils, and other interesting artifacts are displayed along trails around the site, which is open daily for tours. From December through April, you may even see migrating whales near shore. (½ hour)

Originally built for human sacrifices, the remains of 20-foot stone walls surrounding **Mookini Heiau National Historic Site** are reached by a left turn on a bumpy unpaved road at the end of Upolu Airfield's runway. (After a heavy rain, this road requires a four-wheel drive.) Surf pounds against steep cliffs below windswept fields around this sacred site, home of all-powerful gods, once the exclusive domain of *alii* who came to worship here as early as the twelfth century. The remaining foundation is an irregular triangle measuring 125 by 250 feet, with 30-foot-high and 15-foot-thick walls. Offerings (not human, of course) are still to be seen on the altar.

The *heiau* is only a few hundred yards from Kamehameha's birthplace—**Kamehameha Akahi Aina Hanau**. Inside the low stone wall around this historic place are some boulders believed to be the actual stones on which Kamehameha, unifier of the Hawaiian kingdom, was born around 1752. (½ hour)

✩✩ **Kamuela Museum**—Founded by Albert and Harriet Solomon, this museum, located at the junction of Highways 19 and 250, is a collection of Royal Hawaiiana and artifacts from around the world. Featured are stuffed animals and reptiles from four continents, assorted ancient weaponry, pioneer clothing, and Chinese furnishings. It also displays photographs of the Parker family through the years (Harriet's grandfather was John Palmer Parker). Admission is $5.00 for adults, $2 for children under 12. Phone: 885-4724. (½ hour)

★★ **Parker Ranch Visitors Center and Museum**—A frustrated and adventuresome sailor from Newton, Massachusetts, John Parker Palmer jumped ship in Hawaii in 1809 and created a dynasty that changed the history of the Big Island forever. With more than 250,000 acres spreading across North Kona, South Kohala, Waimea, and North Kohala, Parker Ranch today is the largest cattle ranch in the United States, raising one of the largest Hereford herds in the world. Parker imported cowboys from Mexico and South America—*paniolos* (a Hawaiian version of *EspaHawai*)—to work as ranch hands.

The museum at Parker Ranch Visitors Center, first stop on a tour of the ranch, was started by Thelma Parker Smart, mother of the ranch's current owner, Richard Smart. It depicts the history and genealogy of six generations of Parker Ranch owners, displaying old family photos, furnishings, special and day-to-day clothing, old saddles and riding paraphernalia, and other interesting items. One room is dedicated to Duke Kahana-moku, the Hawaiian Olympian and sheriff of Oahu for 25 years who was credited with introducing surfing to Australia.

Shuttle buses take visitors around the ranch to see **Puukalani Stable** and the adjoining horse-drawn carriage museum and two Parker family historic homes: **Puuopelu** and **Mana**. Puuopelu contains a remarkable art collection.

Admission to the visitors center and museum is $5 for adults, $3.75 for children. The two-hour Paniolo Shuttle Tour by mini-van to Puukalani Stables, the working ranch, and the historic homes at Puuopelu costs $15 for adults, $7.50 for children under 12. Another two hours and $39 for adults and $19 for children will take you on the **Paniolo Country Tour** to the original homestead site of Mana and the Parker family cemetery, with lunch included. Hours: Visitors center and museum are open daily from 9:30 a.m. to 3:30 p.m. Phone: 885-7655. (2–4 hours)

★★ **Pololu Valley Lookout**—From the lookout, the valley floor and a black sand beach are visible 300 feet below. Looking down the fantastic coastline of Hawaii's *pali* of hidden valleys, gorges, and luxurious foliage, you see the only access to the shoreline is a dirt trail down to

Pololu Beach, an easy 15-minute walk past thick lauhala growth. (If you're tempted to swim, watch out for currents.) Pololu is five valleys and 12 miles from Waipio Valley. (1–2 hours)

✩ **Hawi**—This former plantation town and the Big Island's northern-most town is full of rustic and derelict charm. Before the Kohala Sugar Company pulled out in the early 1970s, Hawi could boast of four movie theaters. Today there are none. Colorful old houses and false-front stores in Hawi also resemble Makawao and Paia on Maui, or a bustling version of Kauai's comparatively quiet Hanapepe. You'll enjoy the small ways in which Hawi is improving (and especially the Bamboo Restaurant). The large restaurant-entertainment spot next door, **Hale Alii** (889-0206), in the center of town is one visible sign of change. Along the road to the Pololu Valley Lookout stands the original gilt and bronze statue of **Kamehameha the Great**. (The statue of Kamehameha in downtown Honolulu is a replica.) (½ hour)

FITNESS AND RECREATION

For great hiking head for the cool **Kohala Mountains**. Contact **Hawaiian Trail and Mountain Club** (734-5515) for information on trails, and **Hugh Montgomery** (885-7759) to talk about his hiking tours. You can also hike all the way from **Pololu Valley Lookout** to Waipio, starting early in the morning, then hitchhike back.

Snorkelers and beachcombers should visit **Kapaa Beach Park** and **Mahukona Beach Park**.

FOOD

Really good breakfasts are hard to find in Kamuela. The **Waimea Coffee & Country** (Highway 19, 885-4472), across the street from Gallery of Great Things, has the best cup of coffee in town and some decent pastries ("imported" from the French Bakery on Kaiwe Street in Kailua-Kona).

Two of Kamuela's restaurants are among the best in Hawaii: Peter Merriman's **Merriman's** (885-6822) and, across the road, Hans Peter Hager's **Edelweiss** (885-6800, no reservations). Former chef at the Mauna Lani Bay hotel, Peter Merriman is the apostle of local produce: steaks, lamb, fish, vegetables, fruits, herbs, and so forth and the result-ing Pacific Rim cuisine will be long remembered. Next door to leg-endary Merriman's, at **Mean Cuisine** (Opelo Plaza, 885-6325), you'll find one of my favorite chefs (and persons) on the island, Ann Sutherland, former executive chef at the Mauna Lani Resort's Gallery Restaurant (885-7777), whose amazing variety of entrees and desserts are served at even more amazingly low prices. Pick up some delicious picnic items here, such as the Greek spinach pie and Thai chicken.

Drive out to tiny Hawi in North Kohala for one of the best new dining places on the Big Island, Chef Hamel's **Bamboo Restaurant** (889-5555). Chef Hamel took over the old Takata Store, a landmark general store during the sugar plantation era, and serves a wonderous assortment of Pacific Rim dishes at very reasonable prices. While you're in North Kohala, drive about ten minutes to Kapaau for some of Hawaii's best ice cream at the **Tropical Dreams Ice Cream Factory and Café** (889-0505 or 0105).

LODGING

U pcountry Hideaways consists of three B&B cottages, each in a beautiful location, with a different decor, and very hospitable and knowledgeable hosts: Doug and Dodi MacArthur's modern **Puu Manu Cottage** (885-6247, $85), a two-bedroom cottage in a pasture on the "wet side" of Kamuela, with beautiful views of Mauna Kea; Barbara and Charlie Campbell's **Waimea Gardens Cottage** (885-4550, $85) in natural wood, with antique furnishings, located on the "dry side" of Kamuela, near a stream flowing down from the Kohala Mountains in the background; and at the beginning of Highway 250 to Hawi, **Hawaii Country Cottage** (885-7441, $65), with a completely private bedroom, living room, bathroom, and kitchen. All of these B&Bs and many more on the Big Island and throughout Hawaii can be reserved through Barbara Campbell's **Hawaii's Best Bed & Breakfasts** (P.O. Box 563, Kamuela, HI 96743, 885-4550 or 800-262-9912). In Hawi, you will also find the **King's Trail Inn** (889-5606), formerly the Old Hawaii Lodging Company (and previous to that, Luke's Hotel). Catering mainly to local people, the **Kohala Club Hotel** (889-6793) in Kapaau has not changed much in 50 years (and apparently doesn't care).

CAMPING

C amping in North Kohala is available at **Keokea Beach Park**, **Kapaa Beach Park**, and **Mahukona Beach Park**. For reservations and a permit, call the county parks branch office in Kamuela at 885-5454.

KAMUELA AND NORTH KOHALA

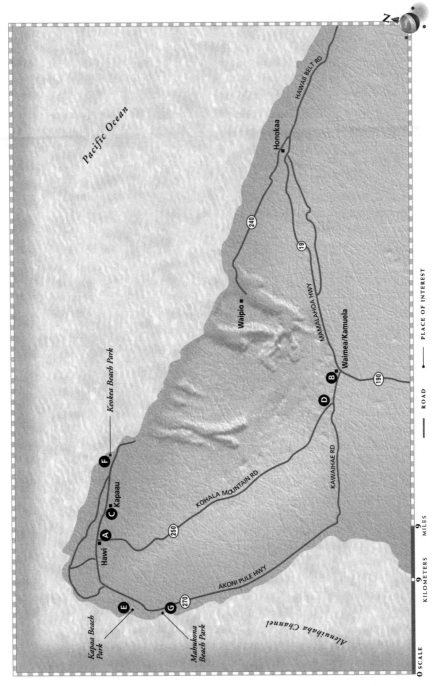

Food

- **Ⓐ** Bamboo Restaurant
- **Ⓑ** Edelweiss
- **Ⓑ** Mean Cuisine
- **Ⓑ** Merriman's
- **Ⓒ** Tropical Dreams Ice Cream
- **Ⓑ** Waimea Coffee & Country Factory and Cafe

Lodging

- **Ⓓ** Hawaii Country Cottage
- **Ⓐ** King's Trail Inn
- **Ⓒ** Kohala Club Hotel
- **Ⓑ** Puu Manu Cottage
- **Ⓑ** Upcountry Hideaways
- **Ⓑ** Waimea Gardens Cottage

Camping

- **Ⓔ** Kapaa Beach Park
- **Ⓕ** Keokea Beach Park
- **Ⓖ** Mahukona Beach Park

Note: Items with the same letter are located in the same town or area

NIGHTLIFE

The ranch's **Kahilu Theater** (885-6017) across from the Parker Ranch Visitors Center brings about a dozen top theatrical, dance, and concert events to Kamuela each season. The current owner of the ranch, Richard Smart, great-great-great-grandson of the founder, is a thespian and responsible for bringing Kamuela theater and performing arts that outshine those found in towns of similar size elsewhere in the United States.

Scenic Route: Kohala Mountain Road— Kamuela to Kawi

Winding through the Kohala Mountains, this very scenic route reaches an elevation of 3,500 feet. With views of the shimmering peaks of Mauna Kea, Mauna Loa, and Hualalai and the plains and ocean below, Highway 250 is a memorable drive from Highway 19 near Kamuela to Hawi at the northern tip of the peninsula. All along this road a succession of spectacular views frame the western shoreline.

KOHALA MOUNTAIN ROAD

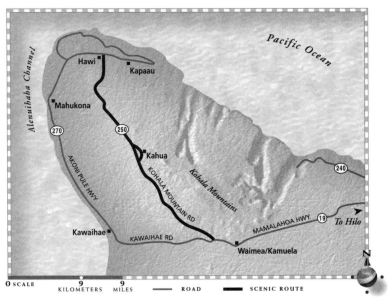

SOUTH KOHALA

According to legend, ancient tribal clairvoyants read the destinies of newly born babies from their umbilical cords placed in circles carved in ropy pahoehoe lava such as you can see in Puako, about 31 miles north of Kailua. Surely none of the ceremonies at these sacred petroglyphs foretold what has occurred along the 20 miles of coastline stretching from Kailua to Kawaihae. Today the shore harbors a half dozen of the world's most attractive and challenging golf courses. Until the early 1960s, nothing grew out of the hardened lava fields north of Kona. Then a Texas oilman sailed into Kahuwai Bay and discovered the abandoned Hawaiian settlement of Kaupulehu. Only 5 miles from today's Keahole Airport, a vision took root of plush, roughing-it, thatched-hut Polynesian bungalows (hale)—Kona Village. At the same time, Laurence Rockefeller built a classic of luxurious refinement, the recently refurbished Mauna Kea Beach Hotel. Rockefeller will never be forgotten for his donation of neighboring Hapuna Beach to the state, which now shares its marvelous beachfront with the new Hapuna Beach Prince. A late development, the Mauna Lani Bay resort offers "bungalows" priced at $2,500 per night. Extra pampering is available at the Ritz-Carlton Mauna Lani. Between the Mauna Lani and Kona Village, on beautiful crescent-shaped Anaehoomalu Beach, the Hilton Waikoloa Village substitutes extravagance for elegance. Guests take a train to their rooms and can swim with dolphins in a huge pool. Thousands of acres of barren lava have yielded fantasies, Hawaiian-style comforts, and Pacific Rim and other exquisite cuisines to suit almost any taste. ◪

SOUTH KOHALA

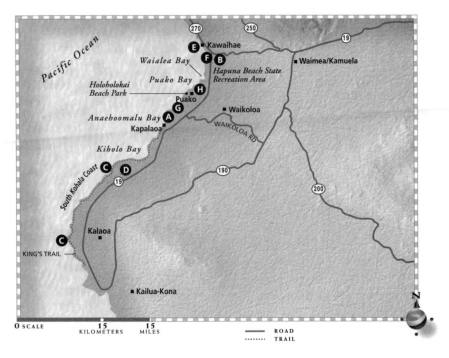

Sightseeing Highlights

A Anaehoomalu Beach

B Hapuna Beach State Recreation Area

C King's Trail

D Kona Village Resort

E Mailekini Heiau

F Mauna Kea Beach Hotel

G Mauna Lani Bay Hotel

H Puako

H Puako Petroglyphs

E Pu'uokohola Heiau National Historical Site

A Waikoloa Beach Resort

Note: Items with the same letter are located in the same town or area

A PERFECT DAY IN SOUTH KOHALA

D rive down the 10-mile long hill to the Kohala Coast enjoying the scenery all the way (while keeping your eyes on the narrow twisting road, too). Kawaihae is to the right and ahead is Pu'uokohola Heiau National Historical Site that Kamehameha built to fulfill a prophecy that he would conquer the islands. Nearby are two older heiaus, the ruins of Mailekini, converted into a fort, and Haleokapuni, dedicated to the shark gods. Drive about a mile south of the Mauna Kea Resort to Hapuna Beach State Recreation Area and enjoy the beautiful beach that Laurance Rockefeller donated when he built the Mauna Kea. After lunch visit Holoholokai Beach Park, just north of the Ritz Carlton Hotel on the Mauni Lani Resort. Spend your afternoon lolling on the beach, snorkeling, or scuba diving—and your evening enjoying a gourmet meal and entertainment at one of the resorts.

SIGHTSEEING HIGHLIGHTS

★★★ **Anaehoomalu Beach**—A long crescent of palm-fringed white sand and one of the Hawaii's most beautiful beaches, Anaehoomalu Beach adjoins the 543-room Royal Waikoloan. Drive into the resort and, just before the Royal Waikoloan, make a left turn to the beach and a nearby field of petroglyphs. (2–4 hours)

★★★ **Beaches of Hapuna and Puak—"69" Beach** (Waialea Bay) is named for a marker on the main highway near Hapuna Beach State Recreation Area. Turn down to Hapuna Beach park, pass the entrance to the park, and stay on the paved road that passes the turnoff to the park. In a little more than ½ mile, turn on the dirt road to the right and take the left fork down the hill to the beach. The same road can be reached by taking a left from Highway 19 at the Puako turnoff and then the next right to reach the dirt road turnoff (to the left this time) described above. Between Hapuna and the Mauna Lani Resort, Puako is a residential community along 3 miles of **Puako Bay**.

Tide pools and snorkeling along this coast are excellent. Deservedly crowded on weekends, **Hapuna Beach State Recreation Area** is one of the nicest beaches in Hawaii. Only 3 miles from Kawaihae, this wide white sand beach is bordered by kiawe, hala, and coconut trees (now surrounded by Mauna Kea resort development). Above the beach, six very basic screened A-frame shelters sleeping four people each can be rented for a nominal fee from the Division of State Parks. (2–4 hours)

✵✵ **King's Trail**—Invisible along the coastline is a trail—the Ala Kahakai—of smooth rocks built by ancient Hawaiians to ease the trip across the island over rough lava. Later, cattle were run on the trail to docks at Kawaihae, and donkey caravans carried salt to and from Kailua. The King's Trail passes along the edge of Kona Village Resort—past ponds, tide pools, and lava tubes filled with clear water, and Loretta Lynn's house and other private estates at Kiholo Bay—and inconspicuously hugs the coastline past all South Kohala and North Kona coastal resorts. (1–2 hours)

✵✵ **Kona Village Resort**—Built on the site of an ancient fishing village, the Kona Village Resort, 15 miles north of Kailua and 7 miles north of the airport, consists of 125 "plush primitive" thatched-roofed huts (*hales*), fashioned after seven different styles of Polynesian island accommodations. Among all of South Kohala's resorts, Kona Village is the most complete escape from reality. All meals are provided. The hales contain no television sets, radios, air-conditioners, or even keys for doors. The resort is barely visible from Highway 19 except for a new golf course shared with the neighboring Four Seasons Hotel, another oasis speck on the ocean surrounded by black volcanic rumble.

✵✵ **Mauna Kea Beach Hotel**—The hotel's collection of more than 1,500 art treasures from the Pacific and Asia is a museum in a beautiful resort set in 500 manicured acres. For a hotel that is as expensive and exclusive as the Mauna Kea, its rooms are surprisingly simple in decor and furnishings. Art tours are conducted twice a week for guests and others. (1–3 hours)

✵✵ **Mauna Lani Bay Resort**—The resort is set in a historic area known as Kalahuipua, along the King's Trail, where Kamehameha I built a small village and canoe landing at Keawanui Bay.

In addition to its fantastic golf courses, the pristine white sand beach on a lovely cove below the 6-story structure, historic fish ponds in a beautifully landscaped area, ten tennis courts in a garden pavilion, and other amenities make this one of the top resorts in the world. With these attractions, the Mauna Lani can rent two-bedroom ocean-side "bungalows" with their own swimming pool and Jacuzzi for $2,000 a night (including a chauffeured limousine, a butler around the clock, and a maid on call). Luxurious two- and three-bedroom condominiums at **Mauna Lani Terrace** (800-882-4252) and **Mauna Lani Point** (800-642-6284) are run like a self-contained hotel, with all of the services of the main hotel. Mauna Lani Bay Resort now includes the 542-room **Ritz Carlton-Mauna Lani Bay** (800-241-3333) that, in addition to elegant public areas, plush rooms, and beautifully landscaped courtyards, adds three more restaurants to the wealth of previously existing restaurants at the resort. (2–4 hours)

✭✭ **Puako Petroglyphs**—Ordinary people, not artists, seem to have made the linear and triangular figures—warriors, canoes, paddles, spears, and other objects. These rock carvings, more than 3,000 of them, were made as part of ritual or prayer, and speak of spiritual phenomena—*mana*. (½ hour)

✭✭ **Pu'ukohola and the Mailekini Heiau**—One mile south of Kawaihae, where Highway 270 turns into Highway 19, is a National Historic Site (Pu'ukohola) preserving Mailekini Heiau and the John Young House. Mailekini Heiau is the last major temple built on the Big Island. Kamehameha built this sacrificial temple in 1791 for his war god, Ku, after a prophet told him to conquer all of Hawaii. When it was completed, he invited his chief rival, Keoua Kuahuula, to the dedication and slew him before he reached shore. In the next four years he conquered all the islands except Kauai. John Young, an English seaman who became Kamehameha's close adviser, taught Hawaiians how to use cannon and musket, converted Mailekini Heiau into a fort, and became a Hawaiian chief. (½ hour)

✭ **Waikoloan Resort**—The Waikoloan Resort features the 1,241-room Hyatt Regency Waikoloa (800-223-1234) on 62 acres landscaped with protected lagoons for swimming instead of a beach. Various wings of the hotel, its shopping areas, seven restaurants, and other facilities are connected by a monorail and motorized passenger boats operating on parallel canals and tracks. Oriental art fills the grounds and lines a mile-long walkway that parallels the monorail and canal route. (1–2 hours)

Waikoloa—At mile marker 74 on Highway 19, look for Waikoloa Road weaving up Mauna Kea's lower slopes for 13 miles, connecting coastal Highway 19 with the more scenic and winding upper Highway 190. About halfway to Highway 190, you pass Waikoloa Village and Waikoloa Stables (883-9335). Short-term rentals in Waikoloa Villas (800-367-7042) would put you closer to the middle of the South Kohala and North Kona resorts. The sunshine in Waikoloa is more predictable than in Kamuela (Waimea) in inland South Kohala, but Waikoloa is windier. In a contest between staying in Kamuela or Waikoloa, Kamuela wins hands-down for economy rentals, excellent B&Bs, restaurants, shopping, and scenery.

FITNESS AND RECREATION

Drive to the **Mauna Lani Hotel** to explore the historical **King's Trail** along an old lava flow that winds around two fish ponds and along the coast. Driving down to the 76-mile point, you'll find more petroglyphs in a large lava field next to the Royal Waikoloan's golf course and Anaehoomalu Bay where you can walk along several large fish ponds. Drive south to the 82-mile point and, if you have at least an hour, you can walk down the jeep trail to the coconut-fringed, black-sand beach of **Kiholo Bay**.

Mauna Lani Resort Golf Course (885-6655) and **Mauna Kea Beach Hotel Golf Course** (882-5888) are legendary. The **Waikoloa Beach** (885-6060) courses (Beach and King) both are beautiful, with oceanfront holes. For the panoramic ocean views on any of these courses, I'll suffer the lava and any other hazards.

The South Kohala Coast has some of the best swimming beaches anywhere in the islands: **Spencer Beach Park**, near Kawaihae and just below the Pu'ukohola Heiau; **Hapuna Beach**, one of the finest white sand beaches in the hemisphere; **Anaehoomalu Beach**, one of the most beautiful, fronting the Royal Waikoloan Hotel; and **Kaun'oa Beach**, which fronts the Westin Mauna Kea Hotel. All of these beaches have public access.

Scuba diving and snorkeling are outstanding off of **Spencer Beach**, **Hapuna Beach**, **Puako Beach**, and **69 Beach**. The water is very clear and calm, protected from trade winds by Mauna Kea and Mauna Loa. The lava rock reefscapes are home to colorful red pencil urchins, moorish idols, lionfish, butterfly angelfish, green and yellow trumpetfish, and spotted moray eels.

FOOD

On the first level of the Kawaihae Shopping Center, **Café Pesto** (882-1071, Kawaihae) serves some of the best pasta, pesto, and pizza on the Big Island. The latest addition to the South Kohala Coast, the **Bistro** (880-3200) at the Hapuna Beach Prince Hotel, was guaranteed success when Chef Albert Diederisks moved over from the Mauna Kea Beach Hotel. If you're prepared to splurge, wear a dinner jacket, and be totally spoiled for dining experiences for a long time to come, dine à là carte or *prix fixe* on meat, fish, or fowl. Just to make the choices unbearably difficult, **The Coast Grille** (880-1111), also at the Hapuna Beach Prince Hotel, has an even better view, especially at sunset, and the cuisine is comparably superb.

Sitting at an outside table at sunset at the Mauna Lani Bay Hotel's **The Canoe House** (885-6622), anticipating the Pacific Rim cuisine of Chef Alan Wong (who actually has moved to Le Soleil in the same hotel), is one of my favorite total experiences in Hawaii. The **Bay Terrace** (breakfast, lunch, and dinner) is less formal but also delicious, and you'll find superb, creative meat and seafood dishes at the **Gallery** (885-7777).

The Dining Room (885-2000) at the **Ritz-Carlton Mauna Lani** has changed executive chefs since I was at its grand opening, and Chef Amy Ferguson-Ota has been performing wonders with local produce, beef, and fish. Another dining room in which to experience Chef Ferguson-Ota's talent is **The Grill Restaurant and Lounge** (885-2000). From inventive appetizers to exquisite desserts, both of the Ritz-Carlton culinary experiences are quite different. **The Café** (breakfast and dinner) and the poolside **Ocean Bar and Grill** (lunch) are more casual gastronomical options at the Ritz-Carlton.

My favorite resort escape on the Big Island still is the **Kona Village Resort** (325-5555). There are no phones, no TVs, or radios in the thatch-roofed bungalows (*hales*). Chef Glenn Alos presides over one of the finest Pacific Rim menus on the Big Island but outdoes himself at the hotel's luau with a buffet that is unsurpassed for variety and quality in Hawaii, combining Hawaiian, Tahitian, ethnic, and other foods.

For dining options in nearby Kailua-Kona, see the next chapter.

LODGING

Hapuna is one of my favorite beaches in the world. When Prince Hotels announced that they would build a resort at Hapuna (next to Mauna Kea), I was dismayed. However, the 4-story oceanfront building of the **Hapuna Beach Prince Hotel** (882-1111 or 800-882-6060) is not intrusive. Looking from the inside out, you need a room on the upper floors to enjoy the magnificent views.

The 38 one- to three-bedroom units of the **Puako Beach Condominiums** (3 Puako Beach Drive, Puako, 882-7711) start at $80 per night and will put you near Spencer, Hapuna, and Anaehoomalu beaches.

SOUTH KOHALA

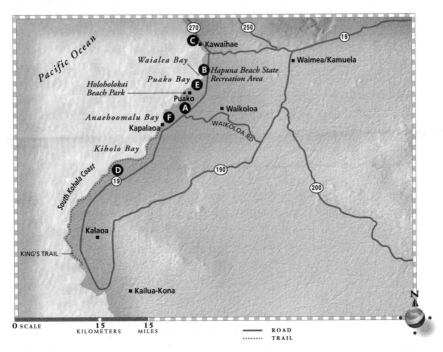

Food

- **A** Bay Terrace
- **B** Bistro
- **A** The Cafe
- **C** Cafe Pesto
- **B** The Coast Grille
- **A** The Dining Room
- **A** Gallery
- **C** The Grill Restaurant and Lounge
- **D** Kona Village Resort
- **A** The Canoe House at the Mauna Lani Bay Hotel
- **A** Ocean Bar and Grill

Lodging

- **B** Hapuna Beach Prince Hotel
- **E** Puako Beach Condominiums
- **A** Mauna Lani Bay Hotel
- **A** Ritz-Carlton Mauna Lani
- **F** Royal Waikoloan Hotel

Note: Items with the same letter are located in the same town or area

No, I admit I haven't stayed at the **Mauna Lani Bay Hotel**'s (885-6622 or 800-367-2323) 4,000-square-foot bungalows with butler service. In combination with one of the best golf courses in the world, I heartily recommend it anyhow. Nor have I stayed on the concierge floor of the **Ritz-Carlton Mauna Lani** (885-2000 or 800-241-3333), which I also recommend without reservation.

The Anaehoomalu Beach and two adjoining 18-hole golf courses (and a third one available up in Waikoloa, 8 miles away) are some of the outstanding attractions of the **Sheraton Royal Waikoloan Hotel** (885-6789 or 800-462-6262). With these assets, garden units with lanais are a bargain at around $125.

For accommodations in Kailua-Kona, see the next chapter.

NIGHTLIFE

Check on schedules for local luaus if you haven't seen them on other islands. The luau at the **Kona Village Resort** on Friday nights is special. A good opportunity to visit the **Mauna Kea** and its **Café Terrace** is provided by the luau or nightly Hawaiian music. The resort's **Batik Room** features dance music. The jazz band at the bar in the **Mauna Lani Bay Hotel** provides nightly entertainment. You'll also find live music, dancing, and entertainment in Kailua-Kona (see next chapter).

12

KONA COAST

Perched on the seawall that borders Kailua-Kona's Alii Drive (the "Nobles' Drive"), which runs 8 miles to Keauhou Bay, you can view almost 200 years of tangled history and savor a wonderful moment of well-being. Marlin and other deep-sea fish are unloaded from charter boats at popular Kailua Wharf. Triathalons begin next to the Ahuena Heiau, a temple near the spot where Kamehameha died. Hulihee Palace, filled with the furnishing of Hawaii's last royalty, stands across the street from Mokuaikaua Church. Above its familiar spire, striving vainly to maintain some vestige of decorum in the town's motley mix, hills of Kona coffee trees and their precious trees lead steeply up to the 8,200-foot Hualalai volcano. The area south of Kailua, along both coastal and coffee country routes, is truly one of the most remarkable and charming parts of Hawaii. Within a scenic stretch of only 15 miles, funky shops, eating places and accommodations in Holualoa, Kealakekua, and Captain Cook provide an extraordinary variety of traditional and contemporary crafts, enjoyable meals and unpretentious places to stay. Nowhere else on the islands can you find a more complete restoration of sanctuary for Hawaiian warriors than the Place of Refuge National Historical Park. Nearby is the monument to Captain Cook's fatal and, for Hawaii, fateful misadventures. Tucked above it is one of the most ornately decorated Catholic churches outside of Spain. Even adventuresome travelers will find something special in this area to stumble upon. ◪

KONA COAST, KAU & SOUTH POINT

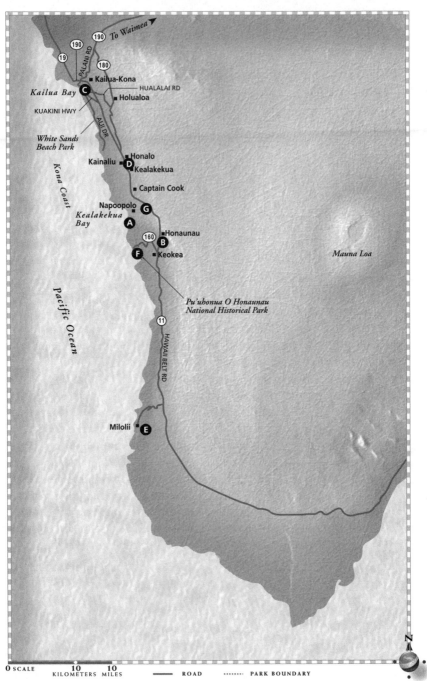

O SCALE   10   10   ━━━ ROAD   ⋯⋯⋯ PARK BOUNDARY
KILOMETERS MILES

Sightseeing Highlights

Ⓐ Hikiau Heiau

Ⓑ Honaunau

Ⓒ Hulihee Palace

Ⓓ Kainaliu and Kealakekua

Ⓐ Kealakekua Bay

Ⓒ King Kamehameha's Royal Palace

Ⓔ Milolii

Ⓒ Mokuaikaua Church

Ⓕ Pu'uhonua O Honaunau National Historic Park

Ⓖ Royal Kona Coffee Mill

Ⓑ St. Benedict's Painted Church

Note: Items with the same letter are located in the same town or area

A PERFECT DAY ON THE KONA COAST

After breakfast (how about Lava Java?), take a walking tour of historic sites in Kailua-Kona: King Kamehameha's Royal Palace, Hulihee Palace, and Mokuaikaua Church. Teshima's in nearby Honalo, or the Aloha Theatre Café in Kainaliu, are tempting for lunch, but even more so will be a dip at Magic Sands Beach; if you like snorkeling, relax next to St. Peter's Catholic Church. Wind your way down the Kona Coast. Stop at the Royal Kona Coffee Mill, Kealakekua Bay (pay a visit to Misha Sperka at the Old Hawaii Coffee Farm; you'll learn an amazing amount about coffee in a short time), Napoopoo Beach Park, Pu'uhonua O Honaunau National Historic Park, and St. Benedict's Painted Church. Return to Kailua-Kona for dinner at Edward's at the Terrace. Afterwards, stroll along the harbor seawall to Kailua Pier and the Kamakahonu Beach.

GETTING AROUND THE KONA COAST

If you haven't already, you may want to rent a car in Kailua-Kona. Your best choices are Phillips' U-Drive (329-1730), United Car Services (329-3411), Tropical Rent-A-Car (329-2437), Ugly Duckling (329-2113), Rent and Drive, Inc., (329-3033), American International Rent-A-Car (329-2926), National Rent-A-Car (329-1674), Dollar Rent-A-Car (jeeps, too; 329-2744), Avis (329-1745), Hertz (329-3566), and Budget Rent-A-Car (jeeps, too; 329-8511).

As you enter Kailua-Kona, Highway 19 becomes Highway 11 a few miles south of the intersection with Palani Road (Highway 190). Palani Road passes two shopping centers before crossing Kuakini Highway to become Alii Drive. Directly ahead on the right, as Alii Drive curves past Kailua Pier, is the King Kamehameha Kona Beach Hotel.

South of the pier along Alii Drive, the Hulihee Palace and Museum is on the bay side, and across the street is the 112-foot steeple of Mokuaikaua Church. St. Michael's Church is another 2 miles south, beyond the intersection of Hualalai Road (Highway 182) with Alii Drive and Highway 19. Magic Sands Beach (a.k.a. White Sands Beach) is south on Alii Drive; from there, you can take Kam III Road to Highway 11 through the small villages of Honalo, Kainaliu, and Kealakekua, turning to Kealakekua Bay on Napoopoo Road for about 3 miles to Middle Keli Road. Turn right to get to the Royal Kona Coffee Mill and Museum. From near the mill, follow the winding road down to Kealakekua Bay, where you can see the Captain Cook Monument. A rough, unmarked one-lane road continues south through lava fields to Pu'uhonua O Honaunau National Historic Park, 29 miles south of Kailua-Kona on Highway 160. Nearby Keei Beach is a secluded gem with wonderful views of Kealakekua Bay. Follow Highway 160 back to Highway 11, and watch for a turnoff to the left for St. Benedict's Church.

Tour bus companies offer standardized rates. Jack's Tours, Inc. (329-2555) offers a circle-island tour for $40; likewise, Akamai Tours (329-7324). Gray Line Hawaii (329-9337) and other companies provide round-the-island, half-day, and full-day tours. Ask about van tours of Kona ($30).

SIGHTSEEING HIGHLIGHTS

★★★ **King Kamehameha's Royal Palace**—This was the home of King Kamehameha the Great before he died in 1819. The restored palace grounds adjacent to the King Kamehameha Kona Beach Hotel include Ahuena Heiau, a lava rock platform with thatched buildings and wooden gods on its own small island adjacent to the shore and connected by a footbridge. (The King Kamehameha Hotel, by the way, has its own museum in the lobby.) Free guided tours of the displays and royal grounds are offered Monday through Friday at 1:30 p.m. (½ hour)

★★★ **Pu'uhonua O Honaunau National Historic Park**—Four miles along a rough and bumpy coastal road from Kealakekua Bay is Pu'uhonua O Honaunau ("City of Refuge") National Historical Park, restored by the National Park Service to the way it looked in the late 1700s. (The other way to reach Pu'uhonua O Honaunau is to drive on Highway 11 to mile marker 104 where Highway 160 goes down to this historic site.) Just ½ mile down this road, turn right onto a lava bed road for **Keei Beach**. This narrow salt-and-pepper beach has hardly enough room to pitch a tent, the swimming is decent, but the main attraction is a channel through the coral to an underwater sea grotto. Pu'uhonua O Honaunau Park itself has excellent dive spots. Entrance to the park is $1 per person, free to those under 16 and over 61. Pick up a brochure from the visitor's center. Hours: Visitors center open daily 7:30 a.m. to 5:30 p.m., park open daily 7:30 a.m to midnight. Phone: 328-2288. (2 hours)

★★ **Hulihee Palace**—A gracious 2-story building stands in the middle of town just down Alii Drive from the King Kamehameha Hotel. It was used as a vacation home for royalty since the time John Kuakini, the Big Island's first governor, built it more than 150 years ago. Restored to its former elegance, it features nineteenth-century furnishings and artifacts. The most fascinating exhibit is the poem written by Robert Louis Stevenson to Princess Kaiulani. Admission is $4 for adults, $.50 for children. Hours: Open 9:00 a.m. to 4:00 p.m. (½ hour)

★★ **Kealakekua Bay**—At the bottom of the hill is **Napoopoo**, a former fishing village, and Kealakekua ("Road of the God") Bay at road's end. The bay is a Marine Life Conservation District with a fine swimming beach and fantastic snorkeling out of **Napoopoo Beach Park**. Diving is even better near the **Captain Cook Monument**, a white obelisk at the northern end of the bay. (Don't swim over in the early evening when sharks come to feed.) Near the park's parking lot is the well-preserved **Hikiau Heiau**. (1–2 hours)

⭐⭐ Milolii—Five miles off Highway 11 south of Kailua, this is an authentic South Seas fishing village with marvelous tide pools. Built on lava rubble, this active fishing village's houses of old lumber and corrugated iron are relics of a past era. Outrigger canoes are powered by outboards, but the method of fishing for opelu, a type of mackerel, hasn't changed. (1 hour)

⭐ Hikiau Heiau—In Kealakekua Bay is a reconstruction of the temple, Hikiau Heiau, where Captain Cook was killed in 1779. Dedicated to the god Lono, the *heiau* is carved into the *pali* and affords a marvelous view of the bay. (½ hour)

⭐ Honaunau—Near this charming village, enjoy a free, fresh-brewed cup of Kona coffee along with a breathtaking view of Kealakekua Bay at the Captain Cook Coffee Company. Afterward drive south on Highway 11 and stop at Mrs. Fields Macadamia Nut Factory, the Honwanji Buddhist Temple, the Central Kona Union Church, or the Lanakila and Christ churches.

⭐ Kainaliu and **Kealakekua**—Just past the former Fujino Mill (one of Kona's oldest, operated by the Captain Cook Coffee Company), visit **Tom Kadaooka's** for orchids. Less than a mile south of Kealakekua on Highway 11, the historic **Greenwell Store** of the former Greenwell Ranch coffee operation houses the **Kona Historical Society Museum**. Built in the mid-1800s by H. N. Greenwell, the masonry uses native stone joined with lime made from burned coral. The museum's reference library and archive contains photographs, manuscripts, maps, and a few artifacts of old Kona. Hours: Open weekdays 9:00 a.m. to 3:00 p.m. (1 hour)

⭐ Mokuaikaua Church—Directly across Alii Drive from the Hulihee Palace, this is the oldest church in the islands. Completed in 1837, 17 years after the first missionaries arrived, the lava and coral structure with the white steeple is a local landmark. Browse around the back of the church to learn about its history. The most intriguing display is easily passed over: a stick chart made by the Polynesians showing the currents, swells, and drift lines that shows how these incredibly observant navigators could sail the vast Pacific. (15 minutes)

⭐ Royal Kona Coffee Mill—On Napoopoo Road near the town of Captain Cook, this mill has been grinding and roasting Kona coffee for nearly a century. The coffee trees are grown on just a few thousand acres, spread over 600 farms between 700 and 2,000 feet, with perfect temperature and soil. A highlight of the visit is the collection of old photographs showing harvests in the days when "Kona nightingales" (mules) carried the coffee beans to the mill. The nearby **Mauna Kea Mill and Museum** (328-2511) also tells the story of Kona coffee processing to frequent waves of tour buses and vans. If you're not ready for more coffee, wait for **Konakai Coffee Farms**, just before the turnoff to Kealakekua Bay, or **Bong Brothers Coffee Company**, a mile before Pu'uhonua Road (Highway 160). (½ hour)

☆ **St. Benedict's Painted Church**—Off Highway 160 (heading up to Highway 11), past the turnoffs for the Dragonfly Ranch and Wakefield Botanical Garden and Restaurant, this church was decorated inside in the early 1900s by Father John Berchmans Velghe, a Belgian priest. The walls, ceiling, and pillars bear copies of medieval religious works and six biblical scenes with Hawaiian motifs, for the benefit of parishioners who couldn't read. (½ hour)

FITNESS AND RECREATION

If you're looking for a hidden gem in North Kona, drive almost to the 88-mile marker on Highway 19 (past the Kona Village Resort) and take a 20-minute hike to **Maniniowali Beach** on Mahaiula Bay. Past Keahole Airport and the new Onizuka Space Center, you can get to the **Old Kona Airport Park**, **Honokohau Beach**, and the new **Kaloko-Honokohou National Historical Park** with a fish pond, burial mounds, and other ancient remains to explore. South of Kailua-Kona, during your visits to the **Captain Cook Monument** and the **Pu'uhonua O Honaunau National Historic Park**, plan to walk on the trails. Contact Hugh Montgomery (885-7759) at **Hawaiian Walkways** to talk about his hiking tours.

Rent bicycles in Kailua-Kona at **Ciao Activities** (326-4177) or at **Dave's Triathlon Shop** (329-4522). An easier and fun way to see the Kona Coast is by moped from **Kona Fun 'n Sun** (329-6068), **Freedom Scoots** (329-2832), or **Rent Scootah** (329-3250). Mopeds rent for $5 per hour, $25 per day, or $125 per week.

The water off the Kona Coast is very clear and calm, protected from trade winds by Mauna Kea and Mauna Loa. The lava rock reefscapes are home to colorful red pencil urchins, moorish idols, lionfish, butterfly angelfish, green and yellow trumpetfish, and spotted moray eels. There are many excellent beaches for scuba diving and snorkeling up and down the coast. Two miles north of Kailua, **Honokohau**, better known for nude sunbathing, has snorkeling, too (stay out of the shark-frequented harbor). Very near Kailua-Kona, yet one of the better kept secrets for tourists, the **Old Airport Beach** has still waters and underwater wonders protected from turbulence by its rocky entrance to the ocean; nudibranchs, cowries, puffers, and scorpionfish hide in the coral heads. South of Kailua-Kona, between Kailua and Keauhou, is beautiful **Magic Sands Beach** (a.k.a. White Sands Beach). This is about the only place I would bodysurf on the Kona side; snorkeling is good here, too. If you are a veteran snorkeler or ready to learn, don't miss **Kealakekua Underwater State Park**'s marine preserve, with its myriad tropical fish and spectacular coral growths. You'll find outstanding snorkeling at **Hale Halawai**, **Kahaluu Beach Park**, **Napoopoo Beach**, **Pu'uhonua O Honaunau Park**, and **Hookena Beach Park**. When you see the sign for Hookena Beach Park near the 100-mile point, it's 2 miles down a narrow, bumpy road to a good beach for swimming and snorkeling, nearby **Kealia Beach**. One of my favorite places for snorkeling also happens to be a favorite beach for swimming and one of the most beautiful beaches on the island: **Milolii**, way past Captain Cook and 5 miles down to the shore, which makes up in tide pools and authentic fishing village charm what it lacks in sand. For novices, the best snorkeling tours are aboard the **Fair Wind** (322-2788) and **Captain Cook Cruise** (329-6411), which combine lessons for those who need it with snorkeling activities.

Many boat charters leave from Kailua-Kona for diving in the nearby waters. However, for learning about each site's natural and cultural history between two dives, it's hard to find a better experience than **Kona Kai Diving** (P.O. Box 4178, Kailua-Kona, HI 96745, 329-0695). The 65-foot submarine **Atlantis** (329-6626) takes passengers 80 to 100 feet below Kona Bay to explore an underwater world that even most scuba divers don't see. The cost of the dive is steep, $67 for adults and $33 for children, and $87 for Wednesday night dives (or day and night dives packaged for $99), but the price is worth the unique experience. (For underwater photography, be sure to bring 400 ASA film.)

About an hour on a **Captain Bean's Cruises** (329-2955), which includes viewing marine life through a glass-bottom boat with hula dancing and entertainment, is $10 for adults, $5 for children. Boats departs daily from Kailua-Kona Pier at 5:15 p.m. for a two-hour sunset cruise, all-you-can-eat buffet, dance and other music; adults only $42. With **Captain Zodiac Cruises** (329-3199) you can explore the Kona coastline, from Honokohau Yacht Harbor to Honaunau Bay, in a 23-foot raft, watch humpback whales January to April, and snorkel in Kealakekua Bay, maybe accompanied by spinner dolphins. Two trips a day, 8:00 a.m. to noon and 1:00 to 5:00 p.m., $57 for adults and $47 for children ages 2 to 12.

The first whales off the Big Island are sighted in November, and whalewatching cruises begin in December. There is no better whale-watching year-round than with research biologist Captain **Dan McSweeney** (322-0028). Besides the humpback whales in winter, there are a half-dozen other types of whales in summer-fall that are just as fascinating; call **Hawaiian Cruises** (329-6411).

Marlin fishing and other game fishing off the Kona Coast is reputedly the finest in the world. Charters operating out of Kailua-Kona usually charge $350 for a full eight- to nine-hour day or $85 per person for a half-day (4–5 hours). Reserve your charter as far ahead as possible, paying a 25 percent deposit. Contact: **Kona Coast Activities** (329-3171), **Pamela Big Game Fishing** (329-1525), **Roy Gay** (329-6041), **Kona Charter Skippers' Association** (329-3600), **Twin Charter Sportfishing** (329-4753), **Seawife Charters** (329-1806), **Lucky Lil Sportfishing** (325-5438), **Aloha Charter Fishing and Activities** (329-2200), **Omega Sport Fishing** (325-7859), or **Marlin Country Charters** (326-1666).

FOOD

In Kailua-Kona one would expect lots of great little places to have delicious coffee and a sandwich or light lunch. They exist but many of them are hidden. For one of the best breakfasts in Kailua-Kona, try the **Kona Ranch House** (329-7061), on Kaukini Highway. For great sandwiches on home-baked bread and the best desserts in town for a picnic lunch, stop at **Jill's Country Kitchen** (Kona Bali Kai Condos, 329-6010). **Island Lava Java** (Alii Sunset Plaza, 327-2161) has caught on with locals, and it's a great place to start the day. Don't miss the cinnamon rolls and the Lava Java cake. (I won't tell you what's in it.)

A Piece of the Apple (Sunset Plaza, 329-9321) has brought classic huge deli sandwiches from Broadway to Alii Drive. Big portions of pasta are standard fare at **Basil's** (326-7836) practically next door on Alii Drive. In the Lanihau Shopping Center, **Buns in the Sun** (326-2774)

KAILUA-KONA

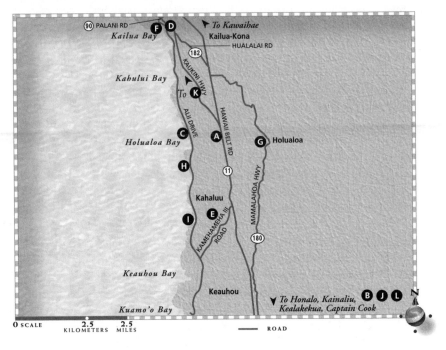

Food

- **A** A Piece of the
- **B** Aloha Theater Cafe
- **C** Basil's
- **D** Buns in the Sun
- **E** Edward's at the Terrace
- **F** Fisherman's Landing
- **G** Holuakoa Cafe
- **A** Island Lava Java
- **H** Jameson's by the Sea

- **C** Jill's Country Kitchen
- **I** Keauhou Beach Hotel
- **D** Kona Ranch House
- **A** La Bourgogne
- **J** Manago Hotel Restaurant
- **F** Oceanview Inn
- **F** Sibu Cafe
- **K** Sam Choy's Restaurant
- **L** Teshima's Restaurant

Note: Items with the same letter are located in the same town or area

offers huge deli sandwiches with really good bread baked on the premises. If you can find your way into the Kanaloa Condominiums (off Kamehameha II Road), the breakfast, lunch, and dinner specialties with a Middle Eastern touch at **Edward's at the Terrace** are as good as you find in Kailua.

In a nondescript building, Kuakini Plaza South on Highway 11, **La Bourgogne**'s (329-6711) chef, Guy Chatelard, prepares French dishes comparable to the best on the island. **Fisherman's Landing** (326-2555) has to be praised for the most spectacular view of the bay. Sit in one of three outside dining rooms, enjoy the delicious food, and most of all the view. The best buffet in South Kona (seafood, $17.95, Friday, Saturday, Sunday; Chinese, $10.95, Monday– Thursday) is at the **Keauhou Beach Hotel** on Alii Drive. For as long as I can remember I've recommended **Sibu Café** (329-1112) at the Kona Banyan Court for tasty and inexpensive Indonesian food. A seaside restaurant with ambience and romance, outdoor tables and candlelight, is **Jameson's by the Sea** (77-6452 Alii Drive, 329-3195), excellent for steak or seafood. The **Oceanview Inn** (Alii Drive, 329-9998) has a tremendous variety of island and Chinese dishes for breakfast, lunch, and dinner and specializes in fresh fish. Go early for dinner to avoid crowds. Look for **Sam Choy's Restaurant** (Kauhola Street, 326-1545) in a Kailua-Kona warehouse for one of the outstanding eating experiences on the Big Island. Chef Choy's talent is legendary.

Not long ago, you couldn't even buy a cup of coffee in Holualoa. Now you can get coffee, pastries, and snack lunches at the **Holuakoa Café** (322-2233, Holualoa). South of Holualoa, past the Hualalai Road junction, after winding through coffee groves on both sides of the road you arrive at Kuakini Highway (11). Both Mamalahoa Highway and Kuakini Highway take you to Honalo. The town's claim to fame is unpretentious, booth-lined **Teshima's Restaurant** (332-9140, Honalo), which has been open continuously since 1943. Breakfast is served starting at 6:30 a.m. Stop for a bento take-out lunch with teriyaki beef and fried fish. Teshima's is next to the Daifukuji Buddhist Temple, worth a peek to see the altar.

In Kainaliu, about ½ mile from Teshima's, very visible on the *makai* side of Highway 19 as you enter town, is the **Aloha Theater Café** (322-3383, Kainaliu). Between 8:00 a.m. and 8:00 p.m. (except Sunday, when Kainaliu is shut down), the Aloha Café serves real Kona coffee (versus diluted blends), huge healthy salads, tasty vegetarian meals, great corn bread and whole grain pancakes, smoothies, carrot cake, and other pastries, at reasonable prices. Get a table at the Aloha

Café on the outside lanai toward the back for the panoramic view over the hills stretching to the ocean.

It's 10 miles and light years from Kailua-Kona to the **Manago Hotel Restaurant** (323-2642) in Captain Cook.

LODGING

Hale Maluhia B&B is only ten minutes up Hualalai Road (Highway 182) from Kailua-Kona, but it is a world away. Lovingly built on old coffee land at the 900-foot elevation of Hualalai Mountain, Ken and Ann Smith have spent 20 years making it attractive and comfortable inside and out. Large rooms with private baths are $75 with breakfast. A three-room guesthouse that sleeps eight people is $125 (without breakfast). Write to Hale Maluhia, 76-770 Haulalai Road, Kailua-Kona, HI 96740, 329-5773 or (800) 559-6627.

Soak in a hot tub while watching a gorgeous sunset, munch on the macadamia nuts grown right on the property, watch whales in winter from a telescope on the lanai, or enjoy wild canaries, parakeets, and other birds year-round. It sounds like paradise. **The Three Bears' B&B** is a comfortable new Hawaiian-style, all-cedar home surrounded by papayas, bananas, flowering hibiscus, bougainvillea, and macadamia trees, at 1,600-feet above Kailua Town. Just uphill from the white sand swimming beach of the new state park, Anne Stockel will loan you beach chairs, towels, mats, a cooler, a boogie board, and snorkel gear. Ann also runs a reservation service specializing in B&Bs for all of the islands, so talk to her first when making travel plans. Garden and Hula Rooms rent for $75 and $85 per day, $10 less for multiple nights. Write Anne Stockel, 72-1001 Puukala Street, Kailua-Kona, HI 96740, 325-7563 or (800) 765-0480.

The 4-story **Uncle Billy's Kona Bay Hotel** (75-5739 Alii Drive, Kailua-Kona, HI 96740, 935-7903), with pool, restaurant, and bar situated in the middle, has nicely furnished, large rooms with mini-kitchenettes and an appealing and relaxing atmosphere. It qualifies as inexpensive to moderate, $72 to $79 single or double with car and breakfast. The **Kailua Plantation House** (329-3727) sits on lava rock overlooking the ocean in Kailua and its five rooms are comfortable, private, and have great views. For one-third the price of most condo units (and no air conditioning) and still a great ocean view, try the **Kona Tiki Hotel** (329-1425) in Kailua-Kona.

Sea Village has spacious, beautifully furnished apartments, kitchens with modern appliances, and ultra-nice bathrooms, with one-bedroom garden view units at $80 to oceanview at $110 going up another $20 in high season (Sea Village Condominium Resort, C/o Paradise Management Corporation, Kukui Plaza C-207, 50 S. Beretania Street, Honolulu, HI 96813, 538-7145 or 800-367-5205).

Frequently overlooked, the **Kona Surf Resort** (322-3411 or 800-367-8011) has panoramic views from its rooms that are as wonderful as any coastal resort. The hotel is between Kailua-Kona and Captain Cook. In the same vicinity, another missed or overlooked location, for both the restaurant (Edward's at the Terrace) and the excellent condo units is **Kanaloa at Koa** (322-2272 or 800-777-1700). Rent an ocean-view room with a jacuzzi.

One of the finest B&Bs in Hawaii is the **Holualoa Inn** (P.O. Box 222, Holualoa, HI 96725, 324-1121 or 800-392-1812), about 5 miles from Kailua-Kona, on 40 acres of pastureland. Amidst coffee groves and lush growth, it has four lovely guest rooms, each with a different theme and decor, for $100 to $200, with choices of king, queen, and twin beds, shared and private bathrooms. Goro and Yayoko Inaba's more than 60-year-old **Kona Hotel** (Mamalahoa Highway, Holualoa, HI 96725, 324-1155) has 11 clean and airy rooms, the best accommodations bargain on the Big Island at $23 per night for two, $15 for one person.

In Honalo, at 1,300 feet above sea level, a very different low-budget choice is the very charming, Japanese-style retreat at **Teshima's Inn** (322-9140), $30 single and $35 double.

Past Kona Kai Farms, on your left, between the old white gas station and Sakamoto Electric (between the 110 and 111 mile markers), turn uphill 0.2 mile and then make a left on a paved road for about 350 feet to **Merryman's B&B** (P.O. Box 474, Kealakekua, HI 86750, 323-2276) $65–$80 double. This is a new house in a lush setting. You'll find comfort, privacy, an excellent breakfast, and a central location for visiting attractions from Kailua-Kona to Captain Cook.

A step up from the Kona Hotel and Teshima's but still in the budget category, the **Manago Hotel** (P.O. Box 145, Captain Cook, HI 96704, 323-2642) on Highway 11 in Captain Cook has 42 individual accommodations, some with a great ocean view and their own bathrooms in the newer wing for $29 to $32 single and $35 to $55 double. On Highway 11, the fifth house on the right after the green 103 mile marker is **Adrienne and Reg Ritz-Batty's B&B** (85-4577 Mamalahoa Highway, R.R. 1, Box 8E, Captain Cook, HI 96704, 328-9726 or 800-242-0039); $50 to $70 for a single or double, and a

KONA COAST, KAU & SOUTH POINT

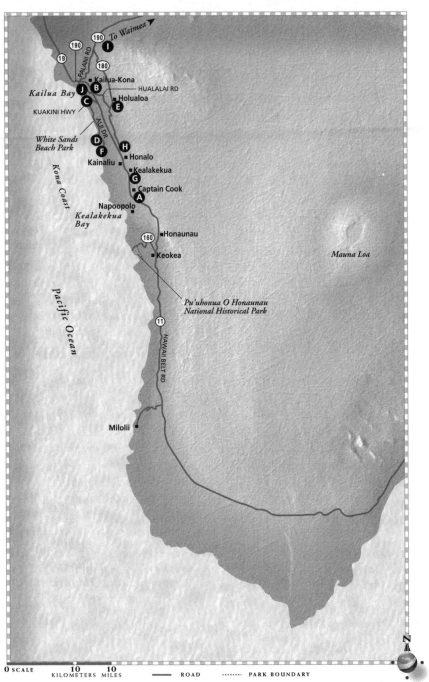

To Waimea

190

190

19

PALANI RD

180

Kailua-Kona

HUALALAI RD

Kailua Bay

J B

C

KUAKINI HWY

ALI DR

Holualoa

E

White Sands
Beach Park

D

F

H

Kona Coast

Kainaliu

Honalo

Kealakekua

G

Captain Cook

A

Napoopolo

Kealakekua
Bay

160

Honaunau

Keokea

Mauna Loa

Pu'uhonua O Honaunau
National Historical Park

Pacific Ocean

11

HAWAII BELT RD

Milolii

N

0 SCALE   10   10
         KILOMETERS MILES   ROAD   ········ PARK BOUNDARY

Lodging

A Adrienne and Reg Ritz-Batty's B&B

B Hale Maluhia B&B

B Holualoa Inn

C Kailua Plantation House

D Kanaloa at Koa

E Kona Hotel

F Kona Surf Resort

G Kona Tiki Hotel

A Manago Hotel

G Merryman's B&B

C Sea Village

H Teshima's Inn

I The Three Bears' B&B

J Uncle Billy's Kona Bay Hotel

Note: Items with the same letter are located in the same town or area

loft for $35 with a shared bath. From their lanai in back of the house, you have an unobstructed view of the slopes above the City of Refuge and the ocean. This B&B is an excellent base for exploring the South Kona area or an overnight stay before heading for South Point and Volcano.

I've spent the night (by myself) on the Outdoor Waterbed Honeymoon Suite at **The Dragonfly Ranch** (328-2159 or 800-487-2159) fantasizing about what the great view of Honaunau Bay would be like with a partner.

NIGHTLIFE

Watching the sunset over the Kailua Pier is a good start to your night. At the luau at the **King Kamehameha Kona Beach Hotel** on Sundays, Tuesdays, and Thursdays, you eat by torchlight at the Kamakahonu restoration. The **Kona Surf Resort** offers a free Polynesian revue nightly and dancing in the **Puka Bar**. Disco at the chrome deco **Eclipse Restaurant**, on the Kuakini Highway across from Foodland. For live bands in Kailua-Kona, the action is on Alii Drive at the **Spindrifter**. Even if the soft rock or jazz music doesn't satisfy you, the views of the bay will. If there's a moon to watch, take a stroll from the pier along Alii Drive.

SIDE TRIP: KAU DISTRICT

Vast tracts of lava rubble in South Kona give way to high forests on the slopes of Mauna Loa, becoming green pasturelands edged by black sand beaches in the Kau District, home of Ka Lae ("South Point"), the southernmost tip of the United States. The 53-mile drive from Kailua-Kona to South Point along Highway 11 passes through land covered with vegetation except for patches or swaths of lava flow. Past Hookena, Highway 11 crosses the 1919, 1936, and 1950 Mauna Loa lava flows and passes a huge macadamia nut orchard. A narrow, winding, bumpy, 6-mile spur road leads down to Milolii, a Hawaiian-Filipino fishing community about 2,000 feet below the highway.

After tranquil **Manuka State Wayside**, a lovely botanic park several thousand feet above the ocean, is a secluded collection of green and black sand beaches (Humuhumu Point and Awili Point) at the end of the 7-mile **Road to the Sea**. The road leads to several cinder cones as well. Drive slowly and park above the last slope. Trails offer hiking possibilities for panoramic views.

The narrow road to **South Point** branches off Highway 11 6 miles west of Naalehu. Experts dispute when the first ancient Polynesians arrived here—A.D. 700, 300, or even 150. Once the most populated part of the island chain, few people live here now. **South Point Road** passes through about 12 miles of grassland, roaming cattle and horses, and the **Kamoa Wind Farm**, to the southernmost point in Hawaii and the nation.

From the **Kaulana Boat Ramp** at South Point, it's 2½ rough miles along the waterline to reach famous **Green Sand Beach** over a rutted road requiring four-wheel drive or two feet supplied with good hiking boots. Hiking round-trip takes two hours. This volcanic sand beach acquires a greenish tint from olivines eroding from the cinder hill, **Puu Mahana**, behind the beach. Avoid climbing down the cinder cone since it crumbles easily underfoot. (1–2 hours)

The countryside and its small country towns convey the feeling of an earlier, quieter, more peaceful era. Returning to the Belt Road, pass through **Waiohinu**, past a monkeypod tree growing from the roots of one planted by Mark Twain in 1866 which was downed by high winds in 1957.

Six miles past the turnoff to South Point is **Naalehu**, the southernmost town in the United States. A former plantation town with a touch of cosmopolitan feeling, Naalehu is situated against a backdrop of very scenic hills. Drop into the **Naalehu Fruit Stand** (929-9009) in Naalehu, and say hello to John and Dorene Santangelo. Pick up one of their famous pineapple breads and a glass of fresh-squeezed pineapple juice. The **Naalehu Coffee Shop**'s (929-7238) banana bread is known far and wide.

One mile off Highway 11 north of Naalehu, **Punaluu Beach Park** may be your best chance to see a black sand beach. This beautiful beach in a palm-fringed lagoon setting, has a visitors center, a museum, and nearby Seamountain Resort with the Punaluu Black Sands Restaurant overlooking the beach. Camping is allowed with a permit. To escape tourist crowds, head about ⅓ mile south to **Ninole Cove** for more privacy. On the hill above the beach is a tiny church with a graveyard shrine to Henry Opukahaia, the Punaluu boy who sailed to America in 1809 and persuaded Christian missionaries to come to save the souls of his people.

Beyond Pahala's Ka'u Sugar Mill and its tall smokestack, the countryside turns to rolling green hills and sugarcane fields, macadamia nut orchards, and beautiful valleys with *ohia* forests.

If you want to stay the night in the area, you have several choices.

Take Highway 11 to mile marker 77 and, shortly thereafter, turn onto Donala Drive to Bruce and Robin Hall's **South Point Bed & Breakfast** (Hei 92-1408 Donala Drive, Captain Cook, 96704, 929-7466). Singles and doubles are $60 per night. In Naalehu, **The Nutt House** (929-9940) sits in an 8-acre macadamia orchard. Nearby **Whaling's Hideaway** (929-9755) was built in a remote valley that requires a four-wheel drive (which the owner will lend you). **Kilauea Lodge** (967-7366) has a fine cottage that I prefer over the other rooms, and the breakfasts are exceptional.

13

HAWAII VOLCANOES
NATIONAL PARK

The Kilauea Caldera, spurting lava on and off since 1983, is center-piece of the spectacular show in Hawaii Volcanoes National Park, even when it's ominously quiet. Beneath your feet, you can sense the endless sinister activity. The park feels even more strange, like the bizarre end of a pilgrimage through other time-zones, when you arrive from Hilo, perhaps after exploring the backroads of Puna, or after traveling through the tiny communities that dot the southwestern route from Kailua around South Point and Punaluu. The eerie coastline, where hundreds of homes have vanished under lava flows, is a reminder of the tremendous destructive power unleashed by the volcano goddess, Pele. Most people follow the 11-mile Crate Rim Drive around the Kilauea Caldera from the Volcano House and back. Others take foot trails to lava tubes, steam vents, scars, and other remains of various eruptions. For another entirely different experience of the volcano, helicopter tours explore Puna and the tranquil Kau farm district on the southwest flank of Mauna Loa, site of some of the earliest Hawaiian settlements. Once a path to the sea, Chain of Craters Road is blocked by a 1972 eruption; but it still offers an outdoor museum dedicated to Pele's wrath from pre-historic times to the present. Even though the Park is the most popular tourist destination in Hawaii, all local accommodations are modest and simple, including some of Hawaii's most enjoyable B&Bs. ◪

HAWAII VOLCANOES NATIONAL PARK

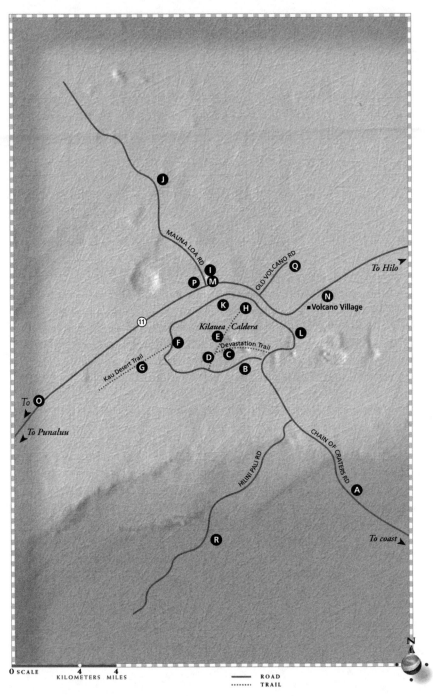

Sightseeing Highlights

A Chain of Craters Road

B Crater Rim Drive

C Devastation Trail

D Halemaumau Crater

E Halemaumau Trail

F Jaggar Museum

G Kau Desert Trail

H Kilauea Visitors Center

I Kipuka Puaulu

J Mauna Loa Road

K Sulphur Banks

L Thurston Lava Tube

M Tree Molds

N Volcano Art Center

Lodging

N Carson's Volcano Cottages

N Chalet Kilauea

N Hale Ohi'a Cottages

N Kilauea Lodge

N My Island B&B

N Volcano B&B

Camping

P Namakini Palo Campground

Q Niaulani Cabin

R Kipuka Nene

Food

N Kilauea Lodge Restaurant

O Punaluu Black Sands Restaurant

O Seamountain Golf Course & Lounge

Note: Items with the same letter are located in the same town or area

A PERFECT DAY IN
HAWAII VOLCANOES NATIONAL PARK

D rop by the Kilauea Visitors Center on your way into Hawaii
Volcanoes National Park (go early to avoid crowds). Follow
Crater Rim Drive to Halemaumau Crater, then visit the informative
Thomas A. Jaggar Museum. Turn left on Mauna Loa Road to visit
Tree Molds, hollow areas filled with lava when koa trees burned
away, and the serene bird park, Kipuka Puaulu. This is a good place
for a picnic, or continue another 10 miles up the mountain for a
great view of Kilauea. Return to browse at the Volcano Art Center,
which displays the work of many of the island's best artists and
craftspeople. Dine at the Kilauea Lodge Restaurant in front of the
"fireplace of friendship."

SIGHTSEEING HIGHLIGHTS

✸✸✸ **Crater Rim Drive**—Circling the Kilauea Crater, this drive
passes through 11 miles of rainforest, desert, lava flows, and pumice
piles. You'll see two types of lava: smooth-looking ropy lava called
pahoehoe and, lower down the slope, the rough cindery type known
as *aa*. (2–4 hours)

✸✸✸ **Halemaumau Trail**—This trail can be entered from two locations: next to the Visitors Center, for a 6-mile, five-hour round trip;
or from the opposite side of Crater Rim Drive, where it's only
¼ mile down. Before leaving this area, be sure to visit the **Thomas
A. Jaggar Museum** (967-7643), in a former volcano observatory on
the crater rim, which opens up a great view of **Halemaumau Crater**,
Pele's firepit, a crater within the crater that drops several hundred
feet down to the lava floor. In the museum, a series of exhibits on the
history and volcanology of Mauna Loa and Kilauea provides a much
better understanding of what you're about to see (or have just seen).
(2 hours)

✸✸✸ **Kilauea Visitors Center**—The visitors center is an essential
stop for maps and books. A film shown daily on the hour, starting at
9:00 a.m., explains how volcanoes are formed and traces the eruptions
that began in 1986. The park entrance fee is $5 per car. Hours: Open
daily 7:45 a.m. to 5:00 p.m. Phone: 967-7311. (½ hour)

⭐⭐ **Chain of Craters Road**—There is no water or gas along this paved two-lane road, which winds 27 miles down the southern slopes of Kilauea Volcano to the ruins of the Wahaula Visitors Center on the Puna Coast. You'll see wonderful coastline vistas, fingers of aa and pahoehoe lava reaching down to the sea, and craters with different stages of life, from none to thickly forested ones. Follow the road as far as park rangers say is permissible. (4 hours)

⭐⭐ **Devastation Trail**—This ½-mile elevated boardwalk crosses a desolate black lava field through a skeletal forest of *ohia* tree trunks entombed during the 1959 eruption of Kilauea Iki ("Little Kilauea"). Gradually returning to life, the trees sprout unusual aerial roots. (½ hour)

⭐⭐ **Halemaumau Crater**—Just past the Hawaiian Volcano Observatory, this crater steams and shows its latent power. Along the trail a series of plaques tells about the area's geology and history. (20 minutes)

⭐⭐ **Kau Desert Trail**—This trail is on Highway 11 about 4 miles south of the Mauna Loa Road. The 1.6-mile round-trip leads across desolate pahoehoe and aa to where about 80 warriors were crossing the desert to battle Kamehameha's warriors when Kilauea erupted. Toxic gases engulfed them and killed them in their tracks. This incredible event was seen as a sign from the gods, endorsing Kamehameha. (½ hour)

⭐⭐ **Mauna Loa Road**—Follow Highway 11 past the Sulphur Banks and the Volcano Golf Course (away from the volcano center) to the Mauna Loa Strip Road. Turn right at **Tree Molds**. Lava flowing through an *ohia* forest encircled and ignited tree trunks, leaving holes in the ground, some of them quite deep. Tree Molds resembles a reverse of Lava Tree State Monument to the east in Punain—in other words, pits instead of tree stumps.

Continue up Mauna Loa Road to **Kipuka Puaulu** ("Bird Park"), an oasis created when the Mauna Loa lava flow divided and left about 100 acres of native plants untouched. The park contains picnic grounds, exhibits about the park's plants and birds, a mile-long nature trail among some of the world's rarest plants, and a bird sanctuary. See if you can spot a bright red iwi or apapane.

Continue along the 10-mile paved road up to the 6,682-foot level to a parking area and lookout. The road then climbs 18.3 miles to the south rim of Moku'aweoweo Caldera at 13,250 feet. (3 hours)

✯✯ **Thurston Lava Tube**—A short trail through the most accessible lava tunnel (450 feet long and 10 feet high), this lava tube is enclosed at the entrance and exit by a fern jungle. (20 minutes)

✯ **Sulphur Banks**—Here, Kilauea releases water into cracks or fumaroles to rise as sulphur gases. The nearby Steam Vents don't contain the sulphur. (10 minutes)

✯ **Volcano Art Center**—This art center, housed in the original Volcano House, sells local paintings, handicrafts, and jewelry from 8:30 a.m. to 5:00 p.m. The selection is the best on the island for Big Island art. (45 minutes)

FITNESS AND RECREATION

Walk as much as you like around the **Crater Rim Trail**, or take the **Halemaumau Trail** across the crater floor. A lovely nature trail loops 1 mile through the **Kipuka Puaulu** bird park. The **Kau Desert Trail** takes you over lava flow to the Kau Desert Footprints. Rent your bicycle in Volcano Village at **Volcano's Best Gallery** (967-8644). Tour bus companies (such as **Jack's Tours, Inc.,** 961-6666, **Gray Line Hawaii,** 935-2835, and **Hawaii Resorts Transportation,** 885-7484) offer tours of Hawaii Volcanoes National Park.

FOOD

In Punaluu, right at the beach, the **Punaluu Black Sands Restaurant** (928-8528) has lunches and dinners at moderate to expensive prices. (Order a box lunch to eat in the picnic area at Kipuka Puaulu in Volcanoes National Park.) The nearby **Seamountain Golf Course & Lounge** (928-6222, Punaluu) serves simple breakfasts, lunches and dinners with excellent views of the volcanoes over the golf course. One of my very favorite restaurants on the Big Island, a great place for a delicious meal on a rainy, cold night, is the **Kilauea Lodge Restaurant** (967-7366, about 2 miles from the park in Volcano Village). In a warm, friendly atmosphere, Chef Albert Jeyte serves a gourmet continental dinner under the high-beamed ceiling. Try the Seafood Mauna Kea or the Fettuccini Primavera, with Kilauea Lodge coffee for dessert and Sunday Surprise at the marvelous Sunday brunch, 10:30 a.m. to 2:30 p.m., closed for lunch in off-season. Reservations essential.

LODGING

There are several B&Bs in the volcano area. **My Island B&B** (P.O. Box 100, Volcano Village, HI 96785, 967-7216) is a historic 100-year-old home sitting in a marvelous tropical garden. Rates range from $30 shared bath to $55 private studio with bath. **Volcano B&B** (P.O. Box 22, Volcano Village, HI 96785, 967-7779; located at Konelehua and Wright roads) has three rooms with shared bath, two up and one down, that range from $45 to $55 depending on season and number in the party. Brian and Lisha Crawford's **Chalet Kilauea** (P.O. Box 998, Volcano Village, HI 96785, 967-7786 or 800-937-7786, $75 double) has three guest rooms that come with a hot tub on the deck and the kind of decor and pampering you'd expect at twice the price. Ask for the Treehouse Suite. Plan ahead and make reservations early at the **Kilauea Lodge** (and restaurant, see above; P.O. Box 116, Volcano Village, HI 96785, 967-7366), located 1 mile (Hilo-side) from Hawaii Volcanoes National Park. It offers uniquely decorated rooms with fireplaces, private baths, and one of the best B&B breakfasts on the Big Island, from $85 to $125. It was built in 1938 as a YMCA camping and lodging facility, and recently Albert and Lorna Jeyte remodeled the lodge and restaurant. Seven new rooms have been added to the four existing rooms of one of the best B&Bs in Hawaii. **Carson's Volcano Cottages** have some of the coziest cottages in one of the loveliest landscaped settings on the Big Island. After a day at the volcano and some time in their hot tub under the stars, you feel at peace with the world. Rates are only $55 to $75 for two. Contact Tom Carson, P.O. Box 503, Volcano Village, HI 96785, 967-7683 or (800) 845-LAVA. You have a choice of a delightful three-bedroom or a one-bedroom house at **Hale Ohi'a Cottages** (967-7986 or 800-455-3803, Volcano Village) on the former Dillingham estate.

CAMPING

Namakini Palo Campground (Hawaii Volcanoes National Park, HI 96718, 967-7321) behind the Hawaii Volcano Observatory requires a permit from park headquarters to camp free for up to seven days. Cabins can be rented through Volcano House for $24 to $31 for up to four people, including sheets, pillows, towel, soap, and blanket. **Kipuka Nene**, 10 miles south of park headquarters, also requires a permit and is free. The **Niaulani Cabin**, rented by the

Division of State Parks, Hilo, on Old Volcano Road about ½ mile from the Volcano General Store, costs from $10 for a single person to $60 for six people.

14
PUNA COAST

More people used to travel on Route 11 from Hilo to Keaau, the aging sugar town, when Route 130 led through Pahoa along the coast to the Chain of Craters Road. They also used to flock to two of the island's most famous black sand beaches, eliminated by the fiery 1990 lava flow that engulfed the town of Kalapana. Pahoa's colorful strip of false-front shops and restaurants quickly reveals that the town is a gathering place for alternative life-styles reminiscent of the 60s and New Agers from the 70s and 80s. Pahoa offers more than another time zone. Local Thai, Mexican and Italian meals are worthy of a detour on the way to Volcano or as the first stop while exploring Puna. There is no more vivid monument to the destructive power of Madame Pele than Lava Tree State Park, nor clearer evidence of Pele's compassion than the lighthouse at Cape Kumukahi where, as legend goes, lava parted to spare the generous occupants. Here, where the sun's first rays greet the Aloha state, you may see a kahuna ("one who knows the secrets") leading prayers. Puna is strange and sacred territory. The "night marchers," a ghostly group of ancient Hawaiians is supposed to walk during the new moon through MacKenzie State Park. Perhaps this phenomenon partially accounts for the fact that the coastal parks along Route 137 and beautiful Kehena Beach are not visited by many tourists. In the midst of this spiritual and natural power is Kalani Honua, an artists' retreat that captures and projects Puna's charisma from another era. ∎

PUNA COAST

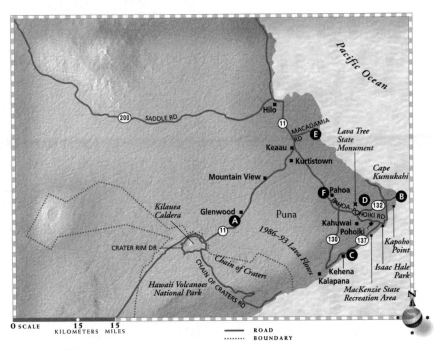

Sightseeing Highlights

Ⓐ Akatsuka Tropical Orchids and Flower Gardens

Ⓑ Cape Kumukahi Lighthouse

Ⓒ Kehena Beach

Ⓓ Lava Tree State Monument

Ⓔ Mauna Loa Macadamia Nut Orchards and Mill

Ⓕ Pahoa

A PERFECT DAY ON THE PUNA COAST

Drive down Highway 11 through Mountain View and Kurtistown to Keeau, turn right on Highway 130 and drive about 10 miles to Pahoa. Detour into the town and have a look at the commercial strip that speaks of new age alternative lifestyles and offers some of the Big Island's best little restaurants. Pick up a picnic lunch for the Puna coast or make note of where to return for a Thai, Italian, or Mexican lunch. Turn on Highway 132 and visit Lava Tree State Park. Stay on Highway 132 when it forks, cross the 1955 lava flow and the spot where Kapoho stood in 1960. Continue to Cape Kumukahi to the lighthouse at the end of the road which miraculously was spared destruction. Return to Highway 137, turn left and, at the Kapoho Kai turnoff, turn left to the Kapoho Tidepools extending out to the reef and along the coastline. (Hopefully you brought snorkeling gear.) If you have the time, bathe in the warm spring just outside of Isaac Hale Park and picnic at MacKenzie State Park in the ironwood grove. After lunch, stop by the Kalani Honua property before heading for Hilo. Drive through macadamia nut orchards and enjoy a free sample at the Mauna Loa Macadamia Nut Orchards and Mill before heading to Hilo for dinner.

SIGHTSEEING HIGHLIGHTS

★★★ **Puna Coast**—Take a right on Pohoiki Road just past Lava Tree and you'll pass the controversial geothermal power station, which may or may not be in operation depending on politics and economic feasibility. Pohoiki Road brings you to the coast at Isaac Hale Beach Park. The main attraction of Isaac Hale is a volcanically heated freshwater pond. Camping (with precautions) is preferable in the ironwood grove at beautiful MacKenzie State Park, bordered by black lava seacliffs. Visit these parks after taking a short but worthwhile side trip. At the intersection of Highways 132 and 137, take a right if you are coming from the lighthouse (or a left if traveling from Pahoa) on paved Old Government Road, which shortly turns to a single-lane packed dirt road. Drive 1.5 miles on this road through beautiful hau jungle to a turnoff to your right between two large mango trees. Return to Highway 137 and drive down the coast to the Kapoho Tidepools for excellent snorkeling. (3 hours)

★★ **Cape Kumukahi Lighthouse**—Highway 132 ends 10 miles from Pahoa at Cape Kumukahi ("First Beginning"). Along the way, *HVB Warriors* mark the lava flows of 1955 and 1960. The 1960 Puna eruption, on the east rift of Kilauea, 28 miles from the Kilauea Caldera, destroyed 70 buildings in Kapoho and added 500 acres to Puna. The former sugar town of Kapoho that used to border both sides of Highway 137 no longer exists; it is covered by lava that erupted for 31 days from the cinder cone. Stay on Highway 132 (Kapoho Road) across Highway 137 to Cape Kumukahi, turn left to the Kukii Heiau site, adjacent to a memorial for a burial ground itself buried by the 1960 lava flow. Continue to the end of this cinder road to Cape Kumukahi Lighthouse, amazingly spared by Madame Pele's lava flow, which split around the lighthouse. Local legend says that on the fateful night in 1960 when lava spared the lighthouse, Pele, disguised as an old woman begging for food, was befriended by the lighthousekeeper and turned away by residents of devastated Kapoho. (15 minutes)

✺✺ **Kehena Beach**—Three miles from the more famous Kaimu Black Sand Beach, wiped out by volcanic flow in 1990–91, Kehena's beach actually consists of two black sand pockets. There's good shore fishing for ulua, papio, mountain bass, red bigeye, and other fish, but the beach is dangerous for swimming and snorkeling. For picnicking, head for a smaller black sand beach on the northern end of the Kehena, more protected and partially shaded by coconut trees (and especially favored by nude bathers). Nearby **Kahuwai**, one of the best-kept secrets on the Puna Coast, is a former center for canoe building and residence of alii. The beautiful black sand beach formed by the 1960 Kapoho lava flow is tucked between two low seacliffs on the rugged shoreline pounded year-round by surf. The area has many sites of historical and archaeological interest. (20 minutes)

✺✺ **Lava Tree State Monument**—The pahoehoe lava that poured through this *ohia* forest in 1790 left hardened tree-shaped shells after cooling which today stand in the midst of lovely new lehua tree growth. A loop of less than a mile circles through the park, passing numerous wild tropical plants and flowers when they're in bloom. (Bring mosquito repellent with you.) (½ hour)

✺ **Akatsuka Tropical Orchids and Flower Gardens**—At mile marker 22½ on Highway 11 on the right side of the road, a few miles beyond Glenwood, is Akatsuka Tropical Orchids and Flower Gardens. A dozen mixed sizes of anthuriums shipped Federal Express to the mainland costs only about $25. Hours: Open 8:30 a.m. to 5:00 p.m. Phone: 967-7660.

☆ **Mauna Loa Macadamia Nut Orchards and Mill**—Ten miles south of Hilo, at the junction of Highways 130 and 11, is Mauna Loa Macadamia Nut Orchards and Mill, home of the world's largest producer and processor of macadamia nuts. Enjoy free samples, watch mill operations, or buy gift boxes. Phone: 966-8612.

☆ **Pahoa**—Pahoa is quaint and ramshackle, colorful and drab. Stop even for a few minutes to walk along the raised wooden sidewalks in front of false-front shops. At shops selling local fruit and vegetables, pick up a picnic lunch. Pahoa is the kind of town where you can order tofu enchiladas for breakfast (unless for some reason you prefer whole grain pancakes and eggs). In the past, Pahoa has been bypassed by heavy bus traffic heading on Highway 130 to Kaimu Black Sand Beach. Now, with Kaimu filled with lava, even that magnet for traffic is gone. The **Pahao Artist's and Crafts Guild** (965-7335), a cooperative venture of about 20 artists, is the only outlet outside of Hilo and Volcano on this side of the island that displays the work of local artists.

The first anthurium plants arrived in Hawaii from London more than 100 years ago. With proper care, anthuriums will last three to four weeks as cut flowers. Visit the **Hawaiian Greenhouse** (965-8351) or **Hawaiian Anthuriums of Pahoa** (965-8247). More than 100 genera and 2,000 species of anthuriums in the Araceae family (a "cousin" of philodendrons) can be seen at these two greenhouses. (1 hour)

FITNESS AND RECREATION

You can hike at **MacKenzie State Park** at **Lava Tree State Monument**. Walking and picnicking are favorite activities at **Kehena Beach** and **Kahuwai Beach,** but neither is safe for swimming or snorkeling.

FOOD

Across from Keaau Town Center shopping area, **Keaau Natural Foods and Bakery**, one of the most complete on the island, adjoins **Tonya's** (966-8091, Keaau), my favorite eatery in that part of the island. It is a very good, tiny (five tables) vegetarian restaurant (11:00 a.m.–7:00 p.m., Monday–Friday, closed on the weekend), specializing in vegetarian Mexican dishes and smoothies.

PUNA COAST

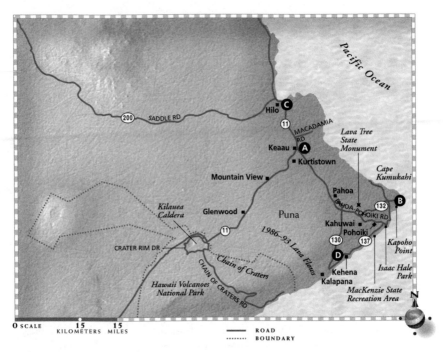

Food

Ⓐ Keaau Natural Foods and Bakery

Ⓐ Tonya's

Lodging

Ⓑ Champagne Cove

Ⓑ Huliaule'a B&B

Ⓒ Dr. Keith or Norma Godfrey - rental home

Ⓓ Kalani Hanua

Ⓐ Rainforest Retreat

Note: Items with the same letter are located in the same town or area

LODGING

Y ou may decide to stay overnight or longer in Puna, especially when you see the accommodation choices. Just 2 blocks from the lighthouse turnoff on the left (Route 137, toward Kalapana) is the entrance to Kapoho Beach Road and two private homes at **Champagne Cove**. This is one of the loveliest, most unspoiled get-away vacation spots on the Big Island. On the Puna coast, **Huliaule'a B&B** (965-9175) sits on more than 20 acres not far from the beautiful black sand Kehena Beach. If you like privacy, comfort, feeding friendly sea turtles, picking bananas off trees in your yard, and a warm tide pool and swimming pool at the doorstep to your three-bedroom oceanfront house, then call **Dr. Keith or Norma Godfrey** (1714 Lei Lelua Street, Hilo, HI 96720, 959-4487, $75 per day, three-day minimum). About 5 miles north of Kalapana is a unique retreat, cultural center, and health spa for "New Age" vegetarian travelers: **Kalani Hanua** (Box 4500, Pahoa, HI 96778, 965-7828). Children are very welcome at this 20-acre oceanfront center. Activities and services include yoga classes, a summer camp, a dance program, resident artists, language courses, and business training. The communal atmosphere is very relaxed. Facilities include a swimming pool, Japanese spa area with sauna, classrooms, massage available, bicycle tours, and four cedar lodges with cooking facilities, private or shared baths, private rooms, and a relatively new three-bedroom, two-bath guesthouse that sleeps six. A room with a shared bath for three nights or more is $52 a night single or double, $62 to $75 with private bath, $85 for a cottage. The **Rainforest Retreat** (982-9601) in Keaau is one of the most unusual B&Bs on the Big Island—two cottages in an orchid nursery within a rainforest.

15

LIHUE AND WAILUA RIVER STATE PARK

A race of tiny people possessing superpowers, the Menehune are supposed to have built fishponds overnight near Lihue, one of the least likely places on earth for idle boasting. Perhaps best known worldwide as a cane shipping port, and to noodle-eaters for Hamura's saimin (noodle soup), Lihue is as unpretentious as its Kauai Museum which displays local art, culture and, with obvious pride, Koa and Kou woodcarving skills. About a hundred years ago, Lihue had its first hotel on well-protected Nawiliwili Bay. The obvious reason is beautiful Kalapaki Beach. Like the good king's beautiful daughter in so many memorable fables, Kalapaki attracted one of the world's gaudiest theme parks cum fantasy resorts. Locals speculate that perhaps the gods were deeply offended. Hurricane Iniki's damage closed the resort indefinitely. After all, Hawaii's royalty, the Alii, totally claimed Kauai's East Coast for themselves. It was a very wise and regal choice, indeed, for it included a beautiful river valley, superb beaches, and calm seas. South and west of Lihue, Kilohana is a restored plantation home full of fashionable and interesting shopping, while to the north of Lihue is a plantation life museum, Grove Farm Homestead. Both provide several good reasons for catching Lihue's infectious unhurried pace of life. Highway 56, lined with shopping malls and development, hugs the Coconut Coast for 10 miles and reveals ancient fishponds encircled by royal coconut groves at the Coco Palms Resort, also badly damaged by Iniki. At the mouth of the Wailua River State Park is the first of seven ancient sanctuaries that line the valley and lead to an arboretum and scenic hiking trails. ◢

LIHUE AND WAILUA RIVER STATE PARK

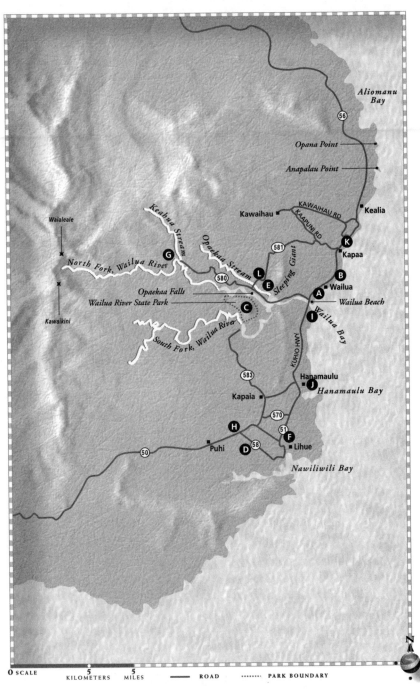

Aliomanu Bay

56

Opana Point

Anapalau Point

Waialeale

KAWAIHAU RD

Kawaihau

KAAPUNI RD

Kealia

Kealua Stream

Opaekaa Stream

581

North Fork, Wailua River

G

580

L

E

Sleeping Giant

K

Kapaa

B

Wailua

A

Opaekaa Falls

Wailua River State Park

C

Wailua Beach

Kawaikini

South Fork, Wailua River

Wailua Bay

I

KUHIO HWY

583

Hanamaulu

J

Hanamaulu Bay

Kapaia

570

H

51

F

50

Puhi

D

58

Lihue

Nawiliwili Bay

N

O SCALE   5   5
        KILOMETERS   MILES   ——— ROAD   ·········· PARK BOUNDARY

Sightseeing Highlights

- Ⓐ Coco Palms Resort
- Ⓑ Coconut Plantation Resort
- Ⓒ Fern Grotto
- Ⓓ Grove Farm Homestead
- Ⓔ Kamokila Hawaiian Village
- Ⓕ Kauai Museum
- Ⓖ Keahua Arboretum
- Ⓗ Kilohana Plantation
- Ⓘ Lydgate State Park
- Ⓔ Opaekaa Falls and Lookout
- Ⓒ Wailua River Area

Food

- Ⓗ Gaylord's
- Ⓕ Hamura Saimin Stand
- Ⓙ Hanamaulu Restaurant
- Ⓚ The King and I
- Ⓚ Kountry Kitchen
- Ⓚ Mark Gomez's Café Expresso
- Ⓚ Michelle's
- Ⓚ A Pacific Café
- Ⓕ Tip Top Café & Bakery

Lodging

- Ⓒ Fern Grotto Inn
- Ⓚ Lani Kai
- Ⓚ Kauai Resort Hotel
- Ⓚ Kauai Sands Hotel
- Ⓛ Makana Inn

Note: Items with the same letter are located in the same town or area

A PERFECT DAY AROUND WAILUA RIVER STATE PARK

After breakfast at the Kountry Kitchen in Kapaa, take a walk at Lydgate State Park's beach to the remains of the Hikini o Kala Heiau, the ancient sanctuary at the mouth of the Wailua River. Next visit Coco Palms Resort, the queen of Hawaii's tourist (and wedding) industry, built around ancient fish ponds and encircled by coconut palm trees. Kuamoo Road (Highway 580) climbs between the Wailua River and Opaekaa Stream to a marvelous scenic lookout over Wailua Valley. At the next stop up Kuamoo Road, Opaekaa Falls is on one side and a view of the Valley on the other overlooking Kamokila Hawaiian Village. Keep driving. Ignore road signs that warn of "unimproved road." When the road crosses Keahua Stream, stop and walk through the Keahua Arboretum. Turn left on Highway 581 to Kaapuni Road and Kawaihau Road for more off-the-beaten track sightseeing. Return to Highway 56 and follow it toward Hanamaulu and Lihue. No restaurant on the Coconut Coast will be more relaxing than the Hanamaulu Restaurant & Tea House.

GETTING AROUND KAUAI

From the airport terminal, you can get bus or limousine service to all hotels for between $7 and $25. Check with Gray Line Kauai (245-3344), Kauai Island Tours (245-4777), Robert's Hawaii Tours (245-9558), or Trans-Hawaiian Kauai (245-5108). The cost of a taxi (Aloha Taxi, 245-4609) to your hotel versus a bus or limousine is also negligible. Poipu Beach costs about $30; Coco Palms resort, about $20.

Otherwise, most people will rent a car from a major U-drive company or a local company. The difference in cost between national and local companies is negligible, especially if you make reservations beforehand. You'll need a rental car for active sightseeing on Kauai. Across the street from the terminal at Lihue Airport is a string of car rental booths. Car rentals with a flat rate start at $21.95 a day, unlimited mileage. Rent-A-Wreck, Rent-A-Jeep Kauai (245-9622), and Beach Boy (245-2913) in Lihue have rentals at $16.95 or lower but may tack on a mileage charge. You won't need a four-wheel drive on Kauai.

Biking around Kauai is easy except for Kokee, the narrow shoulders on the roads, and increasingly heavy traffic. Cycling on Highways 50 and 56 (the Belt Road) is downright hazardous. Rental shops are Bicycles Kauai (1379 Kuhio Highway, in Kapaa, 822-3315) and Aquatics Kauai (822-9213, Kapaa). Rentals cost $4 per hour or $12 to $20 per day or $100 per week.

SIGHTSEEING HIGHLIGHTS

★★ **Kauai Museum**—This museum has a permanent natural history collection and changing Hawaiiana exhibits. The book and gift shop is a good place to pick up souvenirs of your trip. Admission is $3 for adults, children free. Hours: Open Monday through Friday from 9:30 a.m. to 4:00 p.m. Address: Rice Street, Lihue. Phone: 245-6931. (1 hour)

★★ **Kilohana Plantation**—About 2 miles west of Lihue on Highway 50, Kilohana ("Superior" or "Not To Be Surpassed") completely contrasts with Kukio Shopping Center and lives up to the meaning of its name. This elegant plantation home once was the most expensive house built on Kauai. Owner Gaylord Wilcox, nephew of the founder of Grove Farm Homestead, made it the center of uppercrust social, cultural, and business life in the mid-1930s heyday of Hawaii's sugar industry. Open to the public as a house/museum and posh shopping place, Kilohana has been painstakingly restored with many of its original furnishings and artifacts. Phone: 245-7818. (1 hour)

★★ **Wailua River Area**—A really pretty beach lies hidden behind the Wailua Golf Course, reached by a dirt road along the southern end of the links off Highway 56. Lengthy **Wailua Beach** provides many enjoyable places for swimming, picnicking, and unofficial camping. The remains of an ancient place of refuge and one of many *heiaus* along the river are found in **Lydgate State Park** at Leho Drive, just south of the Wailua River. Along a rugged stretch of coast fringed by magnificent ironwoods, you can swim safely (even children) and snorkel in clear water fronting Lydgate Park's white sand beach.

One of the most popular—and beautiful—tourist attractions in Hawaii, the **Fern Grotto**, a huge rock amphitheater draped by ferns under a cascade of water, is 3 miles up Wailua River, reachable only by a 20-minute boat ride ($10 for adults, half price for children). Contact **Smith's Motor Boat Service** (822-4111) and **Waialeale Boat Tours** (822-4908) for a 2-mile ride up the Wailua River.

Smith's Tropical Paradise, a 30-acre botanical garden, is filled with a marked collection of Kauai's ordinary, rare, and exotic foliage. Plywood facsimiles of Japanese, Philippine, and Polynesian villages can be bypassed, but the botanical garden is worth seeing. A guided tram tour costs $7. Admission for adults is $3 and $1.50 for children. (The luau/musical show in the evening—$12 for the show and $45 for the food—is as good as any that you'll see on the island with the exception of the incomparably spirited and unpretentious luau at the Tahiti Nui in Hanalei.) Hours: Open 8:30 a.m. to 4:30 p.m.

From Highway 56 at Coco Palms, take a left on Highway 580 toward Opaekaa Falls. Several miles up Highway 580, Wailua State Park protects the river, and across the road is lovely **Opaekaa Falls and Lookout**. Across the road at the Lookout, a Hawaiian family has put together **Kamokila Hawaiian Village**. The road down on the left just before getting to the falls leads to the village on an island above the Wailua River. Restored thatched homes, a sleeping house, an eating house with utensils, herbalist's house, taro patches, ancient implements, demonstrations of poi-pounding and preparation of medicinal plants all are part of the guided tour. Hula dancing and other Hawaiian entertainment are scheduled at regular intervals. (2–3 hours)

☆ **Grove Farm Homestead**—In Nawiliwili, about halfway up Nawiliwili Road (Highway 58), the Grove Farm Homestead was founded as a sugarcane plantation in 1864 by the son of a Hanalei missionary family. Today the main house, plantation office, workers' cottages and outbuildings, orchards, and gardens are well preserved for tourists. Seeing the homestead requires more preplanning than most other attractions. Tours are provided only on Monday, Wednesday, and Thursday at 10:00 a.m. and 1:15 p.m. and last about two hours. The cost is about $3. Write to Grove Farm Homestead, P.O. Box 1631, Lihue, Kauai, HI 96766, or call 245-3202 at least a month in advance. (1 hour)

☆ **Kapaa and Waipouli**—**Coco Palms Resort**, situated amid 45 acres of coconut trees and including a lagoon, is renowned for its nightly torchlight ceremony. On the *makai* side of Highway 56, the **Sheraton Coconut Beach** with lovely grounds and a popular nightly luau is the northern anchor of **Coconut Plantation Resort**. Kapaa Village stretched along Highway 56 begins just north of the Plantation. Coconut Plantation includes other hotels, condos, and the Market Place at Coconut Plantation. The more than 70 shops in the **Market Place** include some of the more interesting shopping for art and crafts on Kauai. (1–2 hours)

FITNESS AND RECREATION

Three miles up the Wailua River, **Keahua Arboretum** is an ideal place to hike, picnic, and swim. (There's a relatively unknown swimming hole here). Take Highway 580 to the University of Hawaii

Agricultural Experiment Station, and drive about 2 miles to the Keahua Stream where the trailhead starts just past the stream. The **Keahua Trail** is about ½ mile long through a forest reserve maintained by the Division of Forestry where marked posts identify many varieties of native and exotic plants and trees. From the Keahua Trail, a panorama of the coastline opens to the east and the Makaleha ("Eyes Looking About as in Wonder") Mountains to the northwest. The trail through the Arboretum is ½ mile long. Follow Highway 580 for 6.6 miles from Highway 56 to the trailhead of **Kuilai Ridge Trail**, a two-hour hike past waterfalls and orchids to two spectacular coast view points.

Farther north, Sleeping Giant mountain behind Coco Palms shelters an undulating valley and beautiful forest reserve trails on the perimeter reached by Highway 581 or 58 to the end of Waipouli Road. **Nonou Mountain Trail** (east side) begins off Haleilio Road, 1.2 miles from the junction of Highways 56 and 580, in the Wailua House lots behind Sleeping Giant and climbs 1,250 feet to its summit. The west side trail starts on Highway 581 and joins the east side trail at a picnic area about 250 feet below the summit in the **Nonou Forest Reserve**.

Kauai Lagoons Golf Course and the larger, tournament-class **Kiele Golf Course** (241-6000) offer the gamut of challenges.

CAUTION! Starting at **Nukolii Beach**, north of Lihue, beaches on the east coast can be extremely treacherous for swimmers. **Wailua Beach** is beautiful, but heavy surf causes a strong backwash. **Kapaa Beach** is all right at low tide, thanks to reef protection, especially north of the Waikaea Canal, but beware at high tide. The bays on either side of **Anapalau Point**, reached by the old coast road paralleling Kealia Beach, and **Opana Beach** north of Opana Point, have some of the island's best snorkeling, using appropriate caution. Rough waters, surface currents, and backwash make most of the east coast and North Shore beaches dangerous. This is true at **Kealia Beach, Aliomanu Beach, Kukuna Beach, Moloaa Beach, Kaakaaniu Beach, Waipake Beach**, and others to Kilauea Bay. **Kalapaki Beach** and **Hanamaulu Bay** are your best bets in the Lihue area for bodysurfing and beachcombing.

Kauai Canoe Expeditions (245-5122), at the Kauai Canoe Club, near the Menehune Fishpond, and **Island Adventures** (245-9662), both in Nawiliwili, will take you canoeing for two hours up the Huleia River and along the fish pond into a wildfowl refuge. **Kauai by Kayak** (245-9662) offers the same trip. **Kauai River**

Expeditions (826-9608) instructs you in the use of a combined canoe and kayak called a royak, then leads you up the Kalihi Wai River.
Lady Anne Cruises (245-8538) has a two-hour whalewatching cruise for $35, leaving Lihue at 9:00 a.m. with an expert commentator from the Pacific Whale Foundation.

There is no better way to see Kauai, its Na Pali cliffs, Waialeale Mountain, and the island's wilderness interior than by helicopter. Helicopter companies charge about $130 for a 50-minute whirlibird ride. **Jack Harter Helicopters** (245-3774), has a helipad at the Westin Kauai; **Papillon Helicopters** (826-6591) at Princeville Airport offers two tours that land in the wilderness for a swim and picnic lunch ($150) or a champagne lunch ($250); **Niihau Helicopters** (335-3500) offers two tours ($185 and $235) departing from the Port Allen Airport for Niihau. Others are **Ohana Helicopters** (245-3774), **Will Squyres Helicopter Service** (245-7541), and **South Seas Helicopters** (245-7781).

FOOD

I've made it through a long day on **Tip Top Café & Bakery**'s (245-2511, Lihue) *loco moco* (eggs, rice, and beef), fresh bakery items, or pancakes and coffee. In Kapaa my breakfasts usually consist of delicious muffins and coffee at **Michelle's**. When I'm really hungry, I'll eat at the nearby no-ambiance **Kountry Kitchen**. I don't eat eggs too often but I enjoy building my own omelet there with a choice of more than a dozen fillings. For people like me who crave superb capuccinos and muffins in the morning, **Mark Gomez's Café Expresso** in the Coconut Marketplace in Kapaa is the only place I can guarantee.

A visit to Kauai would not be compete without a bowl of saimin at the charmingly funky **Hamura Saimin Stand** (245-3271) in Lihue. The restaurant that stands out from the rest on the island is Jean-Marie Josselin's **A Pacific Café** (822-0013) in Kapaa, one of the most creative dining experiences. Just read Jean-Marie's *A Taste of Hawaii* cookbook and you'll know what mouthwatering dishes await you.

Gaylord's (245-9593, 1 mile west of Lihue, in Kilohana) might stretch the dwindling remainder of your budget for dinner, but for lunch it is reasonable. Dine alfresco in the courtyard. Fish of the day, chicken, duck, or vegetarian dishes, pasta, or Gaylord's Papaya Runneth Over (stuffed with baby shrimp), with Chocolate Decadence Cake or other delicious desserts, make for a fitting feast. Before or after dinner, browse through Kilohana shops such as the Kilohana Galleries Artisan's Room to see Niihau shell jewelry. Even better than Gaylord's for a combination of delicious Chinese and Japanese cuisine and ambiance is the **Hanamaulu Restaurant** (245-2511, 4 miles north of Lihue on Highway 56, in Hanamaulu). Yes, they have the best plate lunch on the island but you really want a cushion overlooking the lovely garden, complete with stone pagoda and a carp pond. The setting is the nondescript Waipouli Plaza in Kapaa, but the Thai food is the best on Kauai at **The King and I** (822-1642, Kapaa).

LODGING

Susan and Don Akre (822-1075), hosts of the **Makana Inn**, have a one-bedroom guest cottage with a king-size bed, overlooking Mount Waialeale and lovely pastures, for $60 per night for a couple or a private one-bedroom apartment downstairs with kitchenette at $50 per night per couple. Providing lovely views over the lush river, the **Fern Grotto Inn** (822-2560) is the only private property in the middle of the Wailua River State Park. Breakfast at the Plantation Room (overlooking the river) consists of fresh Kona coffee, tropical fruit and juices, croissants, bagels, muffins, and a variety of other tempting choices. Sharon Knott offers three rooms from $80 to $100 with private bathrooms and bathtubs, down/feather queen-size beds, and lots of pampering. Write to 4561 Kuamoo Road, Wailua, Kauai, HI 96746.

In Kapaa, the winners are **Kauai Resort Hotel** (245-3931 or 800-367-5004) and the **Kauai Sands Hotel** (822-4951). Right on the ocean, large units, beautifully decorated, expensive but good value, give the **Lani Kai** a try (822-7700 or 800-426-6367).

NIGHTLIFE

The place to go in Lihue for disco and live music Wednesday through Saturday after 10:00 p.m. is the **Club Jetty Restaurant** (245-4970) in Nawiliwili. Or, your excuse for visiting the Westin Kauai Hotel in Nawiliwili could be dancing at **The Paddling Club**, a three-level disco. In Kapaa and Wailua, if you have the energy, you can dance until 4:00 a.m. at the **Vanishing Point**'s disco in Waipouli Plaza or to live music at the **Kauai Beach Boy's Boogie Palace**. Time for one last luau? Try the **Sheraton Coconut Beach** (822-3455) or the **Aston Kauai Resort Hotel** (245-3931) for live entertainment a few nights a week.

16

KAUAI'S NORTH SHORE
AND HANALEI VALLEY

There are few tourist accommodations and not much nightlife along the North Shore, and residents intend to keep it that way. They prefer that visitors and the golf-and-tennis-set stay overnight at Princeville, on the plateau above Hanalei Bay or elsewhere and make short trips to their town where the greatest attraction is sunset from the end of its pier. Admittedly, rooms and restaurants at the Sheraton Princeville Hotel have some of the best views of Hanalei Bay and Bali Hai Mountain, but the view of Bali High Peak over breakfast from the Hanalei Bay Resort is certainly not shabby. Just past Princeville, Hanalei Valley Lookout marks the entrance to another world between Hanalei Bay and the Na Pali Coast. The one-lane bridges on the North Shore are intentionally designed not to accommodate tour buses—better for the taro fields and birds. Beaches are among the best in Hawaii but never see crowds. Still offering stretches of solitude, lovely bays are backed by some of the most beautiful mountains on any tropical island, lined by 14 miles of jagged, dazzling green cliffs. Every promotion for Kauai includes a photo of Na Pali's awesome cliffs shimmering in the distance, but none of them can reveal the truth as seen from its trails, by boat, or by helicopter. The Kalalau Trail traversing the Na Pali challenges hardy hikers, mocks the imagination, and will forever tantalize tourists. ◼

KAUAI'S NORTH SHORE AND HANALEI VALLEY

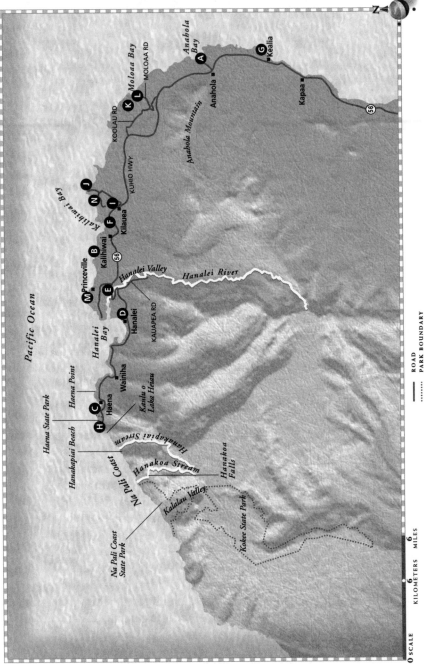

Sightseeing Highlights

Ⓐ Anahola Bay Beach Park

Ⓑ Anini Beach

Ⓒ Haena Beach Park

Ⓓ Hanalei

Ⓔ Hanalei Valley Lookout

Ⓕ Kalihiwai Beach

Ⓖ Kealia Beach

Ⓗ Kee Beach

Ⓘ Kilauea

Ⓙ Kilauea Lighthouse and Bird Sanctuary

Ⓘ Kong Lung Store

Ⓚ Larson's Beach

Ⓛ Moloaa Beach

Ⓜ Princeville

Ⓝ Secret Beach

Note: Items with the same letter are located in the same town or area

A PERFECT DAY ON THE NORTH SHORE

Drive along the base of the beautiful Anahola Mountains and turn off Highway 56 on Koolau Road to discover hidden Anahola and Moloaa beaches, both beautiful and treacherous. (At the risk of getting a little lost, follow the dirt cane road to even more secluded Larsen's Beach.) Return to Kuhio Highway and one of my favorite little towns in Hawaii, Kilauea. The Kilauea Point National Wildlife Refuge at the end of Lighthouse Road is a great place for a coastal walk to see a booby, albatross, frigate, and other sea birds. Explore other beaches as you continue along the North Shore. In Hanalei stop at the Hanalei Museum for a tour of the property and at Hanalei

Gourmet for a delicious picnic lunch at Kee Lagoon, one of my favorite places for snorkeling or a swim. After lunch hike the 2 miles on the Kalalau Trail to Hanakapiai Beach. Return to Hanalei Town through the lush rainforest from Kee Beach to Haena Beach. Besides Kee Beach, the Hanalei Pier may be the best place on Kauai to watch the sunset. Take Weke Road to Black Pot Beach Park for a sunset dip near Hanalei Pier before dinner and evening entertainment at the fabled Tahiti Nui (and the luau on Wednesday or Friday).

SIGHTSEEING HIGHLIGHTS

★★★ **Hanalei**—Situated on Hanalei Bay below Princeville, Hanalei is reached by a narrow one-lane bridge crossing the Hanalei River that unintentionally serves as a blessed barrier to large, heavy tour buses and construction trucks. Cross the Hanalei River on Highway 56 over **Hanalei Bridge**, a steel bridge prefabricated in New York (of all places), erected in 1912, and now on the National Register of Historic Landmarks. For decades Hanalei has been the center of counterculture on Kauai and a gathering place for escapists of all types. Hanalei's hodgepodge of ramshackle and new buildings, including general stores, restaurants, museums, boutiques, galleries, and shops, appropriately reflects Hanalei's nonconformist charm and mystique. A notable departure from this unplanned pattern is the **Old Hanalei School**, on the National Register and recently refurbished for tourist-oriented shops and restaurants. (2 hours)

On the other end of town, behind Waioli Huiia Church, the **Waioli Mission House Museum** (245-3202) is the former residence of the Wilcoxes and other mid-eighteenth-century Protestant missionaries. Living rooms and bedrooms are full of interesting missionary artifacts and history. Hours: Open Tuesdays, Thursdays, and Saturdays until 3:00 p.m. (1–2 hours)

★★ **Anahola Bay Beach Park**—Just a few miles north of Kapaa, this beach is lovely for relaxation and picnics but hazardous for swimming. (15 minutes)

★★ **Anini Beach**—Just before you reach Princeville on the second Kalihiwai Road, this beach is about a mile past the first one to the right just beyond the Kalihiwai Lookout and Princeville Airport. Turn on Anini Road to miles of white sand beach that is sheltered by the longest exposed reef off Kauai. This beach is great for windsurfing year-round and for summer swimming and snorkeling in the shallow water. (1–2 hours)

★★ **Haena Beach Park**—Just past Haena Point, and across from Maniniholo Dry Cave, this beautiful white sand beach has coconut palms, lush foliage, and tall cliffs that rise from the sea. This beach occasionally gets crowded. More secluded Haena beaches are located off access roads along Highway 56. (1 hour)

★★**Kalihiwai Beach**—Swimming and bodysurfing are ideal at this beach in summer months. Swimming is safe in the lagoon where the river meets the ocean. The quiet little village on Kalihiwai Bay was destroyed by tidal waves in 1946 and 1957. You can walk along the beach from Secret Beach to Kalihiwai. (1–2 hours)

★★ **Kealia Beach**—This is the first in a string of beautiful white sand beaches north of Kapaa. From here take the scenic old coastal road almost to Anahola Bay where it returns to Highway 56. (15 minutes)

★★ **Kee Beach**—This is one of the most perfect beaches in Hawaii for picnicking, swimming, and snorkeling in summer and watching the high surf in winter months. Nearby are the remains of a *heiau*, the temple of the goddess of the hula where sacred dances were taught. Beyond are the cliffs of Na Pali and the beginning of the **Kalalau Trail**. The trailhead to Kalalau Valley is opposite the Kee parking area and clearly marked. Walk about ½ mile up the trail and look back for a wonderful view of Kee Beach and the Na Pali Coast. (2–4 hours)

★★ **Kilauea**—A collection of restaurants, bakeries, and shops off **Lighthouse Road** make Kilauea one of the most delightful places on Kauai for a refreshing break. **Sylvester's Catholic Church** is located just before the turn onto Kilauea Road to the lighthouse. It has an octagonal design made out of lava and native wood with interior murals of the stations of the cross painted by Jean Charlot, a well-known island artist. (1 hour)

★★ **Kilauea Lighthouse and Bird Sanctuary**—Drive straight down Kilauea Road to the lighthouse with the largest "clamshell lens" in the world. It sends its beacon 90 miles out to sea. Permanent and migratory birds fill the peninsula, including the red-footed booby, the white-tailed and red-tailed tropic bird, the Laysan albatross, and the wedge-tailed shearwater. A small museum at the lighthouse has pictures of all the birds. The craggy point is under the protection of the U.S. Fish and Wildlife Service. You can borrow binoculars to look for green sea turtles, spinner dolphins, or whales in season. The Kilauea Point Refuge charges a $2 fee for each adult. Hours: Open daily except Saturday from noon to 4:00 p.m. (½ hour)

★★ **Kong Lung Store**—Located in the Kong Lung Center in Old Kilauea Town, on the way to the lighthouse, this is Kauai's oldest planta-tion general store (1881). One room contains an art gallery with very high quality carvings, pottery, and other Pacific area items. (20 minutes)

★★ **Larson's Beach**—A lovely narrow stretch of secluded sand, this beach is found (with difficulty) down Koolau Road, which you take for another mile past the turnoff to Moloaa Beach. Take a cane road to the right, then switch left for a mile onto a dirt road lined on both sides with barbed wire. Pass through a gate and travel another ½-mile of dirt road until you reach the beach. (½ hour)

★★ **Moloaa Beach**—This beach is reached off the Koolau Road. Take a right turn off Highway 56 at the Papaya Plantation and Information Center. From Moloaa Bay take a right turn on Koolau Road to return to Highway 56. (15 minutes)

★★ **Secret Beach**—Also known as Kauapea Beach, this is one of the most beautiful, longest, and widest beaches in Hawaii. Turn left on Kauapea Road (.8 mile from Kong Lung). Watch on your right for a fence (with a marine reserve notice on it) and a dirt path down a long steep trail through beautiful tropical growth to the beach. Beautifully calm in summer, the waves get wicked in winter. As a secluded camping spot, and a favorite nude beach, it's hard to beat. (2–3 hours)

★ **Hanalei Valley Lookout**—You can't miss it, but be prepared to stop at the Hanalei Valley Lookout for the incredible view of the Hanalei River Valley and mountains in the background. Just past the entrance to Princeville, pull off to the left. The Lookout frames one of the most spectacular and tranquil vistas in Hawaii, looking across terraced taro patches surrounding the Hanalei River as it weaves its way 9 miles toward three magnificent mountains and a 3,500-foot *pali* over which more than a dozen waterfalls cascade. The Hanalei River is a silver loop as it flows placidly to Hanalei Bay. The village, river, and beautiful valley along its bank take their name from Hanalei ("Crescent") Bay. (20 minutes)

Many taro growers in the valley cultivate their crops under the watchful eye of the U.S. Fish and Wildlife Service, whose mission is to protect wildlife. Preserved as a National Wildlife Refuge, the valley is home to the Hawaiian duck, the stilt, and endangered Hawaiian gallinule. Over 900 acres of Hanalei Valley comprise the Hanalei National Wildlife Refuge. You can drive down Hanalei Valley Road but can't get out of your car except at the restored Haraguchi Rice Mill or at the end of the road.

✩ **Princeville**—On a royal vacation in 1860, Kamehameha IV, Queen Emma, and their son, Prince Albert, visited the rolling plateau overlooking Hanalei Bay. That regal event inspired its naming as Princeville. First a sugar plantation and then Kauai's largest cattle ranch, the 11,000-acre Princeville resort today is built around several championship golf courses, with thousands of acres of development still on the drawing boards. (2 hours)

NORTH SHORE BEACHES

CAUTION! Rough waters, surface currents, and backwash make most of the east coast and North Shore beaches dangerous. This is true at Kealia Beach, Aliomanu Beach, Kukuna Beach, Moloaa Beach, Kaakaaniu Beach, Waipake Beach, and others to Kilauea Bay and Kilauea Point National Wildlife Refuge. Near Princeville, there's no safe swimming until Hanalei Pier, and even there swimming can be unsafe due to rip currents in winter. Stay close to shore. Kahalahala and Lumahai beaches are as dangerous as they are beautiful. They are for gazing at but not for swimming. The same is true for Wainiha Beach, Wainiha Kuau Beach, Kaonihi and Kanaha beaches, and Makua Beach, where you can snorkel inside the reef. Both Haena Beach and Kee Beach are not for swimming. In other words, *don't swim outside protected areas on the North Shore.*

FITNESS AND RECREATION

The Kalalau Trail, Haena State Park, and the park's Kee Beach, begin at the end of Highway 56. A short hike to **Kaulu o Laka Heiau,** sacred to Laka, goddess of the hula, reveals a most important hula shrine where traditionally hula masters express devotion to their hula mistress. Many legends surround this revered *heiau*, located behind the Allerton House. According to the most famous legend, Pele transformed herself into a mortal to join the hula festival and fell in love with Chief Lohiau.

Day hikers can leave their cars at Kee Beach and walk 2 miles to **Hanakapiai Valley,** a few arduous hours of hiking each way. As though by magic, a white sand beach at Hanakapiai appears in summer and disappears again in winter.

For hikes beyond Hanakapiai, permits are required and appropriate camping gear is necessary. Walking the trail to **Kalalau** nonstop takes a long, nine-hour day. This strenuous hike requires good boots, backpack, waterproof tent, a small stove, and light blanket or sleeping bag. Be prepared to boil or chemically treat all water. The trail should be hiked in two parts, with a break at Hanokoa on the way in and Hanakapiai on the way out, and another overnight at Kalalau Beach. (Don't try to return from Hanakapiai in the dark!) Erosion caused by rain can make the 11-mile trail hazardous between October and May and also during June rains. From May to September, the water is calm enough to land on Kalalau Beach in a canoe. On a lovely trail through narrow, sheltered, once thickly settled Hanakapiai Valley, continue to **Hanalapiai Falls,** an easy hike (2 miles) for about an hour. (You pass the turnoff to the falls on the main trail down to the beach.)

Notice the abandoned taro patches, stone walls, and house foundations, and a large stone chimney that is all that remains of a small coffee mill. Guava and mango trees bear succulent fruit here. Occupied a thousand years ago by *kuaaina* (backcountry folk), villages surrounded by sacred temples and elaborate terraced farms existed peacefully between high cliffs surrounding each valley along the Na Pali Coast. Taro farmers and their families worked Kalalau Valley until the 1920s. It is one of the last untamed parts of the Hawaiian islands.

Rainy **Hanakoa** is 4 miles and two small valleys away from Hanakapiai. At a leisurely pace, the hike should take less than three hours. Frequent switchbacks pass breathtaking drop-offs. If it's not raining in Hanakoa, many pools in the stream offer delightful places to swim. There are ample camping sites sheltered on old agricultural terraces. Remember that constant rain may cause slides on parts of the trail to **Hanakoa Falls.** Clear pools for swimming at these falls are delightful rewards for weary hikers.

In the Hanalei area, **Pooku Stables** (826-6777) offers horse treks on the beach, to nearby waterfalls, and into the hills overlooking Hanalei Valley for wonderful views. In Hanalei contact **Pedal & Paddle** (826-9069) for bike rental.

Princeville's golf courses—the 27-hole **Princeville Makai** and the 18-hole **Prince**—are legendary (826-3580), and the Prince pro shop and spa are unsurpassed. The 27-hole has a greens fee of $40, plus $26 for a mandatory golf cart, for an exquisite round of golf.

In the summer, you should take advantage of the clear waters of **Hanalei Bay**, and further out, **Anini**, **Haena**, and **Kee** for snorkeling. For swimming with children or people who like calm waters, visit Anini Park on the way to Hanalei. Every surfer knows about Hanalei Bay. Explore **Shell Graveyard**, an underwater cave at Hanalei Bay with **Sea Sage Diving Center**, 4-1378 Kuhio Highway, Kapaa, HI 96746 (822-3841).

From mid-May to early October, take a boat trip in relatively calm seas to see the wonders of the Na Pali Coast. Most tours are on heavy-duty 23-foot inflatable rafts made famous by Jacques Cousteau and started on Kauai by **Captain Zodiac**. Unlike other companies making trips to remote Nualolo and Milolii valleys, **Lady Ann Cruises** sails on a 38-foot boat out of Lihue. Guests can snorkel ashore, tour ruins of an ancient Hawaiian village, and have lunch on a Na Pali Coast beach. This unforgettable tour lasts 5½ to 6 hours. Shorter tours, including whalewatching in season (December 15–March 15), are provided year-round.

For an unusual experience, try a double-hulled canoe sail on Hanalei Bay with **Ancient Hawaiian Adventures** (826-6088). Outfitters that run guided one-day or longer sea-kayak trips along Kauai's Na Pali coastline include **Outfitters Kauai** in Poipu (742-9667) and **Kayak Kauai-Na Pali Outfitters** in Hanalei (926-9844). A full-day excursion costs $125 per person including lunch.

From May to August yellowfin tuna are running. Year-round you might catch marlin, mahimahi, ono, and bonita. Fishing charters run $85 per person for a half day, $145 for a full day. **Sea Breeze Sport Fishing Charters** (245-7504) departs from Anini and Port Allen.

FOOD

Two choices of outstanding bakeries—**The Bread Also Rises** and **Jacques**—around the corner from one another in Kilauea, dispense unsurpassed choices of baked goods. Maybe not healthy, but

KAUAI'S NORTH SHORE AND HANALEI VALLEY

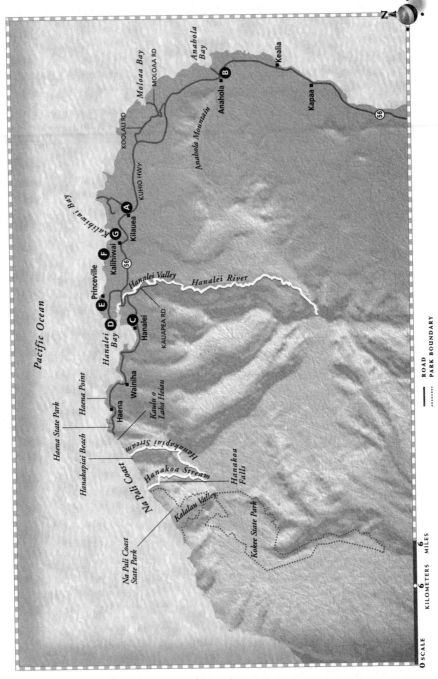

Pacific Ocean

Kailhiwai Bay

Hanalei Bay

Haena Point

Haena State Park

Haena

Hanakapiai Beach

Na Pali Coast

Na Pali Coast State Park

Kaulu o Laka Heiau

Wainiha

Hanakapiai Stream

Hanakoa Stream

Hanakoa Falls

Kalalau Valley

Kokee State Park

Kilauea

Princeville

Kalihiwai

Hanalei

Hanalei Bay

Hanalei Valley

Hanalei River

KAUAPEA RD

KUHIO HWY

KOOLAU RD

MOLOAA RD

Moloaa Bay

Anahola Bay

Anahola Mountain

Anahola

Kealia

Kapaa

A
B
C
D
E
F
G

56

SCALE

0   6
KILOMETERS

0   6
MILES

——— ROAD
········· PARK BOUNDARY

N

Food

Ⓐ The Bread Also Rises

Ⓐ Casa di Amici

Ⓑ Duane's Ono-Char Burger

Ⓐ The Farmer's Market

Ⓒ The Hanalei Gourmet

Ⓒ Hanalei Wake Up Café

Ⓐ Jacques

Ⓐ Kilauea Bakery

Ⓓ Las Cascata (at the Sheraton Mitage Princeville Hotel)

Ⓒ Norberto's El Café

Ⓐ Pau Hana Pizza Pasta

Ⓒ Tahiti Nui

Lodging

Ⓔ The Cliffs

Ⓓ Hanalei Bay Resort

Ⓔ Pali Ke Kua

Ⓓ Sheraton Mirage Princeville Hotel

Camping

Ⓕ Anini Beach

Ⓖ Kalihiwai Beach

Note: Items with the same letter are located in the same town or area

the huge breakfasts that you're not supposed to eat except once a year at **Hanalei Wake Up Café** (Kauhale Shopping Center, 826-5551) definitely will take care of your calories for a day of surfing.

Duane's Ono-Char Burger brings additional glory to the townlet of Anahola with delicious (*ono* in Hawaiian) burgers served from a busy roadside stand. The al fresco **Casa di Amici** (828-1388) in Kilauea serves delicious Italian food, pesto and alfredo sauces, and tasty pasta dishes like pasta with walnuts in a Romano cheese cream sauce. Outdoor dining in Kilauea is one of my favorites, just being near **The Farmer's Market** (where you can get great sandwiches and cookies), the **Kilauea Bakery** and **Pau Hana Pizza Pasta** (the best bread and pizza on Kauai). Pasta and a glass of wine at **Casa di Amici** (828-1388) will do fine.

Norberto's El Café, 4-1373 Kuhio Highway, Kapaa, 822-3362, has opened an inexpensive and delicious restaurant in Hanalei. It doesn't look like much outside, but the food is great, including desserts that Mexican restaurants usually shun. Hanalei comes together day or night at the family-owned and friendly **Tahiti Nui** (826-6277) on Highway 56. Its weather-beaten exterior and thatched-wall interior are just right for a Hanalei beachcomber's watering hole. Nighttime entertainment mostly is spontaneous, mainly Hawaiian songs. Owner Auntie Louise Marston sometimes chimes in with her renditions of Tahitian songs and hula. The luau on Wednesday and Friday nights is deservedly popular, and reservations are essential. The Tahiti Nui's Tahitian owner has created the prime local gathering place, down-to-earth, casual and fun. Chef Jeff Bolman prepares consistently good lunches and dinners that are even better in the colorful, warm, relaxed, beach-shack atmosphere. (Try the fresh fish Polynesian-style.) The live music down the street at the restored old Hanalai School Building comes from **The Hanalei Gourmet** (826-2524). Have them pack a lunch box for you with a thick sandwich on Na Pali bread for a day of beachcombing.

If you want a romantic atmosphere and exceptionally fine dining, **Las Cascata** (826-2761) in the Princeville Hotel is one of your few choices.

LODGING

If you want the magnificent views of Hanalei Bay and the mountains from Princeville, consider the **Hanalei Bay Resort** (5380 Honoiki Road, Hanalei, HI 96714, 826-6522 or 800-827-4427). Princeville offers other first-rate condominiums, such as **Pali Ke Kua** (Ka

Haku Road, Princeville/Hanalei, Kauai, HI 96714, 826-9066 or 800-367-7042), and **The Cliffs** (P.O. Box 1005, Hanalei, HI 96714, 826-6219 or 800-523-0411). The 252-room **Sheraton Mirage Princeville Hotel** (826-9644 or 800-826-4400), practically rebuilt on its old site after Hurricane Iniki, is one of the most elegant hotels in Hawaii in one of the most beautiful settings.

CAMPING

Just past Kilauea down the Kalihiwai Road, you'll come to a dead end at white sand **Kalihiwai Beach**, lined by ironwoods, which is perfect for sheltered camping. Camping at the south end of **Anini Beach**, with facilities, requires a county permit, as does 5-acre Haena Beach Park.

SIDE TRIP: NA PALI COAST

The dazzling Na Pali Coast can be seen by foot, boat, or helicopter. By foot, a short hike from **Haena State Park** is the least you should do; if you're feeling hale and hearty, hike the 11-mile **Kalalau Trail**. **Captain Zodiac Raft Expeditions** (826-9371 or 800-422-7824) offers a $95 full-day trip or a $75 morning or afternoon excursion; and **Blue Odyssey Adventures** (826-9033) has morning, afternoon, and full-day excursions from Hanalei for $75 to $125. Zodiac boats are very tough motorized rubber rafts that are unsinkably safe. **Lady Ann Charters** (245-8538) and **Whitey's Na Pali Cruises** (926-9221) offer cruiser trips with snorkeling along the Na Pali Coast; also from Hanalei Bay.

Na Pali Zodiac helicopter trips (826-9371 or 800-422-7824) are a thrilling (though expensive) way to see the Waimea Canyon and Na Pali Coast, especially early morning and sunset flights. The cost ranges from $100 to $200. Other reliable helicopter operations include **Papillon Helicopters** (826-6591), **Jack Harter Helicopters** (245-3774), and **Will Squire's Helicopter** (245-7541).

17
WAIMEA CANYON

West of Poipu along Route 50, the Hawaiian pioneers of today typically are artists and craftspeople looking for charm, cheap rents and the kind of morning light in abundance around Hanapepe and Waimea. Apart from one of Hawaii's most attractive getaways, the 40 restored plantation homes of Waimea Plantation Cottages, good accommodations here are rarer than orchid farms. Little towns like Eleele and Kaleheo that barely qualify for map imprints will surprise you with their exceptional pizza, Thai food, and not much else besides the hidden gem, Salt Pond Beach Park. All of this nonchalance changes dramatically, however, on the rim of the "Grand Canyon of the Pacific." Drive up Waimea Canyon Road to view the pink and pale green hues of Waimea Canyon from roadside lookouts. Drive down Kokee Road when you've been sated with scenic vistas. A few miles beyond Waimea Canyon, choose one of more than a dozen hiking trails through fragrant pine, koa and redwood forests. At the end of the long mountain road, enjoy the view of the Pacific from Kokee Valley Lookout. Visitors who have the stomach for about five bumpy miles of dirt road west of Waimea will be rewarded by the beautiful desolation of Polihale State Park. Here, according to Hawaiian legend, the souls of fallen warriors depart earth to priestly drumbeats. ◼

WAIMEA CANYON & NA PALI COAST

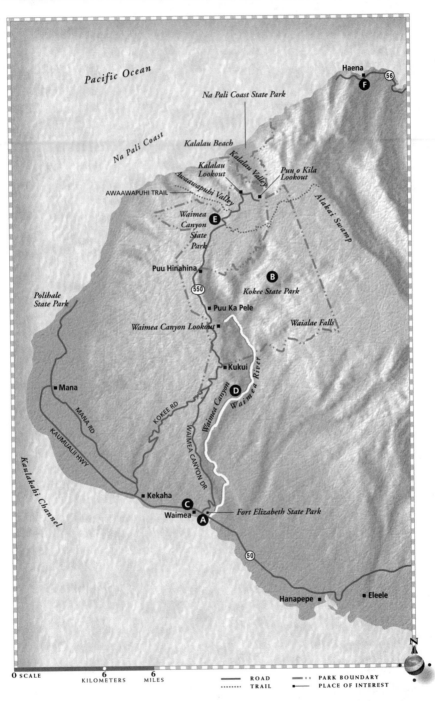

Pacific Ocean

Haena

Na Pali Coast State Park

Na Pali Coast

Kalalau Beach

Kalalau Lookout

Kalalau Valley

Puu o Kila Lookout

AWAAWAPUHI TRAIL

Awaawapuhi Valley

Alakai Swamp

Waimea Canyon State Park

Puu Hinahina

Kokee State Park

Polihale State Park

550

Puu Ka Pele

Waimea Canyon Lookout

Waialae Falls

Kukui

Waimea River

Mana

KOKEE RD

Waimea Canyon

MANA RD

KAUMUALII HWY

Kaulakahi Channel

Kekaha

WAIMEA CANYON DR

Waimea

Fort Elizabeth State Park

50

Hanapepe

Eleele

56

N

0 SCALE	6	6	ROAD	PARK BOUNDARY
	KILOMETERS	MILES	TRAIL	PLACE OF INTEREST

Sightseeing Highlights

Ⓐ Fort Elizabeth State Park

Ⓑ Koke'e State Park

Ⓒ Waimea

Ⓓ Waimea Canyon

Food

Ⓒ The Grove

Ⓔ Koke'e Lodge Restaurant

Lodging

Ⓕ Camp Naue

Ⓑ Camp Sloggett

Ⓔ Koke'e Lodge

Ⓒ Waimea Plantation Cottages

Note: Items with the same letter are located in the same town or area

A PERFECT DAY IN WAIMEA CANYON

At the entrance to the town of Waimea, you'll pass historic Fort Elizabeth State Park. Opposite the library, pick up some homemade sushi at Yumi's for a picnic lunch in the canyon. (Keep your eye out for one of my favorite lodgings in all of Hawaii, the Waimea Plantation Cottages. Couples should plan to have a romantic dinner at The Grove restaurant there this evening.) Take Waimea Canyon Road for the most scenic views. Stop at Waimea Canyon Lookout, Puu Ka Pele (where you'll find picnic tables), and Puu Hinahina. Hike the short Iliau Nature Trail for a glimpse of Waialae Waterfall or take the Cliff Trail to waterfalls where you can take a dip. Have some lunch at Koke'e Lodge and visit the tiny Koke'e Museum for a cram course in local natural history. Continue on Koke'e Road to the Kalalau and Puu o Kila Lookouts, one of Hawaii's great views, Kalalau Beach, and Alakai Swamp. Try the Awaawapuhi Trail for a closer view of this unique environment.

SIGHTSEEING HIGHLIGHTS

★★★ **Koke'e State Park**—This park covers 4,345 acres at 3,600 feet with 45 miles of hiking trails. Pick up a Koke'e Trails map at the **Koke'e Natural History Museum**, which displays the park's flora and fauna. The park is open from 10:00 a.m. to 4:00 p.m. A lush meadow set in a densely forested area is a good spot for a picnic. The view is stunning from the **Kalalau Valley Lookout**, with waterfalls and vegetation cascading 4,000 feet down the deepest valley on the Na Pali Coast. Drive about a mile above the Kalalau Lookout to the **Puu O Kila Lookout** for another spectacular view of the Na Pali Cliffs. (4–8 hours)

★★★ **Waimea Canyon**—The canyon is best seen in early morning light, so beat the tour buses to the three viewing platforms. The 3,000-foot gorge cuts a jagged swath of mossy greens and blues into the reddish brown volcanic walls of the Koke'e Plateau. There are many good hiking trails in Waimea Canyon State Park (see "Fitness and Recreation," below). Your best views will be above Koke'e Camps at **Puu Ka Pele Lookout** at the top of the gorge. Watch the jagged shapes of the gorge change color with the sun. Pick up a trail map at the ranger station or the Koke'e Natural History Museum, in adjoining Koke'e State Park, where you can book for the **Koke'e Lodge** and have lunch. Kauai Mountain Tours, P.O. Box 3069, Lihue, Kauai, HI 96766 (245-7224), has four-wheel-drive tours to Koke'e State Park and around Waimea Canyon. $80 for seven hours, $40 for a half day. (4 hours)

★ **Waimea**—This town is full of history: missionary and English, American, and Russian settlements and churches; the oldest house on the island (Gulick-Rowell House); star-shaped Fort Elizabeth (not much left to see, unfortunately); and, across the river, Captain Cook's 1778 landing site. (20 minutes)

FITNESS AND RECREATION

Easily accessible trails in the **Waimea Canyon State Park** include the ½-mile round-trip **Iliau Nature Loop** (halfway between the 8- and 9-mile markers), offering excellent views of the canyon and Waialae Falls on the other side, and the strenuous 3-mile **Kukui Trail** switchbacking down the west canyon wall to the river below. Koke'e State Park's 45 miles of hiking trails are represented on maps you can pick up at the Natural History Museum.

FOOD

Koke'e Lodge (335-6061), adjoining the gift shop, offers simple, basic, tasty snacks and dinners at moderate prices. After a few hours of walking or hiking, the food tastes very good. In Waimea, next to my favorite Waimea Plantation Cottages, the buffet lunch at **The Grove** (338-1625) is a special treat.

For dining options in nearby Hanapepe, see the next chapter.

LODGING

Koke'e Lodge's dozen cabins are furnished with everything you need for a stay of up to five days. Four newer two-bedroom cedar cabins sleeping up to six rent for $45. Four duplex units containing large studios rent for $35; two other two-bedrooms and two small studios also rent for $35. ($25 cabins are a thing of the past, but these still are among the best deals in Hawaii.) Definitely reserve ahead: P.O. Box 819, Waimea, HI 96796, 335-6061. The former homes of plantation workers have been transformed into a marvelous getaway on a black sand beach in Waimea, **Waimea Plantation Cottages** (800-992-4632).

At the Kauai YMCA's **Camp Naue** in Haena and the YWCA's **Camp Sloggett** in Koke'e you'll find budget accommodations and beautiful hiking trails all around. Purchase a $10 membership card and for $12 per night you get a mattress, space in the dormitory, and kitchen and shower facilities. Write: YMCA, 3094 Elua, Lihue, HI 96766, 245-5959; YWCA, P.O. Box 1786, Lihue, HI 96766, 246-9090.

18
SOUTH SHORE

S unshine and wonderful white sand beaches have attracted crowds and popularity for the southern tip of Kauai at Poipu. Except for recurrent hurricanes which rip through this area, the weather and amenities are predictably pleasant and serene. Poipu also has been fortunate in the hotel and condominium resorts it has attracted over the years. Kiahuna Plantation's 50 acres of lush landscaping have become a tourist attraction. Even the huge Hyatt Regency Kauai is uncommonly tasteful. With advance reservations, there's an ample supply of small and relatively inexpensive hostelries of all types in the vicinity of Poipu. For those who prefer to get away from crowds, the cane roads east of Poipu lead to hidden beaches. Like everywhere else in Hawaii, the end of the era of sugarcane will mean much more tourist and residential development, golf courses, and playgrounds for affluent vacationers. Koloa is an ideal gateway to Poipu, a restored plantation village which maintains its last-century charm even as it adds to its abundance of shops. Poipu's most remarkable attractions, however—the National Tropical Botanical Garden and the adjacent Allerton Estate—offer miles of beautiful landscaping along Lawai Valley's streambeds and hillsides, and a rare chance to see and learn about the world's most exotic flora. ◨

SOUTH SHORE

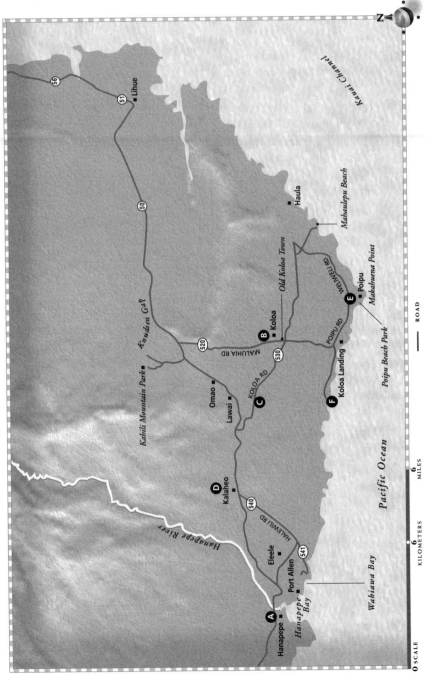

Kauai Channel

Lihue

56

51

50

Mahaulepu Beach

Haula

Old Koloa Town

Knudsen Gap

WELNNELI RD

Poipu

Makahuena Point

B Koloa

MALUHIA RD

POIPU RD

530

Poipu Beach Park

Kahili Mountain Park

520

KOLOA RD

Omao

Lawai

C

F Koloa Landing

Pacific Ocean

D
Kalaheo

540

HALEWILI RD

6   MILES

6   KILOMETERS

Hanapepe River

Eleele

541

Port Allen

Wahiawa Bay

A

Hanapepe

Hanapepe Bay

ROAD

0   SCALE

Sightseeing Highlights

Ⓐ Hanapepe

Ⓑ Koloa

Ⓒ National Tropical Botanical Garden

Ⓓ Olu Pua Gardens

Ⓔ Poipu

Ⓕ Spouting Horn

A PERFECT DAY ON THE SOUTH SHORE

The Plantation Gardens and Café is about as pleasant as you can find for breakfast if you're not staying at one of my favorite B&Bs near Poipu Beach. Drive up Lawai Road to Spouting Horn before the tour buses arrive. At the end of the road, the National Tropical Botanical Garden finally has recovered from Hurricane Iniki and reopened for tours. The beautifully landscaped gardens are unsurpassed in Hawaii. After seeing some of the world's most exotic flora, turn to Poipu Beach or further on Mahaulepu or, a hike of about ½ mile, Haula. Kiahuna Plantation is a lush 50-acre resort landscaped beautifully. Fortunately Koloa had very little damage from Hurricane Iniki and remains a restored plantation village with homes and churches that is always pleasurable to visit. The Hyatt Regency Kauai or Plantation Gardens are excellent places to start the evening with refreshments and relaxation. For a relaxing seafood dinner, the House of Seafood at the Poipu Kai is as good as you'll find in Poipu. For a completely different atmosphere, try pupu platters at the completely rebuilt Brennecke's Beach Broiler.

SIGHTSEEING HIGHLIGHTS

★★★ Koloa—A plantation town that developed in the mid-1800s around a sugar mill, Koloa declined with the demise of the sugar industry until tourism in the early 1970s started the restoration of "**Old Koloa Town**." Along Highway 50 heading for the turnoff to Koloa, the beautiful route from Lihue aims at Knudsen Gap between the Haupu Range and the Kahili Ridge. Kawaikini and Waialeale peaks usually vanish into thick clouds. Highway 520 or Maluhia ("Serenity") Road turns toward Koloa through a mile-long Tree Tunnel lined with Australian eucalyptus trees planted in 1911 by Walter McBride to form a dramatic gateway to his sugar plantation domain. Rusty tin roofs, sagging and bulging walls, dilapidated porches, weathered timber, and other remnants of economic decline still visible in the 1980s have been painted over and prettified into Old Koloa Town. Ruins of Kauai's first sugar mill remain as a picturesque relic of days when owners paid workers in scrip redeemable at the mill's grocery store. Down Hapa Road, off Weliweli Road, in the churchyard of **St. Raphael's Church**, Kauai's oldest Roman Catholic church, are the burial plots of plantation workers and their families. About 3 miles north of Poipu, picturesque Koloa today is a thriving shopping village with more than 40 stores and restaurants. (1–2 hours)

★★★ **National Tropical Botanical Garden**, located on Hailima Road about 2 miles south of Lawai, is the only tropical research garden in the United States. It has a staggering abundance of tropical flora in its collection, adding about a thousand plants each year. A two-hour guided tour of the 186-acre site, only given on Tuesday and Thursday mornings at 9:00 a.m., costs $15 per person and requires advance reservations. The tour includes the estate started by Queen Emma, wife of Kamehameha IV, in the 1870s and developed by the Allerton family. Mailing address: Box 340, Lawai, Kauai, HI 96765. Phone: 332-7361. (2–3 hours)

★★★ **Poipu**—Sun-drenched beaches line Poipu's old sugarcane coast, boasting excellent swimming, snorkeling, diving, and surfing. Hotels and condominiums cluster along Poipu's playground of the alii where Hawaiian fishermen still mend their nets and tell stories at popular **Poipu Beach Park**. The mahimahi T-shirts clinging to so many playful bodies on nearby Brennecke's Beach come from a popular lunch and drinking spot, Brennecke's Beach Broiler. From the lush tropical parklike setting of the condominium **Kiahuna Plantation**, once part of Hawaii's oldest sugarcane plantation, locals beachcomb among shore rocks for edible opihi. Meanwhile, inside deluxe shorefront restaurants, local seafood is served without this delicious tent-shaped mollusk—ironically because opihi is too expensive (almost $200 a gallon). **Mahaulepu**, several miles farther down the main cane road beyond **Shipwreck**, still possesses its "hidden" status. Enjoy scenic views of the coastline and mountains from a beach lined with ironwoods and the pleasures of swimming in tranquil ocean waters during summer months. (3–4 hours)

⋆⋆ **Olu Pua Gardens**—On Highway 50, past the Kukuiolono Golf Course, which has a delightful Japanese garden and outstanding coastal views, Olu Pua Gardens spreads over 12 acres ½ mile past Kalaheo (on the *mauka* side). An estate originally built in the 1930s for the Alexander family, founders of Kauai's largest pineapple plantation, the decor, antiques, and furnishings of the house and its magnificent gardens and tree groves have been delighting visitors for years.

Now Olu Pua Gardens is shaping an exciting new direction as the Hawaiian cultural center for Kauai Ka 'Imi Na'auao Hawai'i Nei, the school of hula and Hawaiian culture. Special tours of the grounds combine Hawaiian lore and botanical information. Don't miss the **Saturday Heritage Garden Tour** (10:00 a.m. and 1:00 p.m., $15 per person) Phone: 332-8182. (1–2 hours)

⋆ **Hanapepe**—En route to Hanapepe, follow Highway 540 toward the McBryde Mill, about a mile east of Port Allen, and turn on the cane road toward the ocean to find **Wahiawa Beach**, one of Kauai's loveliest and most protected beaches. Back to the main road (unless you decide to stay at the beach), a mile past Eleele, a panoramic view opens from **Hanapepe Lookout** over lush and scenic **Hanapepe Valley**. The town is entered past Hanapepe Canyon Lookout at the lush mouth of a green valley planted in taro between red cliffs. The town's wooden buildings hang over the west bank of the river. Besides the canyon view, the best attractions in town are the **Green Garden Restaurant** and several excellent art galleries. This former near "ghost town" is renewing rapidly and will be one of the most interesting tiny towns on Kauai. (45 minutes)

⋆ **Spouting Horn**—In the opposite direction from Poipu Beach, a submerged lava tube regularly produces the Spouting Horn geyser. Old-timers say that this geyser does not spout or moan as vigorously as it used to, but it still remains a major attraction for loads of tourists. Jewelry stands near the geyser's viewpoint offer some of the best deals on the island for coral shell jewelry and Niihau shell leis. (½ hour)

FITNESS AND RECREATION

Bicycle rentals cost $4 per hour or $12 to $20 per day or $100 per week. Contact **South Shore Activities** (742-6873, next to the Sheraton in Poipu). In Poipu, **Outfitter Kauai** (742-9667) will take care of your mountain bike needs.

The South Shore is popular for snorkeling at **Koloa Landing**,

Poipu, Brennecke's Beach, and **Hanapepe**. Most resort hotels and condominiums have snorkeling gear free for guests. Otherwise rentals cost $5 to $15 a day. Dive shops located in Koloa, Wailua/Kapaa, and Hanalei offer one- and two-tank dives for $55 to $75 and certification courses for about $350. Up to three hours of scuba touring costs $55 including equipment, and a half-day dive costs about $75. **Captain Andy's Sailing Adventures** on a catamaran is the best choice for snorkelers and sunset tours. Captain Andy will take snorkelers to Kipukai Bay for good snorkeling and a great beach. **Sport Fishing Kauai** (742-7013) operates out of Kukuiula.

In July and August, surfers gravitate to **Poipu** and **Makahuena Point**, further along the south shore.

FOOD

At the **Koloa Broiler** (742-9122, on Koloa Road, Hanapepe) you order beef or mahimahi, cook it yourself on a central broiler, toast some fresh baked bread, and help yourself to the salad bar. For breakfast or lunch, definitely stop at the **Garden Isle Bake Shoppe** (6:30 a.m. to 9:00 p.m.; 742-6070) in Kiahuna Shopping Village on Poipu Road. The **Beach House** (742-7575), rebuilt after Hurricane Iwa and again after Iniki, has a beautiful setting on Spouting Horn Road but is the place to skip dinner and just have a Malihini Pupu Platter and drinks. The **Plantation Gardens Restaurant** (742-1695, Poipu), at the Kiahuna Plantation Resort, is one of the prettiest restaurants in the area, though you'll pay $20 to $30 per person for dinner, atmosphere, decor, crystal and silver, and the right wine.

LODGING

Near Spouting Horn, facing the surf and rocky coastline, **Gloria's Spouting Horn Bed & Breakfast** (4464 Lawai Beach Road, Koloa, Kauai, HI 96756, 742-6995) offers charming accommodations, mostly with ocean views, tasty and ample breakfasts, and very reasonable rates for Poipu at $50 to $120. Eve Warner and Al Davis, who operate **Hawaii Bed & Breakfast Service**, P.O. Box 449, Kapaa, HI 96746 (822-7771, 800-733-1632, or 800-822-2723) have built their own rental units behind their house near Poipu Beach Park. **Poipu Plantation** (1792 Pe'e Road, Koloa) has four one-bedroom self-contained units at $70 to $80 for a garden view, $75 for an ocean view; and two-bedroom units for $85 with an ocean view, but without breakfast. With a lovely garden, great location, and perfect hosts, you can't go wrong. Write Poipu Plantation, Highway 1, Box 119, Koloa, HI 96756, 742-7038 or 822-7771.

The **Garden Isle Cottages** (2666 Puuholu Road, to your left as you head for Spouting Horn) offers a few of the least expensive local accommodations. Artists Sharon and Robert Flynn have a very comfortable and nicely decorated group of cottages in a garden setting and others scattered around the nearby area, $51 to $83 for a studio and $83 to $115 for a double for two persons. Write Garden Isle Cottages, R.R. 1, Box 355, Koloa, HI 96756, 742-6717. A very special treat at a moderate price is Hans and Sylvia Zeevat's **Koloa Landing Cottages** (27 04B Hooonani Road), with nicely designed, furnished, equipped, and cared for two-bedroom cottages (only two) at $75 single or double and studios at $50 single or double. Write Dolphin Realty, R.R. 1, Box 70, 2827 Poipu Road, Koloa, Kauai, HI 96756, 742-1470.

The Koloa area has some of the more unusual bed and breakfast and alternative accommodations on Kauai, away from the bustle of tourist activities but close to Koloa and Poipu Beach. Rustic **Kahili Mountain Park** (P.O. Box 298, Koloa, Kauai, HI 96756, 742-9921), operated by the Seventh Day Adventist Church, is located 7 miles from Poipu Beach. Cabinettes with hot plates rent for $20 double, and cabins with a two-burner stove and sink rent for $35. Next to Kahili Mountain Park, a few steps from a good snorkeling beach and the Beach House Restaurant, Den and Dee Wilson's **Prince Kuhio Condominiums**, 5160 Lawai Road, Koloa, Kauai, (742-1409 or 800-722-1409) are one of the best hotel or condo deals in Poipu. Their $69 (to $79) double rooms become a $296 weekly rate for a very nicely furnished apartment overlooking Prince Kuhio Park or gardens on the grounds. Prices are higher December 15 to April 15.

SOUTH SHORE

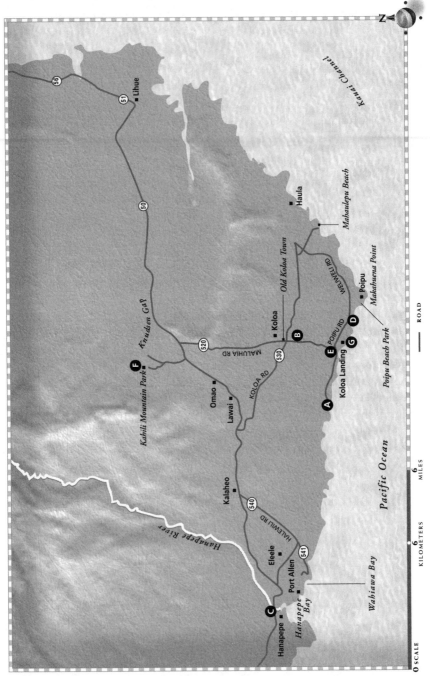

Food

Ⓐ Beach House

Ⓑ Garden Isle Bake Shoppe

Ⓒ Koloa Broiler

Ⓓ Plantation Gardens Restaurant

Lodging

Ⓔ Garden Isle Cottages

Ⓐ Gloria's Spouting Horn Bed & Breakfast

Ⓕ Kahili Mountain Park

Ⓖ Koloa Landing Cottages

Ⓔ Prince Kuhio Condominiums

Ⓓ Poipu Plantation

Note: Items with the same letter are located in the same town or area

APPENDIX

METRIC CONVERSION CHART

1 U.S. gallon = approximately 4 liters
1 liter = about 1 quart
1 Canadian gallon = approximately 4.5 liters

1 pound = approximately $\frac{1}{2}$ kilogram
1 kilogram = about 2 pounds

1 foot = approximately $\frac{2}{3}$ meter
1 meter = about 1 yard
1 yard = a little less than a meter
1 mile = approximately 1.6 kilometers
1 kilometer = about $\frac{2}{3}$ mile

90°F = about 30°C
20°C = approximately 70°F

Planning Map: Hawaii

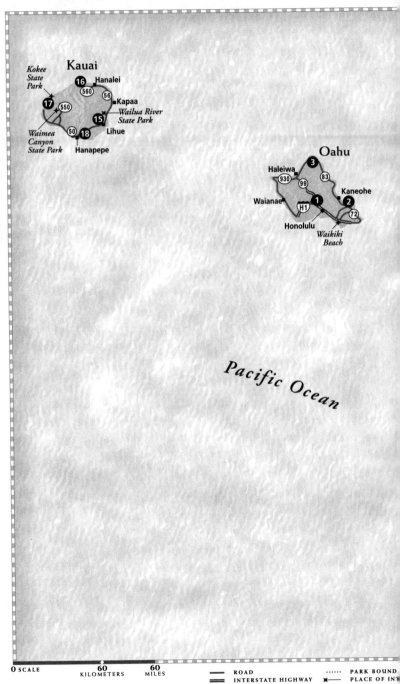

Kauai

Kokee
State
Park

16 Hanalei

560

56 Kapaa

17 550
Wailua River
State Park

15

Waimea
Canyon
State Park

50 18 Lihue

Hanapepe

Oahu

Haleiwa
3

930
99
83

Kaneohe

Waianae
1
2

H1

72

Honolulu

Waikiki
Beach

Pacific Ocean

0 SCALE   60   60
       KILOMETERS MILES

ROAD   PARK BOUND
INTERSTATE HIGHWAY ✕ PLACE OF INT

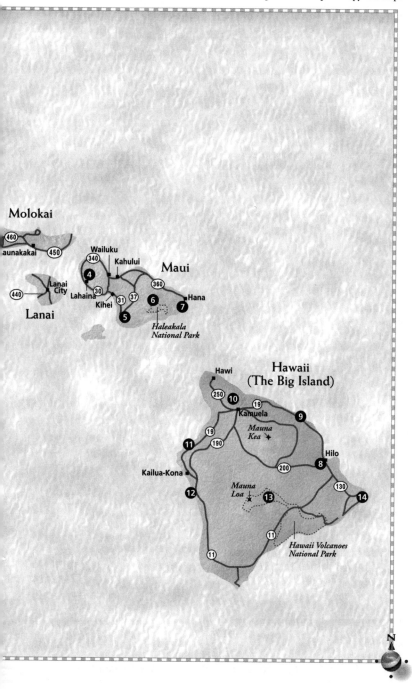

INDEX

Map Index

Other Books from John Muir Publications